CREATIVITY IN SCIENCE

Psychologists, sociologists, philosophers, historians, and even scientists themselves have often tried to decipher the basis for creativity in science. Some have
attributed creativity to a special logic, the so-called scientific method, whereas
others have pointed to the inspirations of genius or to the inevitable workings of the zeitgeist. Finally, some have viewed scientific breakthroughs as the
product of chance, as witnessed in the numerous episodes of serendipity. Too
often these four alternative interpretations are seen as mutually exclusive. Yet
the central thesis of this book is that the chance, logic, genius, and zeitgeist
perspectives can be integrated into a single coherent theory of creativity in science. But for this integration to succeed, chance must be elevated to the status
of primary cause. Logic, genius, and the zeitgeist still have significant roles to
play but mainly operate insofar as they enhance, or constrain, the operation
of a chance combinatorial process.

Dean Keith Simonton is Professor of Psychology at the University of California,
Davis. He is the author of nine books, including *Genius, Creativity, and Leadership* [Harvard, 1984], *Scientific Genius* [Cambridge, 1988], *Psychology, Science,
and History* [Yale, 1990], *Greatness* [Guilford, 1994], *Origins of Genius* [Oxford,
1999], and *Great Psychologists and Their Times* [APA, 2002]

Creativity in Science

CHANCE, LOGIC, GENIUS, AND ZEITGEIST

Dean Keith Simonton
University of California, Davis

CAMBRIDGE
UNIVERSITY PRESS

PUBLISHED BY THE PRESS SYNDICATE OF THE UNIVERSITY OF CAMBRIDGE
The Pitt Building, Trumpington Street, Cambridge, United Kingdom

CAMBRIDGE UNIVERSITY PRESS
The Edinburgh Building, Cambridge CB2 2RU, UK
40 West 20th Street, New York, NY 10011-4211, USA
477 Williamstown Road, Port Melbourne, VIC 3207, Australia
Ruiz de Alarcón 13, 28014 Madrid, Spain
Dock House, The Waterfront, Cape Town 8001, South Africa

http://www.cambridge.org

© Dean Keith Simonton

First published 2004

Printed in the United States of America

Typeface ITC Stone Serif 9/14.5 pt.　　*System* LᴧTᴇX 2$_\varepsilon$　[TB]

A catalog record for this book is available from the British Library.

Library of Congress Cataloging in Publication Data
Simonton, Dean Keith.
Creativity in science: change, logic, genius, and Zeitgeist / Dean Keith Simonton.
p.　cm.
Includes bibliographical references and index.
ISBN 0-521-83579-8 – ISBN 0-521-54369-X(pbk.)
1. Creative ability in science.　I. Title.
Q172.5.C74.S54　2004
500 – dc22　　2003066661

ISBN 0 521 83579 8 hardback
ISBN 0 521 54369 x paperback

To Karen

Contents

Preface • ix

Chapter 1. Introduction: Scientific Creativity • 1

Chapter 2. Creative Products • 14

Chapter 3. Combinatorial Processes • 40

Chapter 4. Scientific Activity • 76

Chapter 5. Creative Scientists • 99

Chapter 6. Scientific Discovery • 137

Chapter 7. Consolidation: Creativity in Science • 160

References • 185

Index • 211

Preface

World history may or may not repeat itself, but personal biography certainly can. Back in 1986 I was asked to contribute a chapter on scientific creativity for a volume on the psychology of science. Although I accepted the invitation with gusto, I soon encountered an unexpected obstacle: The first draft of the chapter was many times larger than the page limitations allowed. Yet it contained lots of ideas that I was reluctant to cut. Moreover, I felt that the draft contained many half-baked ideas that needed more development. My response was to take full advantage of one of the miracles of word processing: I made a duplicate of the electronic file. The original version could be subjected to draconian edits until it reached the permissible length. In contrast, the other copy could be expanded until my ideas on scientific creativity got the attention I thought they deserved. The consequence of that expansion was not one long chapter but seven distinct chapters making up a book-length manuscript. In 1988 Cambridge University Press published this book with the title *Scientific Genius: A Psychology of Science*. Although the book chapter was completed first, it was not published until 1989 in another Cambridge book, *The Psychology of Science: Contributions to Metascience*, edited by Gholson, Shadish, Neimeyer, and Houts. The chapter, titled "The Chance-Configuration Theory of Scientific Creativity," could be considered an abstract for the book.

Preface

Throughout the 1990s the thinking contained in these two publications received a great deal of empirical and theoretical development. After about a dozen years of these developments, the 1988 book and the 1989 chapter appeared to be increasingly obsolete. These publications no longer expressed what I had come to believe about the nature of creativity in science. Rather than wait for another invitation to write a book chapter, I decided to take the initiative by writing a review article that sketched out my revised view. In 2003 this updated version was published in *Psychological Bulletin* under the title "Scientific Creativity as Constrained Stochastic Behavior: The Integration of Product, Process, and Person Perspectives."

Yet, I immediately realized the inadequacy of the presentation even before the article was accepted for publication. The subject again needed book-length treatment. All the time I was going through the review process with the *Bulletin*, I was working on the more elaborate version. This time, rather than simply expand the article into a monograph, I decided to start from scratch. Nevertheless, the writing went very fast. Ideas I had been contemplating for more than a decade crystallized quickly around the core theoretical framework. As a result, the first draft of the book was completed long before I even saw the copyedited manuscript of the *Bulletin* article. However, unlike the previous episode, the book appeared second rather than first. Furthermore, the book's ideas received so much elaboration that the article cannot be taken for its abstract.

In any case, here is the result. It embodies what I consider to be a coherent integration of four divergent perspectives on scientific creativity – chance, logic, genius, and zeitgeist. Moreover, this theoretical integration is based on a large research literature, including many recent studies. In fact, approximately a third of the cited references appeared after *Scientific Genius* was completed. The book is aimed at any reader who has an interest in the place of creativity in science. This readership presumably would include not just psychologists but also practicing scientists in any discipline. All educated laypersons curious about scientific creativity should also find this book instructive, even provocative.

Preface

I would like to thank several individuals who helped me develop the ideas contained in this volume. In particular, my views on scientific creativity have been shaped in various ways by diverse interactions with John Baer, Auguste Brannigan, Donald Campbell, Mihaly Csikszentmihalyi, Kevin Dunbar, Anders Ericsson, Hans Eysenck, Gregory Feist, Liane Gabora, Howard Gardner, Harrison Gough, Howard Gruber, John Huber, John Koza, Colin Martindale, Paul Meehl, Robert K. Merton, Arthur Miller, David Perkins, Derek Price, Mark Runco, William Shadish, Herbert Simon, Robert J. Sternberg, Frank Sulloway, and Tom Ward. Of course, this acknowledgment of influence is not equivalent to the claim that these same individuals would endorse all, some, or even any of the ideas presented in this book.

Mathematical Notation

Although I have tried to keep the mathematics to a bare minimum, sometimes ideas must be presented with the precision that only mathematics provides. To avoid possible confusion, I have adopted a consistent notation throughout the book. This decision has obliged me to alter the manner in which certain concepts are usually presented in the research literature (e.g., Lotka's law). Hence, the definitions of the diverse mathematical symbols are presented here for quick reference.

a The ideation rate for converting creative potential into ideas in development ($0 < a < 1$).

b The elaboration rate for converting ideas in development into finished ideas ($0 < b < 1$).

c The proportionality constant in Lotka's law ($c > 0$).

$C_i(t)$ The number of ideational combinations produced by scientist i at career age t.

e The exponential constant; approximately equal to 2.718.

H_i The total number of high-impact contributions produced by scientist i over an entire lifetime or completed career.

H_{it} The total number of high-impact contributions produced by scientist i at time t.

Mathematical Notation

I The total number of ideas defining the domain of a given scientific discipline (i.e., the disciplinary zeitgeist).

k The proportionality constant relating the number of completed products to the number of ideational combinations generated $(0 < k < 1)$.

n The number of trials in attempting to generate a particular event $(n \geq 1)$.

N The number of scientists active in a given scientific discipline (i.e., the size of the field, where $N \geq 1$).

m_i The total number of ideational combinations that scientist i can generate in an unlimited lifetime $(m_i >> 1)$.

p The probability of a particular event taking place $(0 \leq p \leq 1)$.

$P(j)$ The probability of exactly j events taking place, where $0 \leq P(j) \leq 1$.

r The Pearson product-moment correlation coefficient that gauges the linear association between two variables $(-1.0 \leq r \leq 1.0$, where 0 indicates the absence of a relation).

t Time in years; may represent either career age (e.g., age since Ph.D.) or chronological date, depending on the context.

T Total number of creative products produced over an entire lifetime.

T_i Total number of creative products produced by scientist i over an entire lifetime.

T_{it} Total number of creative products produced by scientist i at time t.

u_i A random "shock" variable pertaining to the expected output of scientist i (with a mean of zero).

u_{it} A random "shock" variable pertaining to the expected output of scientist i at time t (with a mean of zero).

α Parameter in the contagious Poisson having the same function as μ in the simple Poisson.

β Parameter in the contagious Poisson that represents the magnitude of the contagion.

γ Proportionality constant relating the change in I as a function of the product of N and I.

Mathematical Notation

ρ The hit rate or quality ratio – that is, the ratio of high-impact products to total works produced (i.e., H_i/T_i).

μ The mean of a frequency distribution; a parameter in the simple Poisson distribution.

σ^2 The variance of a frequency distribution; $\mu = \sigma^2$ in the simple Poisson distribution.

1

Introduction: Scientific Creativity

Consider the following list: Newton's *Principia Mathematica,* Plato's *Republic,* Shakespeare's *Hamlet,* da Vinci's *Last Supper,* and Beethoven's *Fifth Symphony.* What do these items have in common? The answer clearly is that all five represent creative products, even works of genius. Each can be considered an exemplary contribution to a particular domain of creative achievement. Each of these creations exerted a profound and pervasive influence on the collective repository of human accomplishments that defines world civilization.

Yet in one crucial respect, one of the items on this list does not belong with the rest: Newton's scientific masterpiece. Unlike the others, it is the single work whose merits as a creative product cannot be reasonably assessed by an educated layperson. Any literate person can pull a copy of *Republic* or *Hamlet* off the library shelf and obtain at least some understanding of the logical argument or dramatic development. Likewise, anyone can look at a print of the *Last Supper* or listen to a recording of the *Fifth Symphony* and obtain a good notion of what was being graphically conveyed or musically expressed.

In contrast, it would be rare to find a layperson who could make any sense of the *Principia Mathematica.* Even modern mathematicians and physicists find it tough going, given its obsolete notation and presentational style. Worse still, few people these days read Newton's masterwork for either pleasure or edification. It has become a museum piece largely doomed to collect dust on the bookshelf. In comparison, people continue to read the *Republic*, see performances of *Hamlet*, travel to Milan to see the *Last Supper*, and attend concerts showcasing the *Fifth Symphony*. Indeed, it is telling that I refer to da Vinci's painting and Beethoven's composition by their English-language titles, whereas I refer to Newton's treatise by its Latin title instead of the full English translation, the *Mathematical Principles of Natural Philosophy*. These references are merely following conventional practice. Actually, it is customary to cite Newton's work by the terse title *Principia*, rendering it even more cryptic and remote.

Notwithstanding the stark disparity in intelligibility or appreciation, many would argue that Newton's work rates higher than the others in terms of its significance to world civilization. This differential assessment is apparent in the book *The 100: A Ranking of the Most Influential Persons in History* (Hart, 1987). In the author's assessment, Newton placed second, surpassed by Muhammad alone. Shakespeare came in 36th, Plato 40th, and Beethoven 42nd, with da Vinci receiving a mere "honorable mention," having missed the final cut. In fact, once the religious, military, and political leaders are deleted from the top 100, scientists dominate the residual list of creators. These scientists include Albert Einstein (10th), Galileo Galilei (13th), Charles Darwin (17th), Euclid (22nd), Nicolaus Copernicus (24th), Michael Faraday (28th), James Clerk Maxwell (29th), Antoine Laurent Lavoisier (31st), Antony van Leeuwenhoek (39th), Werner Heisenberg (43rd), Alexander Fleming (45th), Max Planck (54th), William Harvey (57th), Antoine Henri Becquerel (58th), Gregor Mendel (59th), Joseph Lister (60th), René Descartes (64th), Edward Jenner (72nd), Wilhelm Conrad Röntgen (73rd), Enrico Fermi (76th), Leonhard Euler (87th), John Dalton (93rd), Johannes Kepler (97th), and Niels Bohr (100th).

Admittedly, anyone can easily challenge these rankings. Perhaps such a single-handed undertaking is inherently presumptuous. I mention this assessment only because it illustrates the common belief that scientific creativity should be held in higher esteem than other forms of creativity. This status is apparent elsewhere besides this ranking. It is evident in the

2

works counted as "books that changed the world," about half of which are scientific rather than literary or philosophical (Downs, 1983). This differential appreciation is also revealed in the much more extensive public support given to scientists compared with artists. In the United States, for example, the budget of the National Science Foundation far exceeds that of the National Endowment for the Arts. The same disparity is seen in the Nobel Prizes, which now are bestowed in four areas of scientific creativity (physics, chemistry, physiology or medicine, and economics) but in solely one domain of artistic creativity (literature). When *Time* magazine decided to pick the person of the century at the close of the millennium, it identified not an artist, nor even a leader, but rather a scientist – namely, Einstein. If *Time* magazine were published at the end of the 17th century, Isaac Newton might have received that honor.

But what does it take to conceive a masterpiece like the *Principia*? One obvious response is simply to affirm that it represents a concrete consequence of *creativity*. To be more precise, the *Principia* should be called a work of *scientific creativity* and thus distinguish this instance of creativity from whatever process produced the *Republic, Hamlet, Last Supper*, and *Fifth Symphony*. However, this answer really begs the question. What do we mean by scientific creativity? What are its underlying processes? Who has the capacity to produce a work like the *Principia* and who does not? When and where does scientific creativity occur? These issues cannot be addressed without first recognizing that creativity may be viewed from more than one perspective.

FOUR POSSIBLE PERSPECTIVES

Scientific creativity is a topic addressed by many distinct disciplines or what have been termed *metasciences* (Gholson et al., 1989; Simonton, 1988b). The most important of these metasciences are the history of science, the philosophy of science, the sociology of science, and the psychology of science. Not surprisingly, each of these metasciences has a somewhat distinctive outlook on the phenomenon. Part of the disciplinary

3

variation may result simply from contrasts in methodological techniques and substantive interests. Where historians prefer narratives, philosophers favor analyses. While sociologists like to discuss institutions, psychologists like to look at individuals. Nonetheless, some of the differences among the metasciences are also based on the essential fact that scientific creativity can be examined from four principal perspectives: logic, genius, chance, and zeitgeist.

Logic

Philosophers of science have long tried to provide a logical foundation for scientific discovery. These attempts date as far back as Francis Bacon and René Descartes, the former emphasizing inductive reasoning and the latter emphasizing deductive reasoning. To varying degrees, these attempts have attracted great thinkers such as John Locke, Immanuel Kant, and John Stewart Mill. Moreover, the role of logical reasoning is certainly apparent in any high-impact scientific contribution. Newton's *Principia*, for instance, was often taken as a supreme demonstration of the hypothetico-deductive method, a mode of logical analysis that established a paradigm for how best to do science. This view of scientific creativity has the asset of giving science a high degree of incontrovertible inevitability. Provided that the logical deductions fit the empirical facts, it is difficult to challenge scientific truths, and science should continue to accumulate such truths as it extends its methods to all the natural phenomena of the universe.

Some proponents of the psychology of science have adopted the same perspective on scientific creativity (Tweney, Doherty, & Mynatt, 1981). The most conspicuous among these advocates was Herbert Simon, a cognitive psychologist noteworthy for becoming a Nobel laureate in economics. In 1973, Simon published an article in *Philosophy of Science* in which he emphatically argued that scientific discovery betrays a definite logic. This position was based on a general belief that creativity was nothing more than a guise of problem solving, itself a process governed entirely by logical procedures (Newell, Shaw, & Simon, 1958). To strengthen this case, Simon and his colleagues have conducted an impressive number of laboratory experiments and computer simulations that purport to establish the logical underpinnings of scientific discovery (Klahr & Simon, 1999).

Especially provocative are the so-called *discovery programs* (Kulkarni & Simon, 1988; Langley et al., 1987; Shrager & Langley, 1990). These programs claim to replicate the achievements of great scientists by applying logical analyses to empirical data. As if to emphasize the creative prowess of these programs, the software is often named after some big names in the history of science – such as, OCCAM, BACON, GALILEO, GLAUBER, HUYGENS, STAHL, FAHRENHEIT, BLACK, DALTON, PAULI, and GELL-MANN. Of these, BACON may be the most representative. It specializes in the inductive method, yielding data-driven discoveries as advocated in Francis Bacon's *Novum Organum*. By using Baconian induction, BACON reputedly has rediscovered Kepler's Third Law of planetary motion, Black's Law of temperature equilibrium, Ohm's Law of current and resistance, Prout's hypothesis of atomic structure, the Gay–Lussac Law of gaseous reaction, Dulong–Petit Law of atomic heat, and the derivation of atomic weights by Avogadro and Cannizzaro (Bradshaw, Langley, & H. A. Simon, 1983). This impressive list of discoveries appears to make a strong argument for the viewpoint that scientific creativity is the product of mere logic.

Naturally, these simulations often seem to trivialize the achievements of great scientists. If a computer program can duplicate their accomplishments so easily, then it seems like anyone can make significant contributions to science. Nothing really special is required, particularly when computer programs can accomplish in a few seconds what it took real scientists whole careers to achieve. Simon (1973) himself drew this implication. For example, he claimed, "Mendeleev's Periodic Table does not involve a notion of pattern more complex than that required to handle patterned letter sequences" (p. 479). Going beyond mere speculation, Simon even conducted the following informal experiment:

5

On eight occasions I have sat down at lunch with colleagues who are good applied mathematicians and said to them: "I have a problem that you can perhaps help me with. I have some very nice data that can be fitted very accurately for large values of the independent variable by an exponential function, but for small values they fit a linear function accurately. Can you suggest a smooth function that will give me a good fit through the whole range?" (H. A. Simon, 1986, p. 7)

Of the eight colleagues, five arrived at a solution in just a few minutes. In ignorance of what Simon was up to, they had independently arrived at Max Planck's formula for black body radiation – an achievement that earned Planck a Nobel Prize for Physics.

Simon's stance appears to endorse the seemingly outlandish assertion once made by the philosopher Ortega y Gasset (1932/1957). According to Ortega y Gasset,

it is necessary to insist upon this extraordinary but undeniable fact: experimental science has progressed thanks in great part to the work of men astoundingly mediocre, and even less than mediocre. That is to say, modern science, the root and symbol of our actual civilization, finds a place for the intellectually commonplace man allows him to work therein with success. (pp. 110 – 111)

Once a scientist masters the logic of science and the substance of a particular discipline, creativity is assured.

Genius

The idea that discovery features such a straightforward logic appears to contradict the idolizing praise often bestowed on scientific genius. Thus, not only is the *Principia* deemed a model scientific contribution, but its author also is often acclaimed in the most grandiose terms. "Nature and Nature's laws lay hid in night: / God said *Let Newton be!* and all was light," said the poet Alexander Pope (Cohen & Cohen, 1960, p. 285). More explicitly, mathematician Joseph Louis Lagrange called Newton "the greatest genius that had ever existed" (Jeans, 1942, p. 710). Hence, it should come as no surprise that not everyone accepts the limitations of the logic stance. Opponents include philosophers of science such as Karl Popper (1959) as well as Nobel Prize–winning scientists. For example, Max Planck (1949) held that creative scientists "must have a vivid intuitive imagination, for new ideas are not generated by deduction, but by an artistically creative imagination" (p. 109). Similarly, Albert Einstein reported "to these elementary laws there leads no logical path, but only intuition" (Holton, 1971–72, p. 97).

If these testimonials can be taken on face value, then the proposition that discovery has a logic may have been vastly overstated. Instead, scientific creativity might require some special abilities or traits that set the great scientists apart from their lesser colleagues. Individuals who claim these characteristics to the highest degree may even be called geniuses, or at least potentially so (Simonton, 1999a). This is the position advocated by psychologists who represent a separate tradition within the psychology of science (Feist & Gorman, 1998; Simonton, 1988b). For example, some psychologists believe creativity requires the intellectual and dispositional capacity to generate unusual associations and analogies as well as rich, even dream-like imagery (Mednick, 1962; Rothenberg, 1987; Suler, 1980), a contention that dates as far back as Alexander Bain (1855/1977) and William James (1880). This is not a capacity that can be possessed by everyone but rather belongs to a creative elite. Furthermore, these cognitive processes are more illogical than logical. In effect, those who maintain the genius perspective are arguing that great scientists are precisely those who have the ability to dispense with logic. They can thereby come up with ideas that cannot be derived by inductive or deductive methods alone. This contrast is suggested by the manner in which James (1880) described the mental processes of great thinkers:

Instead of thoughts of concrete things patiently following one another in a beaten track of habitual suggestion, we have the most abrupt cross-cuts and transitions from one idea to another, the most rarefied abstractions and discriminations, the most unheard of combination of elements, the subtlest associations of analogy; in a word, we seem suddenly introduced into a seething

7

cauldron of ideas, where everything is fizzling and bobbling about in a state of bewildering activity, where partnerships can be joined or loosened in an instant, treadmill routine is unknown, and the unexpected seems only law. (p. 456)

This description seems a far cry from the linear and discrete logic implemented in the discovery programs.

Chance

If the James (1880) passage has any descriptive validity, then the discovery process might be best described as disorderly, unpredictable, and chaotic. Thoughts tumble over each other willy-nilly, and ideas emerge more by happy accident than by design or deliberation. This implication fits nicely with the third perspective on creativity – the notion that it represents the workings of chance processes. Like the logic and genius perspectives on scientific creativity, this one also has a long history. An early example is the 1896 essay "On the Part Played by Accident in Invention and Discovery" written by the physicist Ernst Mach. Nearly half of a century later Walter Cannon (1940), the physiologist, published a classic article on "The Role of Chance in Discovery." The term that is most frequently applied to these events is *serendipity*, a noun introduced by Horace Walpole in 1754 and defined as "the faculty of making fortunate discoveries by accident" (*American Heritage Electronic Dictionary*, 1992).

Numerous examples of serendipitous events have been documented (Austin, 1978; Roberts, 1989; Shapiro, 1986). Among the more prominent cases are those presented in Table 1.1. Such events often are so unexpected that they can exert an inordinate influence over the course of scientific history, thrusting it in surprising directions (Kantorovich & Ne'eman, 1989). Radioactivity and X-rays provide obvious examples. Serendipity even has a prominent role in the folklore of science. Many schoolchildren have heard the story about how Newton "discovered gravity" after watching an apple fall from a tree.

8

TABLE 1.1. Some Representative Episodes of Serendipity in the History of Science and Technology

Name	Discovery or Invention	Date
Columbus	New World	1492
Grimaldi	interference of light	1663
Haüy	geometric laws of crystallography	1781
Galvani	animal electricity	1791
Davy	laughing gas anesthesia	1798
Oersted	electromagnetism	1820
Schönbein	ozone	1839
Daguerre	photography (daguerrotype)	1839
Perkin	synthetic coal-tar dyes	1856
Kirchhoff	D-line in the solar spectrum	1859
Nobel	dynamite	1866
Edison	phonograph	1877
Pasteur	vaccination	1878
Fahlberg	saccharin	1879
Röntgen	X-rays	1895
Becquerel	radioactivity	1896
Richet	induced sensitization (anaphylaxis)	1902
Pavlov	classical conditioning	1902
Fleming	penicillin	1928
Dam	vitamin K	1929
Domagk	sulfa drugs (Prontosil)	1932
Plunkett	Teflon	1938
de Maestral	Velcro	1948

Note: Several of the dates are only approximate.

To be more precise, however, serendipity assumes many forms, some of which may be better called instances of *pseudo-serendipity* (Roberts, 1989; Simonton, 1999c). In cases of true serendipity, the discovery was not only accidental but also unintended or undesired (Díaz de Chumaceiro, 1995). The individual discovers something he or she was not even looking for. Alexander Fleming's discovery of the antibacterial properties of *Penicillium* is a prime illustration. On other occasions, a scientist discoverers what he or she was looking for, but manages to do so solely via some unexpected route, and usually not without considerable "trial and error."

Nevertheless, to perceive creativity as a chance phenomenon is not equivalent to claiming that creative scientists are merely "lucky." Because some scientists appear to be consistently more lucky than others, it is probably more correct to assert that scientific genius includes a capacity for the exploitation of chance. As Louis Pasteur famously said, "chance favours only the prepared mind" (Beveridge 1957, p. 46). A portion of that preparation could entail the cognitive and dispositional attributes associated with scientific genius.

Zeitgeist

Although the chance perspective is not necessarily inconsistent with the genius perspective, it is strikingly incompatible with the fourth and last viewpoint on scientific creativity. Sociologists of science have argued that discoveries and inventions are the inevitable product of the sociocultural system – often personified as the *zeitgeist* or "spirit of the times." For instance, Robert K. Merton (1961a) maintained, "discoveries and inventions become virtually inevitable (1) as prerequisite kinds of knowledge accumulate in man's cultural store; (2) as the attention of a sufficient number of investigators is focused on a problem – by emerging social needs, or by developments internal to the particular science, or by both" (p. 306). This position is also maintained by historians of science who believe scientific creativity is contextually determined (Boring, 1963; Furumoto, 1989). This view is especially strong among Marxist historians who hold that scientific ideas must instantaneously and irrevocably reflect the underlying materialistic conditions of the society (Bernal, 1971).

Whether advocated by sociologists or historians, such sociocultural determinism seems antithetical to the very concept of serendipity, pseudo or otherwise. How can a discovery or invention result from pure chance and yet at the same time be completely determined by zeitgeist? But it should be equally apparent that the zeitgeist position is also opposed to the genius perspective (Boring, 1963; Kroeber, 1917; Merton, 1961a). If discoveries and inventions are the inevitable result of sociocultural determinism, then the individual scientist or inventor is reduced to being a mere agent of zeitgeist. As a result, his or her personal characteristics may matter not one iota. For instance, Leslie White (1949), a cultural anthropologist, belittled the very idea that any special talents were required to invent the steamboat. "Is great intelligence required to put one and one – a boat and an engine – together? An ape can do this" (p. 212). One reason why he could make this emphatic claim is that the invention of the steamboat is usually credited to more than one independent inventor. The most frequently named candidates for the honors are Jouffroy, Rumsey, Fitch, and Symington (Kroeber, 1963). If so many distinct individuals could be responsible for the same invention, then it appears more likely that the idea for the steamboat was "in the air" waiting for anyone to pick. The inevitability of the event precluded not just chance but also genius.

Of course, one might argue that this instance is too exceptional to exclude so categorically the other two perspectives. But advocates of sociocultural determinism argue otherwise, compiling dozens, even hundreds of cases (Merton, 1961b; Ogburn & Thomas, 1922). Cases like the steamboat are so commonplace that they have even earned a special name, that of *multiples* (Lamb & Easton, 1984; Merton, 1961b). Notable examples of multiples include the creation of calculus by Newton and Leibniz, the proposal of a theory of evolution by natural selection by Darwin and Wallace, and the discovery of the laws of genetic inheritance by Mendel, De Vries, Correns, and Tschermak. Such examples are taken as incontestable proof of sociocultural determinism. For instance, Alfred Kroeber (1917), another cultural anthropologist, believed it was no mere coincidence that De Vries, Correns, and Tschermak all rediscovered Mendel's laws a few months apart within the same year. On the contrary, Mendelian genetics "was discovered in 1900 because it could have been discovered only then, and because

11

it infallibly must have been discovered then" (p. 199). The individual players in this multiples episode were as extraneous as chance was absent.

THEIR POTENTIAL INTEGRATION

By now it should be obvious that these four viewpoints do not form a coherent account of scientific creativity. The logic position appears to contradict both the chance and genius positions, and the zeitgeist position is opposed to the latter two positions as well. Although the logic viewpoint is not obviously inconsistent with the zeitgeist viewpoint, the two viewpoints are more independent than mutually supportive. Perhaps this hodgepodge of unrelated and incompatible perspectives should be expected. After all, to some degree logic, chance, genius, and zeitgeist reflect deeper intellectual controversies that have been going on for centuries if not millennia. Especially pertinent are age-old debates about the relative prominence of rationality versus irrationality, chance versus determinism, and individual versus society (Simonton, 1976d, 2000b). The discrepancies also may have resulted from the contrasts between separate academic disciplines. It certainly makes sense that sociologists would champion the zeitgeist perspective while psychologists favor the genius perspective. Sociology concerns groups, psychology individuals.

It would be tempting, given these intellectual debates and disciplinary divisions, to just give up and resign ourselves to the inconsistencies among the four perspectives. Maybe scientific creativity is too complex a phenomenon to lend itself to a coherent explanation. Alternatively, we can opt to pick one perspective as the "truth" and arbitrarily reject any other perspective that disagrees with that decision. Yet neither of these choices is attractive from a scientific outlook. It would be the height of irony to propose that scientific creativity cannot be the subject of successful scientific study. Consequently, my goal in this book is to offer a scientific analysis that integrates all four perspectives. This integration is attained by subsuming three of the perspectives under the fourth, giving the latter explanatory primacy. In particular, the logic, genius, and zeitgeist positions are subsumed under the chance position (cf. Simonton, 2003b). Although the former perspectives are subordinated to the latter perspective, the analysis preserves the unquestionable findings generated by each point of view. In other words, the best of the contrary positions are incorporated rather than ignored.

This integration begins in Chapter 2, where I discuss the distinctive features of creative products in the sciences. In Chapter 3, these features are provided a theoretical explanation that highlights the probabilistic nature of scientific creativity. This theoretical explanation is then linked to substantive explanations in Chapter 4, where I discuss the probabilistic consequences of certain prominent aspects of scientific activity. The final two chapters take this explanatory elaboration even further. Chapter 5 discusses creative scientists and Chapter 6 treats scientific discovery. The book closes by consolidating the diverse aspects of this integrated account of creativity in science.

In the end, it should become clear that the scientific creativity that produced *Principia* must be the joint product of logic, chance, genius, and zeitgeist – with chance primus inter pares.

2

Creative Products

Of the four major metasciences mentioned in the preceding chapter, the psychology of science has the deepest commitment to understanding scientific creativity. Yet, it should have become apparent that the psychology of science fails to provide a unified perspective on the phenomenon (Simonton, 2003b). In particular, while some practitioners adopt the logic perspective on the phenomenon, others embrace the genius perspective. The reason for this split is that scientific psychology actually consists of two distinct, even antagonistic disciplines (Cronbach, 1957). On the one side are experimental psychologists, who conduct laboratory experiments on the abstract human mind; on the other side are correlational psychologists, who study concrete differences among individual human beings. This split carries over into the psychology of science, the first looking at scientific discovery as a generalized logical process and the second investigating the personal attributes of outstanding scientists. Because the methods and aims are so disparate, the two research traditions find it difficult to agree on a common theoretical language to address the phenomenon. So the data generated by one tradition are often taken as irrelevant to the data generated by the contrary tradition. Thus, Mansfield and Busse's (1981) *The Psychology of Creativity and Discovery*, which represents the correlational tradition, virtually ignored the vast experimental literature on the subject. A more recent overview of scientific creativity contains not a single reference to laboratory experiments or computer simulations (Stumpf, 1995). On the other side of the disciplinary divide, Klahr's (2000) *Exploring Science* reviewed experimental research to the exclusion of correlational studies. Indeed, when Klahr listed what he considered to be the five general approaches to the empirical study of science, he excluded personality and differential research altogether.

Although I believe both research traditions have captured a portion of the truth, their exclusiveness prevents psychologists from acquiring a complete understanding of scientific creativity. If our aim is to reconcile the logic and genius perspectives, then it would seem that our first task is to devise a new psychology of science that avoids the narrow commitments of the two established psychologies of science. This third psychology of science does not concentrate on either the process or the person but rather focuses on the product (Simonton, 2003b). This shift not only may help resolve the disciplinary division, but it also makes good sense. After all, ultimately it is the product that counts, the process and the person providing solely the means to that end. Indeed, the product provides the final criterion of whether the process or the person can be considered creative (Simonton, 2000a). The creative process is defined as those mental operations that result in creative products; the creative person is that individual who has the capacity to generate creative products. Just as important is the fact that science itself cares more about the products than about either the processes or the persons behind those products. What is really important about, say, Albert Einstein, is not how he pondered problems or what kind of personality traits he possessed, but rather his concrete contributions to theoretical physics. When he received the Nobel Prize for Physics in 1921, it was Einstein's ideas that were being honored, not his cognitive processes or character quirks.

In this chapter, I implement this shift in focus by scrutinizing creative products in two contexts. First, I examine the distribution of publications in scientific careers. Second, I investigate the characteristic features of multiple discoveries that emerge within scientific communities. Thus,

15

scientific products are treated from two levels of analysis: the individual and the group.

SCIENTIFIC CAREERS: PUBLICATIONS

In the early stages of modern science, scientists communicated their creative ideas largely by publishing books. This modus operandi is illustrated not only by Newton's *Principia*, but also by Copernicus' *On the Revolutions of the Heavenly Spheres*, Kepler's *The Harmonies of the World*, and Galileo's *Dialogues Concerning the Two New Sciences*. With the advent of scientific periodicals, such as the *Transactions of the Royal Society of London*, books gradually yielded ground to the technical journal article as the chief form of scientific communication. Of course, books were not abandoned altogether, as Darwin's *Origin of Species* shows. Even so, it eventually became possible for scientists to establish a reputation for their creative contributions without publishing a single book-length treatment of their ideas. For instance, the revolutionary ideas that earned Einstein his Nobel Prize – concerning the special theory of relativity, the photoelectric effect, and Brownian motion – appeared as papers in the *Annalen der Physik*. His status as one of the greatest scientists of all time does not depend on the publication of a single book.

This historic change in scientific publication patterns has two important assets.

1. The supremacy of journal articles means that creative ideas are conveyed in smaller packets. Rather than work for years on a single magnum opus, like Newton did for his *Principia* and Darwin did for his *Origin*, contributions could be developed in a series of papers. So instead of having a few hefty monographs to mark creative output, we can investigate hundreds of scientific journal articles. This downscaling of the publication unit enables a more fine-grained analysis of how creative products are distributed across or within creative careers. In particular, smaller parcels permit a more precise determination of the

timing of creative ideas. Newton did not publish the *Principia* until 1687, when he was 45, even though some of the key ideas contained in that work, such as universal gravitation, occurred to him more than 20 years earlier. In contrast, when Einstein first arrived at the idea of special relativity, he could publish the theory almost immediately, in a paper appearing when he was just 26 years old. Afterward he would publish a series of articles developing relativity theory ever further, after about a decade reaching the point where he could propose his general theory of relativity.

2. Journal articles provide an objective basis for defining the creativity of scientific products. To be published in high-impact scientific journals, a submitted paper must first undergo the process of peer review. Moreover, the criteria applied to determine acceptance or rejection are very similar to standard definitions of the creative product (see, e.g., Wolff, 1970, 1973). Specifically, to be considered creative a product must be (1) original, novel, or surprising to those who define a domain of creativity and (2) meet standards appropriate to that creative domain. By the same token, to be accepted by a major journal requires that a submitted manuscript present new theory or research and that it satisfy certain standards of logic and fact. Accordingly, publication by a peer-reviewed journal provides a minimum criterion for counting as a creative product. However, because even published articles can vary appreciably in scientific creativity, this minimum criterion can be replaced by one more rigorous – namely, whether the article received citations in subsequent articles (Garfield, 1987; Price, 1965). This is a more demanding test than might first appear because a very large percentage of scientific publications are never cited at all. For instance, of 783,339 papers published in scientific journals in 1981, 81% were cited 10 times or less, and 47% were not cited at all between 1981 and June 1997 (Redner, 1998). Of course, the cutoff might be raised even higher by requiring that the publication be cited a certain number of times within a specified time interval (e.g., Simonton, 1985).

Given that the journal article provides the primary definition of the creative product, I want to address two questions about scientific careers. First, how do scientists differ in the amount of creativity they display? Second, how does creativity change across the course of any given scientist's career?

Individual Variation

The word "genius" is often used in a misleading manner. Too frequently it is applied as if it were a categorical label. This application assumes that a person either has genius or none at all, without admission of gradations between. Hence, Einstein was a scientific genius, whereas Marcel Grossmann, his onetime college classmate and sometime collaborator, was not. This dichotomous usage overlooks the fact that an underlying continuous dimension connects Einstein and Grossmann. That is, although scientists vary greatly in the influence they exert over their respective disciplines, this variation is a matter of degree rather than kind (Cole & Cole, 1973). One useful means to place a scientist on the implicit scale is to consider the various honors and awards that are listed on his or her curriculum vitae. At the highest level are those who have received international recognition, such as a Nobel Prize (Berry, 1981; Zuckerman, 1977) or at least election to scientific academies or societies in countries other than the nation in which they work (Candolle, 1873). At a bit lower grade are those who have earned national recognition, such as membership in the National Academy of Sciences (Feist, 1993; Over, 1981) or the Royal Society of London (Galton, 1874; Hudson, 1958). Lower still are those who are recognized by discipline-specific honors. An instance within psychology is the Distinguished Scientific Contribution Award of the American Psychological Association (Simonton, 1985). Below this level is recognition like fellow status within a division of a specialized scientific society. Finally, at the bottom are those active scientists who have not earned any special recognition for their work.

This conspicuous variation in recognition has two crucial features. First, individual differences in the scope or prestige in honors correlates highly with alternative indicators of distinction, including expert ratings or eminence gauged by biographical dictionaries, encyclopedias, or histories (Simonton, 1984e, 2002). In fact, alternative indicators of differential impact are demonstrably a function of a single latent variable (Simonton, 1991b). Thus, they all represent the same underlying construct – namely, the differential impact a scientist has on his or her discipline. Second, and even more critical, this cross-sectional variation in disciplinary impact is ultimately grounded in individual differences in creative productivity (Cole & Cole, 1967; Feist, 1997; Feist & Barron, 2003; Simonton, 1991a). For instance, the total lifetime output of a 19th century scientist predicts the probability that he or she will have an entry in a 20th century edition of the *Encyclopaedia Britannica* (Dennis, 1954a; Simonton, 1984c). Similarly, future Nobel laureates can be predicted on the basis of the total number of citations candidate scientists receive to their body of work (Ashton & Oppenheim, 1978), and yet the single most critical predictor of citations is the total number of publications (Cole &Cole, 1973; Simonton, 2002).

Therefore, to comprehend how scientists differ in overall impact, it is essential to understand precisely how scientists differ in output. This understanding involves two key features: the skewed nature of the cross-sectional distribution and the probabilistic relation between quantity and quality.

Elitist Distribution. Great scientists tend to be highly prolific. This is evident in the lifetime publication counts of the following scientists: biologist Charles Darwin, 119; psychologist Gustav Fechner, 267; physiologist, Johannes Müller 285; physicist Albert Einstein, 607; mathematician Leonhard Euler, 856; and chemist Wilhelm Ostwald, 5,545 (Bringmann & Balk, 1983). Admittedly, these specific numbers may be misleading insofar as scientific disciplines vary in the size of the *least-publishable unit.* Some fields favor lots of short publications, others somewhat fewer but longer publications. Nevertheless, even when we restrict the analysis to specific disciplines, the same pattern emerges. Within any given domain, a small number of the scientists account for a disproportionate number of the publications. The dominance of this prolific elite appears because the productivity distribution is highly skewed so that the modal level of lifetime output is a single contribution, ignoring those who published nothing at all. In more formal terms, creative productivity is best described by some variety of lognormal or, better yet, exponential distribution (Huber, 1999; Shockley, 1957; Simon, 1955).

This distinctive distribution is sometimes expressed in the form of Lotka's law (Huber, 2001; Lotka, 1926; Price, 1963). This law holds that the number of scientists who make exactly T total contributions is inversely proportional to T^2. Stated more formally, the law asserts that $f(T) = cT^{-2}$, whare c is a positive constant. Hence according to this "inverse-square law of productivity ... [f]or every 100 authors who produce but a single paper ... there are 25 with two, 11 with three, and so on" (Price, 1963, p. 43). If both sides of this equation are subjected to a logarithmic transformation, we obtain the linear expression $\log f(T) = \log c - 2 \log T$. This implies that if the number of persons producing T contributions as a function of T is plotted on a double-log graph, the data points should closely approximate a straight line. This implication has been confirmed for data sources as diverse as the *Philosophical Transactions of the Royal Society of London* and *Chemical Abstracts* (Price, 1963).

A more dramatic way of depicting the elitist distribution is to calculate the proportion of a discipline's total publications that can be ascribed to scientists of varying degrees of lifetime output. Typically, the most prolific scientists account for the lion's share of the total scientific literature in any given discipline (Dennis, 1954a, 1954b, 1955; Price, 1963). For instance, one empirical study randomly sampled 200 contributors to each of the following four disciplines: chemistry, geology, gerontology and geriatrics, and infantile paralysis (Dennis, 1955). The total number of lifetime contributions was then determined for each scientist. No matter what the discipline, the same pattern emerged (see also Kyvik, 1989). First, the scientists in the elite 10% according to total output were responsible for nearly

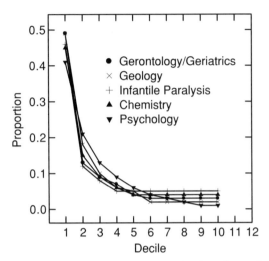

FIGURE 2.1. Proportion of total contributions to the disciplines of chemistry, geology, gerontology and geriatrics, and infantile paralysis produced by scientists in different deciles. Graph constructed from tabular information published by Dennis (1955).

50% of the publications. Second, at the other end of the distribution, approximately half the scientists in each discipline could be credited with just one lifetime contribution. Indeed, the scientists in the bottom half of the productivity distribution account for fewer total publications than the scientists who form the top 10% elite. If all the contributions by the scientists in the bottom half of the distribution were lost to the world, then each discipline would still retain more than 82% of its scientific publications. Figure 2.1 displays the proportions provided for each of the 10 deciles for the four disciplines. The elitism seen in this graph could hardly be more salient.

What makes the above findings so striking is that the probability distribution departs markedly from the normal distribution that has been attributed to human abilities ever since the days of Francis Galton (1869). To put this discrepancy in perspective, suppose IQ exhibited the same skewed distribution as seen in lifetime productivity. Then it would be commonplace to have persons whose IQs were more than 15 standard deviations above the mean (Simonton, 1988b). Clearly, any adequate theory of scientific creativity must account for this prominent incongruity. At first glance, the genius perspective looks most promising. It might even seem reasonable to claim that anyone who rises to the top decile in total output can be unequivocally identified as a bona fide scientific genius.

Equal-Odds Rule. Yet, one objection to the foregoing attribution can be raised: the reported results are based on total quantity of lifetime output regardless of the quality of that output. This emphasis ignores the fact that a very large percentage of publications have no impact on their scientific disciplines. Perhaps the distribution might be less elitist if we confined our attention to just high-impact work. But this objection has no empirical support. The distribution of quality does not differ substantially from the distribution of quantity (Simonton, 1999c). For example, a small proportion of the scientists in any field account for a disproportionate number of citations in the research literature (Helmreich et al., 1980; Myers, 1970; Redner, 1998; White & White, 1978). More significantly, scientists who publish the most highly cited works also publish the most poorly cited works, so that quality is a probabilistic consequence of quantity (Simonton, 1997a). In fact, the ratio of high-impact publications to total output – the *hit rate* – is uncorrelated with total output (Davis, 1987; Platz, 1965; Platz & Blakelock, 1960; Simonton, 1985; White & White, 1978). This has been called the *equal-odds rule* (Simonton, 1997a; cf. Simonton, 1988a).

To better appreciate the claims of this principle, let us consider two alternative scenarios that would contradict the equal-odds rule (Simonton, 2003c). On the one hand, suppose the hit rate were a positive linear function of total output. In other words, those scientists who are most prolific have a larger proportion of hits to misses. If total lifetime output is given by T and the total count of high-impact works is given by H (where $T \gg H$), then the hit rate is $H/T = \rho T$, where ρ is a proportionality constant ($\rho > 0$). It necessarily follows, then, that $H = \rho T^2$. In other words, quality would be a *quadratic* rather than linear function of quantity. On the other hand, suppose the hit rate was a negative function of total output – that is, those scientists who are the most prolific produce a higher proportion of low-quality works (i.e., $\rho < 0$). Then function would remain quadratic, but with a decelerating rather than accelerating curve. Both of these predictions are inconsistent with the empirical evidence gathered to date (Simonton, 2003b); that is, the scientific literature appears to support the conclusion that the quality–quantity relation is best described by the linear function $H = \rho T$ ($0 < \rho < 1$).

Interestingly, the equal-odds rule also applies to gender differences in scientific creativity. Specifically, although female scientists tend to be cited less than male scientists, they also tend to be less productive in an equal proportion, so that the citation-per-publication rate is gender invariant (Long, 1992; Over, 1982, 1990). In other words, within any given discipline, the quality ratio is the same regardless of gender. Hence, attempts to comprehend the differential impact of men and women scientists must focus on the factors that determine their output rates (e.g., Cole, 1987; Kyvik, 1990; Xie &Shauman, 2003; Zuckerman, Cole, & Bruer, 1991). Otherwise, on a publication-for-publication basis, female scientists are just as likely as male scientists to have impact.

Naturally, the equal-odds rule operates only on the average. Some scientists are seemingly *perfectionists* with hit rates higher than average, whereas other scientists are apparent *mass producers* with hit rates lower than average (Cole & Cole, 1972; Feist, 1997). Even so, these departures from statistical expectation are in line with the probabilistic nature of the association (Simonton, 1997a, 1999c). Because the quantity–quality correlation seldom exceeds .70, and often falls closer to .50, the amount of variance shared between the two distributions does not exceed one-half and frequently can be as low as .25. Ample latitude accordingly remains for the existence of considerable scatter around the regression line. Yet, there is no evidence that these residuals or errors represent distinct types of scientists in a taxometric sense (Simonton, 1999c). On the contrary, the departures from statistical expectation are precisely what would be anticipated

23

from a statistical association of this magnitude. For example, suppose the correlation between total publications and the number of highly cited publications is around .50. If the measures of quantity and quality are dichotomized at their respective medians, this correlation implies that 25% of scientists are either high-quality and low-quantity perfectionists or high-quantity and low-quality mass producers. Even so, these "exceptions to the rule" merely confirm the statistical nature of the association. The scientists conforming to statistical expectation still outnumber the exceptions 3 to 1 (Cole & Cole, 1972; Feist, 1997; Helmreich, Spence, & Thorbecke, 1981).

To some extent, the equal-odds rule undermines the genius perspective on scientific creativity. Highly influential scientists do not seem to possess some special ability or skill that permits them to circumvent the "chanciness" of scientific research. Hence, the genius and chance perspectives must somehow be reconciled if we seek a comprehensive view of creativity in science. The urgency of this reconciliation becomes all the more paramount when we turn to the second aspect of creative productivity.

Longitudinal Change

The equal-odds rule has more applications besides the relation between quantity and quality across scientific careers. In particular, complementary results emerge when the inquiry turns to longitudinal fluctuations in output *within* careers rather than cross-sectional distributions of output *across* careers (Simonton, 1988a, 1991a, 1997a). In general, the periods during the course of a scientist's career in which the most total output is produced tend to be those periods in which the most high-impact works appear (Cole, 1979; Oromaner, 1977; Over, 1988, 1989; Simonton, 1984c, 1985). In other words, quality is once again a probabilistic consequence of quantity, as specified by the equal-odds rule (Simonton, 1988a, 1997a). Stated more emphatically, the ratio of high-impact work to total output in any given period neither increases nor decreases across the career course. These conclusions are demonstrated by a statistical analysis (Simonton,

1984c) of data published on the productivity and citation counts of hundreds of chemists, geologists, mathematicians, physicists, psychologists, and sociologists (Cole, 1979). The correlation between productivity and citation counts across consecutive career periods is .77, indicating that 59% of the variance is shared. In addition, the ratio of citations to publications correlates −.02 with the scientist's age at each career period, signifying that amount of shared variance is virtually zero (namely, .004%). These scientists could not improve their hit rate as their careers progressed.

Just as significant is the manner in which output is distributed across the career course. Table 2.1 shows a typical outcome for 10 hypothetical scientists, each of whom made 25 contributions spread over 20 career years. Expressed differently, each scientist averaged 1.25 publications per year (i.e., the mean annual output $\mu = 1.25$). This table illustrates two crucial empirical findings:

1. The output of products tends to be randomly distributed across the career course (Huber, 1998a, 1998b, 2000, 2002; Huber & Wagner-Döbler, 2001a, 2001b); that is, when one scrutinizes yearly time series one rarely discerns significant "runs" at any point in the career, whether at the beginning, middle, or end. This random distribution holds for all alternative definitions of what constitutes a scientific product, such as patents awarded for new inventions or original articles published in refereed journals.

2. Somewhat less obviously, the number of products that appear in any given year is Poisson distributed (Huber, 1998a, 1998b, 2002; Huber & Wagner-Döbler, 2001a, 2001b). This fact has been demonstrated for scientific domains as diverse as mathematical logic, physics, biology, psychology, and technology (Huber, 2001). In the hypothetical example shown in Table 2.1, 22.5% of the years exhibit zero output, 39.5% merely one product, 29.5% two products, 7.5% three products, and merely 1.0% four products.

The significance of the last finding becomes more apparent if I pause a moment to describe the nature of the Poisson distribution, a distribution

TABLE 2.1. Representative Productivity Distributions for Ten Hypothetical Scientists

Scientist	Career year																			
	1	2	3	4	5	6	7	8	9	10	11	12	13	14	15	16	17	18	19	20
1	1	1	0	2	2	1	3	2	0	1	0	3	0	1	2	1	1	0	2	2
2	2	2	0	1	1	2	0	1	2	0	1	2	3	2	1	1	1	2	0	1
3	2	1	1	0	2	0	1	3	0	2	1	2	1	1	2	1	2	2	1	0
4	0	1	2	0	2	0	1	3	1	4	0	0	2	1	1	1	1	2	1	2
5	2	1	0	1	0	1	1	3	2	1	1	2	3	2	1	1	2	1	0	0
6	0	0	1	1	2	1	2	1	2	0	1	1	2	0	1	3	2	2	2	1
7	2	2	0	1	2	0	1	1	2	3	1	2	0	3	1	2	1	0	1	0
8	1	2	0	2	2	1	3	0	1	1	3	2	1	0	0	1	0	1	2	2
9	2	1	0	2	1	1	2	4	0	0	2	1	3	0	1	1	0	2	1	1
10	1	1	2	1	2	1	0	3	2	1	1	1	2	3	2	1	0	0	1	0

Note: Each scientist is presumed to produce 25 contributions randomly distributed over 20 career years, with a Poisson distribution for the number of contributions per yearly unit (where $\mu = 1.25$).

that will become useful later in the next chapter as well (Haight, 1967; Molina, 1942). The Poisson distribution, like the normal distribution, can be derived from the binomial distribution with the parameters p (the probability of an event) and n (the number of trials). However, unlike holds for the normal distribution, the derivation of the Poisson distribution assumes that p is extremely small and n is extremely large. Furthermore, unlike the equation for the normal distribution, which has two parameters, the mean (μ) and the variance (σ^2), the equation describing the Poisson distribution has just one parameter because the mean equals the variance (i.e., $\mu = \sigma^2$, where $\mu = np$ as $n \to \infty$). In particular, the probability of j events occurring within a given time unit is given by

$$P(j) = \mu^j e^{-\mu}/j! \tag{2.1}$$

Here e is the exponential constant 2.718 … and $j! = 1 \times 2 \times 3 \times \ldots \times j$. The main asset of the Poisson distribution is its broad applicability to low-probability events; that is, it applies to events that are so unlikely that they can take place at all only because the number of trials is so large. By implication, the output of a creative product in a given year must be considered a relatively improbable event for the vast majority of scientists.

To illustrate this fact, we can turn to a study of the publication rate of scientists working at a major research laboratory (Shockley, 1957). Of the 162 scientists in the lab, 139 (86%) averaged fewer than one publication per year (i.e., in terms of the Equation 2.1, $\mu < 1$). In fact, 64 (40%) produced not one single publication during a 4-year interval. Moreover, 160, or 99%, averaged fewer than two publications per year (i.e., $\mu < 2$). Of the two remaining scientists, one averaged two publications per year and the other averaged three (i.e., μs of 2 and 3, respectively). Across all scientists in the laboratory, the average publication rate per scientist per year was only .12. Even when the scientists who published nothing are deleted, the per capita annual output increases to just .80. The sole reason why the laboratory was able to produce around 20 publications per year was that it contained so many research scientists, including a few who were reasonably productive.

The above example suggests that the productivity distribution discussed earlier may be even more elitist than suggested by Lotka's law or the proportions given in Figure 2.1. After all, at that point we considered exclusively those scientists who made at least one contribution to science. Hence, the statement that the modal level of lifetime output is solely one product may apply only to those scientists who attained that threshold degree of productivity. It is impossible to determine the exact size of this totally silent group – the purely noncreative scientists of the world. Nevertheless, it is clear that creative scientists represent a subset of the available pool of scientists if the latter is defined by those who manage to earn a Ph.D. in a scientific discipline (Bloom, 1963). Not every Ph.D. in the sciences even manages to publish his or her doctoral dissertation.

Although the last conclusion seems compatible with the genius perspective, that perspective is still challenged by how creative products are distributed across the career. One would expect geniuses to able to improve their hit rate over the course of their career, and produce more "runs" in total output in the latter part of their career. In addition, the Poisson distribution of yearly output is more in line with what would be expected from a chance perspective. Scientific creativity seems more a matter of luck. Of course, these empirical findings are not any more friendly with the logic and zeitgeist perspectives, which tend to have a more deterministic view of creativity in science. To the degree that quantity and quality of output are probabilistic, it is hard to contend that discoveries and inventions are inevitable products of either logical reasoning or the sociocultural system.

SCIENTIFIC COMMUNITIES: MULTIPLES

Psychologists often tend to view scientific creativity as a process that takes place within the individual (Simonton, 2000a). This viewpoint has antecedents in the common myth of the "lone genius," who risks social isolation to produce unprecedented masterworks. For instance, this myth is apparent in Wordsworth's description of Newton as "for ever voyaging through strange seas of thought alone" (Jeans, 1942, p. 711). Yet this image is totally misleading. The individual scientist necessarily works within the context of a larger community of scientists, including those scientists who contribute to the same discipline (Crane, 1972). Even the somewhat solitary Newton maintained contacts with numerous other scientists (Simonton, 1992b). Among the notables who participated in Newton's disciplinary network were Johann Bernoulli, James Bradley, Abraham DeMoivre, John Flamsteed, Edmund Halley, Robert Hooke, Gottfried Wilhelm Leibniz, John Locke, John Wallis, and Christopher Wren. Furthermore, these relationships were often instrumental rather than merely incidental to Newton's scientific creativity. Halley, for one, played a major part in getting Newton to publish the *Principia Mathematica*. Newton may have been introverted, but he was not isolated. Once the analysis is expanded to encompass many scientists working within the same discipline, a new phenomenon becomes possible that has no counterpart at the individual level – the phenomenon of scientific multiples. As pointed out in Chapter 1, multiples occur when two or more scientists independently make the same discovery. I also noted that this phenomenon is often evoked to undermine the role individual genius plays in scientific advance. However, this inference depends on an excessively superficial look at the historical data (Simonton, 1987, 1999c). Specifically, multiples have four critical characteristics that do not lend themselves so readily to a zeitgeist interpretation. These are the distribution of multiple grades, the temporal separation of multiple discoveries, individual variation in multiple participation, and the degree of multiple identity.

Distribution of Multiple Grades

Table 2.2 provides a list of representative multiples from a diversity of disciplines (cf. Kroeber, 1963; Ogburn & Thomas, 1922; Simonton, 1994). Alongside each multiple are the names of the contributors and the dates of their respective contributions. It should be apparent from inspection of this collection that multiples do not constitute a homogeneous phenomenon. Rather, multiples differ along several parameters. Most

TABLE 2.2. Representative Multiple Discoveries and Inventions with Contributors and Approximate Dates

Mathematics
  Equation of the cycloid – Roberval 1640, Torricelli 1644
  Calculus – Newton 1671, Leibniz 1676
  Quadratic reciprocity law – Euler 1772, Legendre 1785, Gauss 1796
  Non-Euclidean geometry – Gauss 1799, Lobachevsky 1826, Bolyai 1832
Astronomy
  Sunspots – Galileo 1610, Fabricius 1611, Scheiner 1611, Harriott 1611
  Stellar parallax – Bessel 1838, F. Struve 1838, Henderson 1838
  Neptune predicted – J. C. Adams 1845, Leverrier 1846
  Hyperion (Saturn satellite) – W. C. Bond 1848, Lassell 1848
Physics
  Law of gases – Boyle 1662, Mariotte 1676
  Leyden jar condenser – E. G. Kleist 1745, van Musschenbroek 1746
  Electromagnetic induction – J. Henry 1830, Faraday 1831
  Conservation of energy – J. R. von Mayer 1843, Helmholtz 1847, Joule 1847
  Liquifaction of oxygen – Cailletet 1877, Pictet 1877
  Wave properties of electron – G. P. Thomson 1927, Davisson and Germer 1927
Chemistry
  Oxygen – Priestley 1774, Scheele 1774
  H_2O – Cavendish 1781, Watt 1781, Lavoisier & Laplace 1783, Monge 1783
  Periodic law of elements – DeChancourtis 1862, Newlands 1864, L. Meyer 1869, Mendeleev 1869
  Stereochemistry of carbon – Van' Hoff 1874, Le Bel 1874
Biology
  Spinal nerve root functions – C. Bell 1811, Magendie 1822
  Evolution by natural selection – C. Darwin 1844, Wallace 1858
  Genetic laws – Mendel 1865, De Vries 1900, Correns 1900, Tschermak 1900
  Bat echolocation – Griffen & Galambos 1942, Dijkgraat 1943

TABLE 2.2. (*Continued*)

Medicine
Ether anesthesia in surgery – C. W. Long 1842, Morton 1846
Puerperal fever contagious – O. W. Holmes 1843, Semmelweiss 1847
Ophthalmoscope – C. Babbage 1847, Helmholtz 1851, Anagnostakis
1854
Plague bacillus – Yersin 1894, Kitasato 1894
Technology
Photography – Daguerre 1839, Talbot 1839
Telephone – A. G. Bell 1876, E. Gray 1876
Incandescent lamp carbon filament – Edison 1878, Swan 1879
Aluminum electrolytic production – C. M. Hall 1886, Héroult 1886

Note. The claims are not all equally secure.

---

obviously, multiples can be categorized along disciplinary lines. But other distinctions are both subtler and more important. Especially significant are the contrasts in the multiple's *grade* (Simonton, 1979). The grade is simply the count of the number of rival claimants to the discovery or invention. The greater the number of independent discoverers or inventors, the higher is the multiple's designated grade. Clearly, the lowest possible grade for a multiple is 2, because grade 1 would indicate that the contribution is a *singleton* (Merton, 1961b). The upper limit, however, is an empirical issue. Although the highest grade multiple may be the telescope, with as many as nine independent claimants (Simonton, 1986d), most multiples are of lower grade (Price, 1963). This is evident in Table 2.2 where most of the multiples are grade 2.

In fact, just as we can scrutinize the distribution of creative productivity, so can we analyze the distribution of multiple grades (Price, 1963). When we do so, it becomes immediately apparent that the frequency of a given multiple declines as the grade increases. Hence, doublets are the most common, triplets the next most common, and so on, with high grade multiples represented by just one or two cases. For instance, the most comprehensive

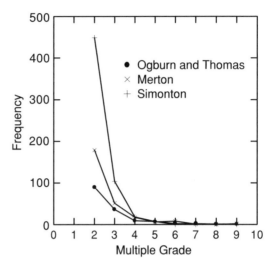

FIGURE 2.2. The frequency of various multiple grades for three data sets: Ogburn and Thomas (1922), Merton (1961b), and Simonton (1979).

collection gathered to date claimed 449 doublets, but only 104 triplets, 18 quadruplets, 7 quintuplets, and 1 octuplet (Simonton, 1979). Less complete samples yield similar results, as is graphically depicted in Figure 2.2. Indeed, it should be evident that the more exhaustive is the sample of multiples, the larger is the disparity between low- and high-grade multiples (Simonton, 1987).

It is not apparent how the zeitgeist interpretation could handle this empirical reality. Indeed, if sociocultural determinism truly guarantees the inevitability of discoveries and inventions, it would seem that higher grade multiples would be far more common than lower grade multiples (Simonton, 1979). This point can be illustrated by using the binomial distribution for $n = 10$ and $p = .9$. These parameters describe a zeitgeist scenario where for any given discovery there are 10 scientists capable of making it, each with a 90% probability of success. Under these conditions, 35% of all discoveries should be grade 10, 39% grade 9, 19% grade 8, 6% grade 7, and 1% grade 6. Those percentages add up to 100% because multiples of grades less than 6 would occur less than 0.2% of the time. One could hardly imagine a distribution more discrepant from what is shown in Figure 2.2.

Temporal Separation of Multiple Discoveries

Advocates of the zeitgeist theory of creativity place great emphasis on the fact that many multiples are not just independently discovered but are also *simultaneously* discovered (Kroeber, 1917; Lamb & Easton, 1984). If two or more individuals make the same discovery at the same time, then surely the discovery must have been inevitable. Thus, it is apparent from inspection of Table 2.2 that many multiples occurred within the same calendar year. Actually, some multiples were more simultaneous than the dates imply. W. C. Bond and W. Lassell independently observed Hyperion, Saturn's seventh satellite, on the exact same night, and Bell and Gray announced their independent invention of the telephone to the U.S. Patent Office within just a few hours of each other. Yet how common are these dramatic episodes of simultaneity? Do all multiples occur within a year's time?

According to one study of 264 cases, fully 20% of the independent contributions took place within a 1-year interval (Merton, 1961b). Nevertheless, that leaves 80% of the multiples with temporal separations of two years or more. Hence, strictly simultaneous discoveries and inventions are the exception rather than the rule. Even more tellingly, 34% of the 264 multiples required at least a decade to transpire before the duplications ceased (Merton, 1961b). Indeed, occasionally hundreds of years divide the first and last instance of a multiple (e.g., the discovery of the Eustacian tubes, the principles of hydrostatics, the transit of Venus across the solar disk). In cases of wide temporal separation it may be more correct to use the term rediscovery rather than multiple. Such rediscoveries are difficult to accommodate within sociocultural determinism. If the discovery of genetic laws was absolutely inevitable in 1865, then why did they have to be rediscovered in 1900? It is not sufficient to claim that Mendel was "ahead of his time" if the times (zeitgeist) determine what can and cannot be conceived. It seems preferable to separate the origination of ideas from the acceptance of ideas. According to William James (1880),

social evolution is a resultant of the interaction of two wholly distinct factors: the individual, deriving his peculiar gifts from the play of psychological and infra-social forces, but bearing all the power of initiative and origination in his hands; and, second, the social environment, with its power of adopting or rejecting both him and his gifts. (p. 448)

The zeitgeist decided whether Mendel's epochal experiments would have a contemporary impact but did not determine the ideas that emerged from those experiments.

Individual Variation in Multiple Participation

Needless to say, involvement in a multiple is often an unpleasant experience. Charles Darwin had been working on his theory of evolution for more than a dozen years only to learn that his labors were about to be preempted by a paper by Alfred Wallace outlining an identical theory. Darwin was understandably upset and ended up taking measures that helped ensure his priority. Although this episode ended amicably for the participants, this is not always the case (Merton, 1961b). Often bitter priority disputes result, such as the nasty charges of plagiarism that Newton raised against Leibniz in the controversy over who should get the credit for inventing calculus. At the same time, it is evident that scientists may vary in the frequency that they see their work anticipated by other colleagues. Just as multiples form a subset of all scientific products, so do scientists involved in priority disputes form a subset of all scientific creators. Furthermore, scientists who participate in more than one multiple would be rarer still.

The question then arises whether scientists who have a propensity to participate in multiples tend to differ systematically from those who exhibit no such inclination. Empirical research has identified two factors associated with such involvement (Simonton, 2003b). First, the higher the number of total contributions an individual makes to science, the larger the number of multiples in which he or she participates (Simonton, 1979). Thus, the same factor that determines the output of high-impact works also determines participation in multiples. Duplication is partly a repercussion of quantity. Second, those scientists who are active in large fields with many active colleagues tend to get involved in multiples at higher rates than do "lone wolves" who carve out a specialty uniquely their own (Hagstrom, 1974). In other words, the proclivity for getting involved in multiples depends on the size of the scientific community to which the scientist belongs.

Sociocultural determinism would have a hard time explaining the first factor. As mentioned earlier in this chapter, prolific output is an individual property associated with genius, not the zeitgeist. On the other hand, the second factor appears more compatible with the zeitgeist interpretation. The zeitgeist presumably is embedded in the scientific community that defines the important problems and the means for their solution. Yet, even here an objection emerges: how can someone be a lone wolf? That implies that creative scientists can escape the constraints of the zeitgeist, a possibility closer to the notion of genius.

Degree of Multiple Identity

Those who claim that multiples establish the creative efficacy of the zeitgeist fail to point out that multiples constitute a very small proportion of all discoveries and inventions. The largest collection of multiples ever compiled consisted of merely 579 cases (Simonton, 1979). That may seem like an impressive figure, but solely if we overlook the fact that this sample was drawn from an initial sample consisting of thousands of contributions. Hence, multiples are extremely rare relative to singletons. To be sure, some have argued that many singletons are actually multiples incognito. According to Merton (1961b), "all scientific discoveries are in principle multiples, including those that on the surface appear to be singletons" (p. 477). For instance, multiples-in-the-making might have been preempted because scientists learn that a problem has already been solved before they managed to reach the solution themselves. Thus, it is highly likely that Linus Pauling eventually would have deciphered the structure of DNA had not Watson and Crick beat him to the punch.

As plausible as this argument may sound, it is just as easy to argue that many supposed multiples are actually singletons (Simonton, 1987). Specifically, many candidates fail to pass one or both of two essential criteria. The first criterion is independence. Thus, Galileo is sometimes credited with the independent invention of the telescope even though he had already heard of its invention by Dutch lens grinders. Similarly, Dolland and C. M. Hall are often given dual credit for devising the achromatic lens even though Dolland probably knew of Hall's prior work on the problem. Naturally, this criterion is a very hard one to apply. Frequently scientists are motivated to hide the fact that they have "borrowed" ideas from their contemporaries or predecessors. Without an overt acknowledgment, it is extremely difficult to establish the intellectual debt. For instance, it was discovered recently that David Hilbert, the great mathematician, had stolen an idea from Albert Einstein, an act of surreptitious plagiarism revealed only after Hilbert's corrected proofs were finally scrutinized (Corry, Renn, & Stachel, 1997). Hilbert had evidently altered the proofs after seeing Einstein's unpublished manuscript introducing the novel concept. Ironically, for a long time it was suggested that Einstein had lifted the idea from Hilbert's published paper! Admittedly, we can never know for sure how many multiples are actually singletons by this criterion. Even so, the longer is the time separation between the duplicates, the lower the odds of their genuine independence.

The second criterion is identity. Strictly speaking, multiples are indeed duplicates. According to the zeitgeist perspective, the ideas are "in the air" like ripe fruit for the picking. It is for that reason that genius is supposed to be so irrelevant. An apple remains an apple no matter who happens to pick it. Yet when the identity criterion is applied to most reputed multiples, a great many cases are found wanting (Patinkin, 1983; Schmookler, 1966). Frequently, the cases are "based on a failure to distinguish between the genius and the individual" (Schmookler, 1966, p. 191); that is, the independent contributions can be lumped together only by imposing extremely inclusive, generic categories that have no precise meaning. For instance, the supposed multiple invention of the "steam turbine" places under one generic category machines that have dramatically different designs and that operate under totally different physical principles (Constant, 1978). Another interesting case is nuclear magnetic resonance, which was independently and simultaneously observed in 1946 by Purcell, Torrey, and Pound at Harvard and by Bloch, Hansen, and Packard at Stanford. Nevertheless, although physicists "have come to look at the two experiments as practically identical," said Purcell, "when Hansen first showed up [at our lab] and started talking about it, it was about an hour before either of us understood how the other was trying to explain it" (Zuckerman, 1977, p. 203).

To be sure, genuinely identical multiples may occur. For example, when Charles Darwin read Wallace's 1858 paper he said, "I never saw a more striking coincidence; if Wallace had my MS. sketch written out in 1842, he could not have made a better short abstract! Even his terms now stand as heads of my chapters. . . . So all my originality, whatever it may amount to, will be smashed" (F. Darwin, 1892/1958, p. 196). Nonetheless, identical duplicates are extremely rare. Most multiples vary greatly in the magnitude of similarity that holds the contributions together under a single generic category. In fact, just as multiples vary regarding their grade and temporal separation, so can they vary according to the degree to which they actually represent similar contributions. This variation is evident in the interference proceedings that take place before the United States Patent Office when one patent application is claimed to infringe upon an earlier patent (Schmookler, 1966). Typically, the overlap involves merely one feature out of over a hundred that may be specified in the application. It is extremely rare for two features to be involved, and genuine duplication practically never occurs.

The rarity of identity lends some support to the genius perspective. Geniuses are usually conceived as possessing some unique vision or style that renders them sui generis. Even scientific geniuses have personal characteristics that give their work an identifiable distinctiveness (Holton, 1971–72, 1982). This personal imprint even shows up in domains as abstract as mathematics. Thus, Boltzmann said, "a mathematician will recognize Cauchy, Gauss, Jacobi, or Helmholtz, after reading a few pages, just as musicians recognized, from the first few bars, Mozart, Beethoven, or Schubert" (Koestler, 1964, p. 265). This recognizable style was illustrated by an episode in which Newton submitted a solution to a mathematical challenge that had been posed to the international community. Although the solution was sent anonymously, the recipient immediately claimed that he recognized "the claw of the lion." It is for this reason that the calculus of Newton was not identical to that of Leibniz. Similarly, Darwin's thinking about evolution was not equivalent to Wallace's, a fact that eventually became apparent to both participants in the hypothetical multiple.

CONCLUSION: STATEMENT OF THE PROBLEM

Judging from the empirical literature just reviewed, a satisfactory theory of scientific creativity has a great deal of explaining to do. Looking at scientific careers, we observed phenomena such as the highly skewed distribution of lifetime output, the equal-odds rule connecting quantity and quality across and within careers, and the random distribution of output within a career as well as the Poisson distribution of output in any time unit of that career. Then, turning to scientific communities, we examined the central features of multiples – namely, the distribution of multiple grades, the temporal separation of multiple discoveries, individual variation in multiple participation, and the degree of multiple identity. This wealth of well-established findings must provide severe constraints on the range of possible explanations. In fact, I made it repeatedly clear that many of the results appear to contradict one or more of the four key perspectives presented in Chapter 1. For instance, the equal-odds rule appears to be inconsistent with both the logic and genius perspectives, while the distribution of multiple grades seems to be incompatible with the zeitgeist perspective.

Does this mean we must despair of ever having a unified theoretical explanation? The answer is negative. None of the reported findings rules out
the chance perspective. At least the perspective is not overturned if it is developed to a degree of sophistication worthy of the phenomenon. Then,
once that development is achieved, the other three perspectives on scientific creativity can be allotted their proper place in the comprehensive
theoretical account.

3

Combinatorial Processes

From time to time creative scientists provide introspective reports about the mental processes underlying their discoveries. These self-observations can lay the foundation of a theoretical explanation for the phenomena reviewed in the preceding chapter. Take, for example, the following description Hermann von Helmholtz (1891/1898) offered regarding his own problem-solving triumphs:

> I only succeeded in solving such problems after many devious ways, by the gradually increasing generalisation of favourable examples, and by a series of fortunate guesses. I had to compare myself with an Alpine climber, who, not knowing the way, ascends slowly and with toil, and is often compelled to retrace his steps because his progress is stopped; sometimes by reasoning, and sometimes by accident, he hits upon traces of a fresh path, which again leads him a little further; and finally, when he has reached the goal, he finds to his annoyance a royal road on which he might have ridden up if he had been clever enough to find the right starting-point at the outset. In my memoirs I have, of course, not given the reader an account of my wanderings, but I have described the beaten path on which he can now reach the summit without trouble. (p. 282)

This report clearly describes a process far removed from step-by-step logical analysis. Yet, it is no less distant from the mythical image of the scientific genius who conjures up great ideas by some effortless act of inspiration or flash of insight. And the picture is equally remote from the implication of sociocultural determinism that the creative idea should be nothing more than a ripe apple ready to pick with the lazy sweep of a hand.

In fact, if we had to select a single adjective to describe his problem-solving process, we might say that it was *stochastic*, at least if we use this word in its general rather than mathematical meaning. According to its nontechnical definition, the process is stochastic if it is "characterized by conjecture; conjectural," "involving or containing a random variable or variables," or "involving chance or probability" (*American Heritage Electronic Dictionary*, 1992). The last part of the definition connects the adjective to the noun *chance*. The latter word can be used to indicate "an accidental or unpredictable event," "a favorable set of circumstances; an opportunity," "a risk or hazard; a gamble" (*American Heritage Electronic Dictionary*, 1992). Other concepts closely connected to stochastic and chance are the adjectives *accidental, fortuitous, random, probabilistic,* and *unpredictable*. In other words, to claim that scientific creativity is stochastic is to assert that it entails much more predictive uncertainty than would be expected from (1) a forthright, rational process; (2) a genius with some mysterious insight into the truth; or (3) a deterministic zeitgeist providing an inevitable sociocultural product.

The subjective reports of other scientists permit us to be even more specific about the nature of this probabilistic process. In particular, creativity is often said to be *combinatorial* – that is, it entails the generation of chance combinations. For instance, Jacques Hadamard (1945), the mathematician, claimed that mathematical creativity requires the discovery of unusual but fruitful combinations of ideas. To find such combinations, it is "necessary to construct the very numerous possible combinations, among which the useful ones are to be found" (p. 29). But "it cannot be avoided that this first operation take place, to a certain extent, at random, so that the role of chance is hardly doubtful in this first step of the mental process" (pp. 29–30).

Probably the best known, most graphic, and most useful example is the introspective report provided by Henri Poincaré (1921). In describing

41

one discovery episode, he observed how "ideas rose in crowds; I felt them collide until pairs interlocked, so to speak, making a stable combination" (p. 387). Poincaré compared these colliding images to "the hooked atoms of Epicurus" that jiggle and bump "like the molecules of gas in the kinematic theory of gases" so "their mutual impacts may produce new combinations" (p. 393). Although this quote suggests a fairly random combinatorial process, it is not completely unconstrained. In particular, Poincaré claimed that the ideas participating in the random collisions are provided during the preparation period of the creative process. "The mobilized atoms are . . . not any atoms whatsoever; they are those from which we might reasonably expect the desired solution. Then the mobilized atoms undergo impacts which make them enter into combinations among themselves or with other atoms at rest which they struck against in their course" (p. 389). As a consequence, "the only combinations that have a chance of forming are those where at least one of the elements is one of those atoms freely chosen by our will. Now, it is evidently among these that is found what I called the good combination" (p. 389).

Poincaré's (1921) introspections also imply that just a tiny portion of the ideas generated by the chaotic mental process pass muster by some scientific criterion. As Poincaré expressed it, "among the great numbers of combinations blindly formed . . . almost all are without interest and without utility" (p. 392). One reason why the odds are so small is that the useful or interesting combinations

are those which reveal to us unsuspected kinship between other facts, long known, but wrongly believed to be strangers to one another. . . . [Accordingly,] among chosen combinations the most fertile will often be those formed of elements drawn from domains which are far apart. Not that I mean as sufficing for invention the bringing together of objects as disparate as possible; most combinations so formed would be entirely sterile. But certain among them, very rare, are the most fruitful of all. (p. 386)

But what does it specifically mean to say that good combinations are so rare? What is the actual probability of coming up with a truly creative idea? Michael Faraday, the physicist and chemist, offered a rough estimate in the following observation:

The world little knows how many thoughts and theories which have passed through the mind of a scientific investigator have been crushed in silence and secrecy by his own severe criticism and adverse examinations; that in the most successful instances not a tenth of the suggestions, the hopes, the wishes, the preliminary conclusions have been realized. (Beveridge, 1957, p. 79)

However, Faraday's probability estimate of 1 out of 10 may be too high. These odds apply only to the ideational combinations that hold sufficient promise to have been actively pursued in conscious thought. According to Hadamard (1945), "the intervention of chance occurs inside the unconscious: for most of these combinations – more exactly, all those which are useless – remain unknown to us" (p. 30). Poincaré (1921) similarly said "the sterile combinations do not even present themselves to the mind of the inventor. Never in the field of his consciousness do combinations appear that are not really useful, except some that he rejects but which have to some extent the characteristics of useful combinations" (p. 386). In the last part of this passage, Poincaré allows for the appearance of false hunches. For every 10 hunches, 9 may be false by Faraday's reckoning.

Admittedly, these introspective reports cannot be considered empirical proof that scientific creativity operates according to a chance combinatorial mechanism. Such impressionistic information is fraught with potential biases and errors (Nisbett & Wilson, 1977; Perkins, 1981). Nevertheless, these observations provide the foundation for an explanatory account of the key phenomena associated with both scientific careers and scientific communities. It is to that explanation that I now turn.

ASSUMPTIONS

The goal now is to outline a chance combination model of scientific creativity. Let us begin by recognizing that each individual scientist operates in a specific disciplinary context. That context consists of two essential components – namely the *domain* and the *field* (Csikszentmihalyi, 1990, 1999).

The domain consists of a large but finite set of phenomena, facts, concepts, variables, constants, techniques, theories, laws, questions, goals, and criteria. These can be collectively referred to as the population of *ideas* that make up a given domain. These ideas are equivalent to the "hooked atoms" in Poincaré's (1921) imagery. For instance, quantum mechanics during the course of its development has been defined by ideas such as the adiabatic hypothesis, anharmonic oscillator, Bell's inequality, blackbody radiation, collapse of the wave function, Copenhagen interpretation, correspondence principle, eigenvalue problem, electron spin, exclusion principle, Heisenberg uncertainty principle, hidden variables, indeterminacy, Josephson effect, line spectrum, magnetic dipole moment, many-worlds interpretation, photoelectric effect, Planck's constant, Planck's radiation law, positron, quanta, quantum electrodynamics, quantum oscillation frequency, renormalization, state functions, the Stern–Gerlach experiment, tunneling, virtual oscillators, wavelength, wave equation, wave-particle duality, wave-particle hypothesis, and X-ray scattering.

The field consists of all those individuals who are also working with the set of ideas that define the domain. These are the scientists who are most likely to read, study, evaluate, and build upon the discoveries and inventions created by others in the same specialty. It is they who ultimately decide the impact of any colleague's contribution (e.g., by their decisions regarding what to cite in their own publications). The field of quantum mechanics was partially defined at different times by variable subsets of the following notable scientists: John Stewart Bell, Hans Bethe, Niels Bohr, Max Born, Louis-Victor de Broglie, Paul Dirac, Paul Ehrenfest, Albert Einstein, Richard Feynman, James Franck, George Gamow, Werner Heisenberg, Pascual Jordan, Brian Josephson, Hendrik A. Kramers, Rudolf W. Ladenburg, John Von Neumann, Max Planck, Erwin Schrödinger, Julian Schwinger, Tomonaga Shin'ichiro, John C. Slater, Arnold Sommerfeld, and John H. Van Vleck.

Given these definitions, the model can be built from just six basic assumptions.

Assumption 1. Each scientist during the course of formal education and professional training acquires his or her *sample* from the larger set of ideas. In other words, each creator who belongs to a given field contains a unique subset of ideas that define the domain. Although a large portion of each creator's ideational sample is usually shared with one or more creators working in the same field, another portion of that sample will be unique to each creator, owing to discrepancies in background and preparation. For instance, the scientist or inventor might have switched disciplines, bringing ideas that are alien to the new domain of choice (Hudson & Jacot, 1986; Simonton, 1984d). Even when two scientists both received their training within the same discipline, there will necessarily exist sampling differences insofar as they took different courses from distinct instructors and institutions. In any event, if the domain and the field are sufficiently large, each scientist's sample can be considered a nearly random subsample from the larger population of phenomena, facts, concepts, variables, constants, techniques, theories, laws, questions, goals, and criteria that define the domain.

Assumption 2. The size of the ideational sample varies across the contributors making up any given field. That is, some scientists possess a large supply of disciplinary phenomena, facts, concepts, variables, constants, techniques, theories, laws, questions, goals, and criteria, whereas other individuals possess a relatively diminutive sample of such ideas. The former may be termed *generalists*, the latter *specialists*. For purposes of discussion, it can be assumed that the distribution of these sample sizes is roughly described by the normal bell-shaped curve so that most scientists fall somewhere between extreme generalists and extreme specialists. This assumption merely reflects the likelihood that the psychological factors underlying the acquisition of this knowledge base are normally distributed (cf. Galton, 1869;

Simonton, 1999d). The most obvious example is intelligence (but see Burt, 1963).

Assumption 3. The disciplinary ideas making up each creator's sample are then subjected to free, relatively unconstrained, or nearly random recombination, with the aim of finding original and useful permutations (Campbell, 1960; James, 1880). For instance, this process may entail what Einstein styled the "combinatorial play," which he considered to be "the essential feature in productive thought" (Hadamard, 1945, p. 142). In any case, because these combinations are "blindly formed," to use Poincaré's (1921, p. 392) phrase, the scientist cannot accurately foresee which ideas will bear fruit and which will prove sterile (Simonton, 1995). Consequently, these ideational variations actually have a relatively low probability of arriving at a creative combination. A large amount of time is spent shifting through useless combinations. Fortunately, however, the low likelihood of success is partially compensated by the large number of trials. Each creator working within a given field presumably engages in this combinatory process across the length of his or her career.

Assumption 4. The ideas generated by the combinatorial process vary greatly in Poincaré's attribute of "goodness." The vast majority fail to pass the scientist's own internal criteria for what can be considered a promising idea. Of those that pass this first criterion, most will not pan out for various reasons. For instance, the hunch may fail to survive initial empirical or logical tests. Even if it does so, it will then have to survive even more rigorous criteria, such as the standards imposed for a paper to be accepted by a peer-reviewed journal. Even after publication, the screening process continues. As noted in Chapter 2, only about half of scientific publications earn at least a single citation, and fewer than 20% earn more than 10 citations (Redner, 1998; see also Price, 1965). Genuine "citation classics" are rarer still, while those ideas that win their creator a Nobel Prize must have the lowest probability of all. Hence, the probability of coming up with a high-impact idea is minuscule.

Assumption 5. The number of individuals making up a field varies considerably from one research area to the next. Some disciplines, specialties, or topics attract many participants – so-called *mainstream* areas – whereas others are far less popular. This means that some disciplines have dozens, even hundreds, of scientists subjecting some of the same phenomena, facts, concepts, variables, constants, techniques, theories, laws, questions, goals, and criteria to the combinatory process, whereas other disciplines may have a half dozen or fewer scientists with overlapping ideational samples. There may even be instances in which scientists are the first to initiate research on a given topic and remain isolated investigators for much of their careers. A classic case would be Anton van Leeuwenhoek's pioneering work in microscropy.

Assumption 6. Since the advent of modern science, scientists have been strongly motivated to publish their results as rapidly as possible. The first to claim a discovery or invention thereby avoids nasty priority disputes. Accordingly, when scientists come across a good combination, they will, as quickly as possible, make others aware of the idea through conference presentations, journal publications, patent applications, or other vehicles of professional communication. The successful dissemination of a particular combination has the asset of preempting others from arriving at that same combination (Merton, 1961b). Once creators in the same field find out they have been anticipated, they move to some other topic or issue, often incorporating the preempting discovery into the repertoire of ideas that will be subject to future combinatory processes. Yet this communication process need not be instantaneous. Publication lags of various kinds, coupled with barriers set up by linguistic, cultural, and perhaps disciplinary boundaries, would cause a certain amount of delay. Nonetheless, as time transpires, the innovation will become more widely disseminated, so that the probability of a duplicate effort progressively shrinks, eventually reaching zero. In addition, it can be safely assumed that the communication process has become more efficient over the course of scientific history. The advent of the printing press, professional journals, scientific conferences, and, most recently, the Internet served to accelerate the diffusion of new ideas in science.

Figure 3.1 illustrates a few features of the proposed explanation. Two scientific disciplines are displayed using Venn diagrams to indicate the corresponding domains and fields. The upper square gives the set of phenomena, facts, concepts, variables, constants, techniques, theories, laws, questions, goals, and criteria that define Domain A, whereas the lower square gives the set of ideas defining Domain B. Each circle then signifies a single scientist's sample from his or her chosen domain. Because

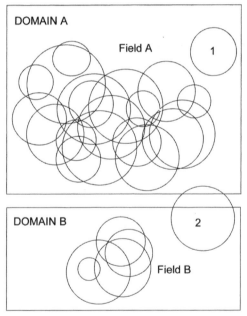

FIGURE 3.1. Schematic representation of two scientific domains with their corresponding fields. Circles represent the ideational samples of individual scientists, the size of the circle indicating the extent of the sample. Overlapping circles signify shared ideational contents.

the size these samples vary appreciably from one scientist to another, the circles have variable diameters. The overlap between the circles indicates the extent to which the scientists' samples share ideational content. The entire cluster of overlapping circles indicates the field for each domain. Yet just as the scientists' sample of domain-specific ideas can vary, so may the number of scientists making up each field vary. Here Field A surpasses Field B. Although these two clusters represent the most typical situation according to the model, Figure 3.1 depicts two crucial departures from the norm. First, circle 1 represents a *lone wolf* whose sample from Domain A does not overlap with any of the other samples in Field A. Second, circle 2 signifies a scientist who has sampled ideas from two different domains. For instance, he or she might have been initially trained in Domain B before moving into Domain A. Such a scientist might be called an *outsider* with respect to the latter domain.

IMPLICATIONS

The six assumptions just enumerated are all that are necessary to account for the critical phenomena discussed in Chapter 2, whether those phenomena concern scientific careers or scientific communities.

Research Publications

Let us begin the explanation with the skewed distribution of total output. According to Assumption 1, each scientist obtains a sample of the ideas representing a given domain. Yet by Assumption 2 the size of the sample varies across scientists making up the same field (see Figure 3.1). As a result, scientists necessarily differ in the total number of ideational combinations they can generate. However, although it was postulated that the sizes of these samples were distributed according to the normal curve, the distribution of the total output of ideas will not be (Simonton, 1989b, 1997a). On the contrary, it must be recognized that the total number of potential combinations increases more or less exponentially with the number of available phenomena, facts, concepts, variables, constants, techniques, theories, laws, questions, goals, and criteria entering the combinatorial hopper (cf. Barsalou & Prinz, 1997). Accordingly, the distribution of lifetime productivity should be closely approximated by a lognormal distribution (Simonton, 1988b). As expected, this distribution is extremely skewed, with a long upper tail, so that a small minority of scientists account for a lion's share of the discipline's creative ideas.

Admittedly, the lognormal distribution would appear to depart from the empirical distribution of lifetime output because it still possesses a lower tail. However, this discrepancy is merely superficial. The lower end of the distribution is so extremely compressed that the lowest score – the scientist with the fewest possible ideas – would be located just a small distance from the mean, median, and mode of the overall frequency distribution. In short, the distribution is extremely asymmetric. Furthermore, this diminutive portion of the distribution can easily be folded into the main portion of the distribution that contains the largest number of scientists. All that is required is to assume that there exists a certain minimum number of combinations necessary before a scientist has enough good combinations to support the generation of at least one creative product. Given this threshold requirement, those with hardly any ideas are indistinguishable from those scientists who, while claiming more ideas, still cannot produce enough to support a single contribution. The upshot is a cross-sectional distribution no different from what is empirically observed.

Now let us return to the upper tail of the distribution of output – the segment of the curve that contains the discipline's most prolific scientists. Although these prolific elites produce the most high-impact work, they also generate the most low-impact work, which brings us to the theoretical basis for the equal-odds rule. If the combinatorial process is truly blind, as specified by Assumption 3, and if the quality of ideas is highly variable, as stated in Assumption 4, then what Poincaré (1921) called good combinations should be randomly distributed across and within careers (Simonton, 1988a, 1997a). Thus, with respect to cross-sectional data, hit rates should be uncorrelated with total output. Those scientists who produce the most ideas deemed worthy of attention by others in their fields also tend to generate the most ideas that are ignored or even criticized by their colleagues. At least this association between quantity and quality holds *on average*. By chance alone some scientists have higher hit rates than average and thus appear as perfectionists, whereas others have lower hit rates than average and thus appear as mass producers. This variation in hit rates ultimately reflects the extent to which each scientist's sample approximates a random selection of ideas from the population of ideas that define the domain.

This argument may be more formally expressed by modifying slightly the formulation of the equal-odds rule provided in Chapter 2. In particular, the argument can be expressed by the equation

$$H_i = \rho T_i + u_i, \qquad (3.1)$$

where H_i is the total output of high-quality (high-impact, highly cited) works by scientist i, ρ is the expected (or average) *hit rate* or *quality ratio* for the scientist's domain, T_i is the total productivity regardless of quality, and u_i is a random (shock) variable uncorrelated with T_i and with a mean of 0 (and with a distribution similar to that of T). Hence, when $u_i > 0$ for a particular scientist, he or she departs from the expected hit rate in the positive direction and becomes an apparent perfectionist. Likewise, when $u_i < 0$, the departure is in the negative direction, rendering him or her an apparent mass producer. If $u_i \approx 0$, then the ith scientist's hit rate is typical for his or her discipline – namely, ρ.

If the combinatorial procedure is truly blind, as stated in Assumption 3, then the equal-odds rule should hold within careers as well (Simonton, 1999c). Those periods in a scientist's career in which he or she happens to generate the most combinations are the periods in which the good combinations most likely appear. Indeed, the more prolific a scientist is within a given career interval the higher the probability that he or she will create a high-impact publication. This longitudinal form of the equal-odds rule may be expressed by slightly modifying Equation 3.1 as follows:

$$H_{it} = \rho T_{it} + u_{it} \qquad (3.2)$$

Here the number of high-impact works at time t is proportional to the total number of works at t plus a random shock at t that is uncorrelated with T_{it}. Because the combinatorial process exhibits no foresight, the hit rate should fluctuate randomly throughout the career course. As a result, the combinations that support high-impact products are also randomly distributed across the scientist's career. Combinations that underlie low-impact products are likewise randomly distributed across the career course.

Finally, because the odds of finding a good combination are so small, the number of hits in any given year should be described by the Poisson distribution. As discussed in Chapter 2, the Poisson distribution naturally emerges whenever the probability of a hit is very small but the number of trials is very high. Accordingly, most scientists must consider themselves lucky if they can claim one publication in a given year. Output of two publications requires even more luck, and output of three publications is luckier still. Nobel laureates, who average a bit over three publications per year, can thus be viewed as very fortunate indeed (Zuckerman, 1977).

To sum up, the central features of productivity across and within careers can be explicated by assuming that creativity operates like a random combinatorial procedure. Admittedly, it can be argued that other factors are not irrelevant. A case in point is genius. The skewed distribution of total output has been derived by assuming that the size of the ideational samples acquired by various scientists was normally distributed. Even so, that normal distribution of domain-relevant expertise must be predicated on the distribution of cognitive and dispositional traits needed to master the knowledge and techniques of a discipline. These traits might include intelligence, energy, and persistence, among other factors (Galton, 1869). Certainly those scientists who are blessed with high levels of all these traits would hold the edge in acquiring a sample sufficiently large to place themselves in the prolific elite of the productivity distribution. If so, there should be no objection to calling these individuals scientific geniuses.

The genius perspective receives more extensive treatment in Chapter 5. Meanwhile, it is now necessary to account for the phenomenon associated with scientific communities.

Multiple Discoveries

The previous explanations required no more than the first four assumptions. A subset of these same assumptions are sufficient to account for many features of multiples as well. In the first place, the duplicate efforts merely reflect the fact that most disciplines consist of several scientists applying combinatorial processes to ideational samples that share a core of domain-specific phenomena, facts, concepts, variables, constants, techniques, theories, laws, questions, goals, and criteria (see Figure 3.1). By chance alone, then, two or more scientists are bound to generate the same ideational combination. Nevertheless, given the low probability of finding a good combination, the frequency of multiple grades should closely follow a Poisson distribution (Price, 1963; Simonton, 1978). Again, the latter distribution is characteristic of combinatorial processes in which the probability of success is extremely low but the number of trials is extremely high. In fact, chi-square goodness-of-fit tests have demonstrated that the Poisson distribution accurately describes every frequency distribution of multiple grades so far published (Simonton, 1978, 1979). Any departures from the frequencies predicted by the Poisson distribution can be attributed to sampling errors. Figure 3.2 displays the degree of congruence for the largest collection of multiples gathered to date (Simonton, 1979). The correspondence between observed and predicted frequencies is as high as can normally be expected for real data.

One curious consequence of fitting a Poisson distribution to the observed data is that it provides predicted frequencies not just for multiples, but for singletons and *nulltons* besides – where a nullton is a discovery or invention that never got made because "luck ran out" in the scientific community. With respect to the data with 579 multiples, for instance, the Poisson distribution predicts 1,361 singletons and 1,088 nulltons

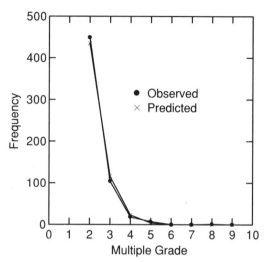

FIGURE 3.2. Graph showing the degree of concordance between observed and predicted frequencies of multiple grades. The observed data were published in Simonton (1979), the predictions coming from a Poisson distribution with $\mu = .8$.

(Simonton, 1979). Hence, multiples represent just 19% of the total possible outcomes according to this interpretation, whereas singletons constitute 45% and nulltons 36%. However, it should not be concluded from the latter figure that the combinatorial explanation requires that more than one-third of all potential discoveries and inventions never be made. On the contrary, we can hypothesize that the combinatorial process runs until it has exhausted all good combinations in the population of phenomena, facts, concepts, variables, constants, techniques, theories, laws, questions, goals, and criteria that define a given domain (cf. Price, 1963). Given this exhaustion provision, all nulltons eventually would be converted into singletons and multiples, yielding proportions of 70% and 30%, respectively (Simonton, 1986b). The prominence of singletons becomes all the more conspicuous.

Turning to a different issue, it should be readily understood why the most prolific scientists tend to participate in more multiples (Merton, 1961a; Simonton, 1979, 1999c). Just as those scientists who generate more ideational combinations tend, on average, to produce more good combinations, so are prolific scientists more likely to come up with combinations similar to those conceived by colleagues working with samples containing roughly the same set of phenomena, facts, concepts, variables, constants, techniques, theories, laws, questions, goals, and criteria. Merton (1961b) recognized this same principle when he observed that those of "great scientific genius will have been repeatedly involved in multiples . . . because the genius will have made many discoveries altogether" (p. 484). Indeed, those of "scientific genius are precisely those . . . whose work in the end would be eventually rediscovered. These rediscoveries would be made, not by a single scientist, but by an entire corps of scientists" (p. 484). The single scientific genius thus becomes, according to Merton, "the functional equivalent of a considerable array of other scientists of varying degrees of talent" (p. 484). The lesser talents at least have the advantage that their negligible creativity serves to minimize the likelihood that they might find themselves entering into priority disputes with scientists far more illustrious.

Still, it is manifest that absolutely identical duplicates would be rather rare. Just as two siblings from the same parents will almost never inherit the same set of genes except when they come from the same fertilized egg (i.e., monozygotic twins), so will the discoveries or inventions constituting a putative multiple consist of a different mix of combinatorial components. In fact, the distinctiveness of the supposed duplicates is all the more assured by the assumption that scientists working within the same discipline seldom possess identical samples from the domain (see Figure 3.1). Therefore, we should predict that the degree of similarity should exhibit a distribution not unlike that found for multiple grades (Simonton, 2003b). Multiples sharing one essential idea would be the most common, followed by those with two ideas, and so forth in a negative monotonic and decelerating curve. True duplicates with 100% overlap in constitutive ideas would be extremely rare. This prediction could be tested by conducting a detailed analysis of a representative sample of multiple discoveries and inventions (e.g., Ogburn & Thomas, 1922).

The last two of the six assumptions are required to account for two remaining characteristics of multiple discoveries and inventions:

Assumption 5 is needed to explain why scientists are most likely to participate in multiples if they are active in large fields with many colleagues subjecting similar samples of ideas to the same combinatorial process (Simonton, 1999c). By chance alone, the more scientists there are who are manipulating the same set of phenomena, facts, concepts, variables, constants, techniques, theories, laws, questions, goals, and criteria the greater the odds that two or more scientists will find themselves anticipated. The lone wolf, in contrast, can pursue a line of inquiry with little worry of being preempted by some colleague (Hagstrom, 1974). Hence, one way highly prolific scientists can avoid priority disputes is to avoid mainstream research questions. Hadamard provided an example from his own professional experience:

The scientist may be and often is discouraged from studying such and such a problem not by the knowledge that it has been solved, but by the fear that it has been solved without his knowing it, a fact which would render his work useless. . . . I even add that, after having started a certain set of questions and seeing that several other authors had begun to follow that same line, I happened to drop it and investigate something else. (Hadamard, 1945, p. 132)

Assumption 6 is needed to explain why multiples vary in the temporal separation of their duplicates. This assumption can be formally expressed in terms of the insertion of a *negative contagion* component to the probabilistic process, yielding a contagious Poisson model (Brannigan & Wanner, 1983a; Simonton, 1986b, 1999c). That is, once a discovery has been made, the probability of a duplicate decreases over time as the new idea becomes successfully disseminated through the scientific community. The specific equation may be expressed as follows:

$$P(j) = \frac{\alpha(\alpha + \beta) \ldots (\alpha + [j - 1]\beta)e^{-\alpha}(1 - e^{-\beta})^j}{j!\beta^j} \tag{3.3}$$

Here α has the same role as does μ in the original Poisson model (see Equation 2.1), whereas β gauges the magnitude and direction of the contagion (as $\beta \to 0$, Equation 3.3 approaches Equation 2.1 in the limit). Because the contagion operates to decrease the possibility of another multiple, β has a negative sign. When this model is fit to the data collected by Simonton (1979), one obtains the parameters $\alpha = .858$ and $\beta = -.079$ (Brannigan & Wanner, 1983a). The value of the first parameter is very close to the $\mu = 0.82$ when the simple Poisson is fit to the same data. The value of the second parameter, in contrast, adds new information – namely, that "once a discovery is made, the probability of it being duplicated is reduced by a factor of 0.079" (Brannigan & Wanner, 1983a, p. 427). As a consequence, higher grade multiples become somewhat less likely than predicted by a Poisson model lacking this theoretical refinement.

Besides predicting the distribution of multiple grades, the addition of a negative contagion also permits us to predict the observed distribution of time lags between the first and last duplicate in a multiple (Brannigan & Wanner, 1983b; Simonton, 1986c). Furthermore, the parameters of this model show that the expected degree of temporal separation has indeed been declining (Brannigan & Wanner, 1983b). To illustrate, the average interval between duplicates declined from around 86 years in the 16th century to a little more than 2 years in the 20th century. Current forms of scientific communication are probably so efficient that independent discoveries must be practically simultaneous for multiples to occur at all.

Naturally, if the temporal opportunity for a multiple is progressively shrinking, then multiple grades must diminish as well. Time will quickly run out and thus terminate the accumulation of duplicates. That implication has been confirmed (Brannigan & Wanner, 1983b). The exchange of scientific information is so rapid and effective that doublets have become even more common relative to higher grade multiples. This trend even provides an explanation for another result reported in Chapter 2: the larger the sample of multiples the greater the predominance of doublets (see Figure 2.2). Because the larger samples also contain more recent exemplars, they include more modern instances of the phenomenon. Hence, whereas doublets made up 61% of the 148 multiples gathered in the early 1920s (Osgood & Thomas, 1922), the proportion of doublets rose to 78% when the sample was expanded to 579 multiples in the late 1970s (Simonton, 1979).

In summary, the critical characteristics of multiples can be explained by assuming that scientific creativity functions according to a procedure that generates chance combinations. It is especially remarkable that all the essential attributes of this phenomenon can be understood without evoking the concept of zeitgeist. Certainly the probabilistic explanation is antithetical to sociocultural determinism. A discovery or invention cannot be both inevitable and improbable at the same time. This is not to say that the zeitgeist has absolutely no role to play whatsoever. On the contrary, the zeitgeist has been simply reduced to a relatively minor player in the event. Its contributions are threefold. First, the sociocultural system defines the communication technologies that can be used for the dissemination of scientific ideas. Each major revolution in such technologies has accelerated the communication of new findings, thereby reducing the time available for multiples to emerge, with corresponding effects on the number of rival claimants. Second, the disciplinary zeitgeist – the collection of phenomena, facts, concepts, variables, constants, techniques, theories, laws, questions, goals, and criteria that define the domain at a particular point in time – provides the essential substrate for scientific creativity. After all, the combinatorial process operates on the ideas that each scientist has sampled from his or her chosen specialty area. Third, the sociocultural system or the disciplinary zeitgeist may influence the number of scientists actively engaged in solving a particular problem. During wartime, for example, investigators may be effectively channeled into defense research, such as the atomic bomb projects supported during World War II. Or special awards or recognition may attract scientists to work on especially intractable problems (e.g., how to determine longitude, the proof of Fermat's Last Theorem, a program that passes the Turing Test).

I elaborate these functions in the next chapter. Before turning to these substantive developments, however, it is first necessary to address a distinct and more urgent explanatory deficiency. I have claimed that the combinatorial model explains the central attributes of scientific careers. That is not completely true. There are certain features of creative productivity in science that have been left out of the interpretative purview. This omission was necessary because I wished to begin with the simplest possible model that could account for both research publications and multiple discoveries. To explain scientific careers more fully requires that the combinatorial model undergo an extension.

EXTENSION

I emphasized in Chapter 2 that creative products tend to be randomly distributed across the career course. That is, if one examines yearly output, the pattern appears to be random (Huber, 1998a, 1998b; Huber & Wagner-Döbler, 2001). Yet this generalization must be qualified. It is possible to obtain a longitudinal pattern that appears far more systematic. This can be accomplished by imposing two conditions simultaneously. First, rather than look at how productivity is distributed within singular careers, the data can be summed, or aggregated, across the careers of dozens, even hundreds, of scientists. Second, rather than use yearly units of analysis, the products can be aggregated into larger time intervals, such as 5-year and even 10-year units. By combining data in this way, the randomness seen in the annual data for individual scientists converts into a smoother agewise trend. The effect of such aggregation is apparent in Table 2.1. If the random output is summed across 5-year periods and summed across the 10 scientists, we get totals of 58, 68, 69, and 55 contributions per career unit rather than an even distribution. The output in the middle two units is greater than that in the flanking units. The implicit nonmonotonic function would become even more pronounced if we included more scientists, including scientists who vary greatly in total output.

Empirical investigations adopting this aggregation strategy have discerned a longitudinal trend that represents the typical career trajectory in science (e.g., Cole, 1979; Dennis, 1966; Lehman, 1953; Zuckerman, 1977). In particular, the result is what may be called an inverted-backward J curve

(Simonton, 1988a, 1997a). That is, the expected level of productivity first increases until it reaches a peak, after which output tends to decline gradually. Departures from this trend account for appreciably less than 5% of the total longitudinal variance in creative output (Simonton, 1988a, 1997a). Again, it must be emphasized that this trajectory is a statistical summary of aggregated tendencies. No scientist's career conforms perfectly to this trend, particularly if output is tabulated into annual time units. It is only through aggregation across scientists and across time that all the unpredictable peculiarities of each scientist's career average out to yield a predictable longitudinal pattern. Specifically, there appears a slight tendency for products to cluster near the career peak. This clustering is too weak to produce verifiable runs in annual data for a single career and yet will emerge once the data are averaged across yearly units and across numerous careers.

The question thus emerges: Can a combinatorial process account for these career trajectories? It can do so and much more besides.

Career Trajectories

Although numerous explanations have been offered for the observed trajectories, only one can be integrated into the combinatorial process already presented (Simonton, 2003b). This model starts with Assumption 1 – that is, each scientist begins with a sample of domain-specific phenomena, facts, concepts, variables, constants, techniques, theories, laws, questions, goals, and criteria. This sample defines the total number of ideational combinations a scientist is potentially capable of making in an unlimited lifetime. Let the number of potential combinations be called the *initial creative potential*, which can be designated m_i for the ith scientist. This creative potential is then converted into actual creative products by a two-step cognitive process: ideation and elaboration. Ideation is the process of generating the good combinations, whereas elaboration is the process of developing those combinations into published ideas. Therefore, there are two rates, an ideation rate a and an elaboration rate b. The model then expresses the ith scientist's annual combinatorial output according to the following equation:

$$C_i(t) = \frac{abm_i(e^{-at} - e^{-bt})}{b - a} \qquad (3.4)$$

Here e is again the exponential constant ($= 2.718 \ldots$). In the special case in which the two information-processing parameters are identical ($a = b$), Equation 3.4 becomes

$$C_i(t) = a^2 m_i t e^{-at} \qquad (3.5)$$

a slightly simpler form, but with essentially the same predicted career trajectory. Because C_i (t) pertains to the production of ideational combinations rather than actual creative products, the model further assumes that the latter is some small but more or less constant fraction of the former (Simonton, 1997a). More precisely, $T_{it} = kC_i(t)$, where T_{it} is defined as in Equation 3.2 and k is a decimal fraction that is determined by the number of ideas that make up a typical publication unit for a discipline. With that assumption, the curves defined by Equations 3.4 and 3.5 can be taken to predict longitudinal changes in the output of creative products after the introduction of the scaling factor k.

However, it is significant that t is not chronological age, but rather *career age*. That is, $t = 0$ at the moment the individual begins generating ideational combinations in a particular domain. Figure 3.3 shows what this curve looks like for $m_i = 100$, $a = .04$, and $b = .05$. These can be considered fairly typical parameters. As is immediately apparent, the model predicts an age function with the following three fundamental attributes. First, the curve is single peaked rather than having two or more maxima. Second, the ascending portion of the curve is concave downward (i.e., decelerating rather than accelerating). Third, the descending portion of the curve eventually exhibits an inflexion point where the curve becomes concave upward and thereafter approaches the zero-output point asymptotically.

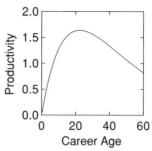

FIGURE 3.3. Typical career trajectory for output per time unit ($m_i = 100$, $a = .04$, and $b = .05$). Figure is taken from Simonton (2002).

All three of these features of the predicted age curve have been success-fully verified against actual aggregate data (Simonton, 1984b). The correla-tion between expected and observed output at the aggregate level is usually in the upper .90s. For example, the correlation between the observed and predicted output tabulated into consecutive decades across 41 American Nobel laureate scientists is .96 (using the data from Zuckerman, 1977).

Besides accounting for the general form of career trajectories in science, the model just presented explains how those trajectories vary according to individual differences and interdisciplinary contrasts. But before con-tinuing with those implications, let me first deal with an assumption that might seem a bit implausible. According to the model, each scientist be-gins with a repository of phenomena, facts, concepts, variables, constants, techniques, theories, laws, questions, goals, and criteria that define his or her domain sample. This initial creative potential is then transformed into published output through a two-step process of ideation and elaboration. During the course of this process, the given supply of ideas is slowly de-pleted, yielding the post-peak decline shown in Figure 3.3. Yet surely no scientific creator constitutes such a closed system as this postulate implies. Indeed, in later chapters I document all the ways scientific investigators are exposed to new ideas in the disciplinary domain. Even so, this influx of new ideational material is severely limited. This limitation has three causes:

1. Because of various professional and personal responsibilities, the rate at which new knowledge is acquired changes dramatically once the career commences. The acquisition of new knowledge and technique then has to complete increasingly with activities such as teaching, administration, public service, marriage, and family (Hargens, McCann, & Reskin, 1978; Horner, Murray, & Rushton, 1994; Kyvik, 1990; Roe, 1965). When in graduate school, top-flight scientists typically devoted 50 or more hours per week to study and research (Chambers, 1964). Such a pace of expertise acquisition is difficult if not impossible to maintain after entering a full-time position. Even a lengthy sabbatical leave cannot compensate for the diminished acquisition rate whose effects accumulate year after year throughout the career. The Hungarian mathematician Paul Erdös was one the few modern scientists ever to escape this hindrance. He managed to devote nearly all his waking hours to research by avoiding virtually all the responsibilities normally associated with a life and a career. Having no genuine job, nor family obligations, and living out of a suitcase that held almost everything he owned, Erdös spent much of his time as the guest of fellow mathematicians who relished the opportunity to collaborate with him on papers. Not only did this enable him to publish well over 1,400 papers, but also his unique eccentricity allowed him to maintain an exceptional rate of output right up to the year of his death at age 83.

2. After a scientist launches his or her research program, the scope of expertise acquisition tends to become narrower. Reading and study become increasingly confined to what is most immediately relevant to current investigations (Dennis & Girden, 1954). To be sure, scientists vary in the degree to which they become so specialized, as is discussed in later chapters. Even so, the time and attention devoted to extraneous intellectual activities become appreciably constricted, certainly much more so than the breadth apparent during undergraduate and graduate education. Most active scientists usually deem themselves fortunate if they can just keep up on the research being

published in their specialty area. This impediment becomes particularly problematic when a scientist is part of a rapidly growing field and domain (Price, 1963).

3. A certain amount of this reduced openness may be attributed to what is known as *Planck's Principle*. Planck (1949) expressed the principle as follows: "A new scientific truth does not triumph by convincing its opponents and making them see the light, but rather because its opponents eventually die, and a new generation grows up that is familiar with it" (pp. 33–34). In other words, as scientists get older they tend to become less receptive to new ideas emerging in their discipline (for evidence, see Diamond, 1980; Hull, Tessner, & Diamond, 1978; Sulloway, 1996; Whaples, 1991). Planck came up with this principle upon observing the reactions of his fellow physicists to his quantum theory, a theory that was picked up and extended almost exclusively by younger colleagues. Among those youths was Einstein, whose 1905 paper on the photoelectric effect showed that it had unexpected explanatory utility. Ironically, Einstein himself eventually failed to accept the full implications of the quantum revolution as developed by Bohr and Heisenberg. Einstein's rejection eventually had disastrous consequences for his attempts to develop a unified field theory. His domain sample was missing some ideas that were absolutely essential for any advance in this direction.

These three causes taken together suggest that, for the vast majority of scientists, individual creative potential is consumed faster than it can be replenished. As an additional justification for this conclusion, the current model makes some distinctive predictions that have survived the empirical test – as becomes apparent immediately below.

Individual Differences

Two features of this model enable to account for individual differences in career trajectories. First, because productive output is a function of career rather than chronological age, the model allows for variation in *age at career onset* (Simonton, 1997a). That is, early bloomers begin the combinatorial process at a relatively young age, whereas late bloomers commence at an older age. In part, this variation reflects differences in when the scientist managed to complete the acquisition of domain-specific expertise (e.g., age at receiving a Ph.D.). Second, scientists can vary in their initial creative potential (m_i). This variation is based on variation in the size of the acquired disciplinary sample. We accordingly distinguish between low- and high-creative scientists (Simonton, 1991a). Because these two individual differences are largely uncorrelated with each other, it becomes possible to generate a typology of scientific careers (Simonton, 1997a). In other words, we can speak of *low-creative early bloomers, low-creative late bloomers, high-creative early bloomers,* and *high-creative late bloomers.* These four career types are graphically represented in Figure 3.4.

It should be apparent that variation in age at career onset does nothing more than shift the career trajectory earlier or later with respect to chronological age. Otherwise the predicted curve is unaffected. Variation in initial creative potential, in contrast, has a direct effect on how output changes across the course of the career. The larger the value of m_i, the higher is overall height of the curve. In other words, the greater a scientist's initial creative potential, the higher is his or her output rate across the career course. This expectation leads to two predictions. First, the career peak is located at the same career age no matter whether the scientist is high or low in creative potential. Therefore, highly prolific scientists should reach their maximum output rate at the same career age as their less productive colleagues. This prediction is confirmed by empirical data (Christensen & Jacomb, 1992; Horner, Rushton, & Vernon, 1986; Lehman, 1958; Simonton, 1991a, 1992a; Zuckerman, 1977). Second, because the output rate in any given career interval (e.g., 5- or 10-year periods) is a direct function of creative potential, then the productivity in any given period should be highly correlated with that in any other period. In fact, the correlation matrix should be adequately explained by a single underlying factor (latent variable) that can be identified as a proxy

65

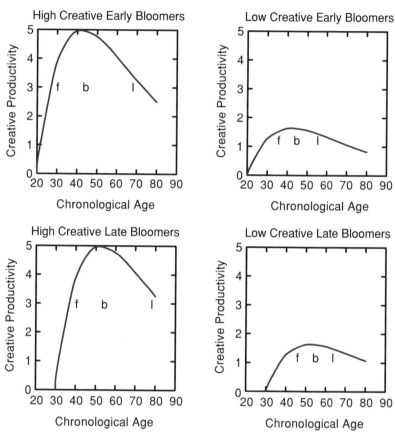

FIGURE 3.4. Fourfold typology of career trajectories and landmarks according to a combinatorial model of creative productivity. The predicted locations of the three career landmarks are indicated by letters, where f = first major contribution, b = best contribution, and l = last major contribution. Figure is taken from Simonton (2002).

for creative potential. This prediction has also been verified (Simonton, 1997a). For instance, when a single-factor model was fit to the careers of 435 mathematicians (from Cole, 1979), the output in any given age period correlated between .74 and .88 with the general factor that represents the level of creativity.

The model's predictions can be extended yet further once we recognize that three career landmarks highlight the lifetime output of any productive scientist. These landmarks are the *first major publication*, the *best publication*, and the *last major publication* (Raskin, 1936; Simonton, 1991a; Zusne, 1976). Here *major* means that the publication has had some impact on the field (e.g., as assessed by some threshold level of citation) and *best* identifies the publication with the highest impact (i.e., the most cited work). The question then arises as to where these three landmarks are most likely to appear over the career course. The answer is provided by the equal-odds rule. According to the rule, the odds of producing a high-impact work is a probabilistic function of the total number of works produced. Moreover, the most influential work of all will most likely appear around the time when the output of ideas maximizes.

The consequences of applying this principle are illustrated in Figure 3.4. It should be clear that the best work appears at the same career age no matter where the scientist is placed in the typology (namely, early or late bloomer, high- or low-creative). In addition, for highly creative scientists, the first high-impact work appears at a younger career age and the last high-impact work appears at older career age compared with their less creative colleagues. More subtle predictions can also be derived from the model (Simonton, 1991a, 1997a). For instance, the model predicts that if age at high-impact work is statistically controlled, then age at first high-impact work correlates negatively with the age of the last high-impact work. All these predictions have been empirically confirmed on large samples (Simonton, 1991a, 1992a, 1997a).

Interdisciplinary Contrasts

So far we have been operating under the assumption that the career trajectory is essentially the same under a wide range of conditions. Early bloomers may commence their career at a younger age than late bloomers, but their peak output appears at the same career age. Highly creative scientists may maintain a higher rate of output throughout their career, but the general shape remains the same, including the location of the productive maximum. Yet it is highly unlikely that the expected career trajectories are identical across all scientific disciplines. On the contrary, some disciplines may exhibit earlier career peaks relative to other disciplines. Theoretical physics offers an example. According to Paul Dirac, who won the Nobel Prize for research he had published in his mid-20s,

> Age is, of course, a fever chill
> that every physicist must fear.
> He's better dead than living still
> when once he's past his thirtieth year.
> (Jungk, 1958, p. 27)

Although empirical research on this question shows that Dirac exaggerated quite a bit, the fact remains that the various sciences have very distinct career trajectories (e.g., Adams, 1946; Dennis, 1966; Lehman, 1953; Simonton, 1989a). For instance, Figure 3.5 shows the typical chronological ages for the three career landmarks for eight broad domains (based on data reported by Simonton, 1991a). Notice that mathematicians and physicists are most likely to have the first career landmark appear in the late 20s, the second landmark in the late 30s, and the last landmark in the early 50s. In contrast, astronomers and geoscientists are most likely to attain the same three landmarks in the early 30s, the early 40s, and the late 50s. Significantly, not only are such differences statistically reliable, but in addition they survive control for all relevant contaminating variables (Simonton, 1991a). Hence, the interdisciplinary contrasts must be accommodated by any comprehensive theory of scientific creativity.

The current model explicates these differences quite readily. The differences follow directly from the model's ideation (a) and elaboration (b) rates. Unlike m_i, which is characteristic of the scientist, a and b are attributes of the discipline in which the scientist acquired his or her creative potential (Simonton, 1984b, 1989a). These rates depend on the nature of the domain-specific phenomena, facts, concepts, variables, constants, techniques, theories, laws, questions, goals, and criteria; the requirements

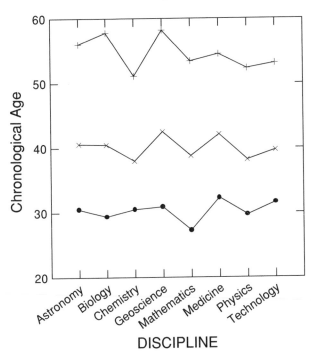

- ● First Major Contribution
- × Best Contribution
- + Last Major Contribution

FIGURE 3.5. Typical chronological ages for the three career landmarks for eight broad domains. Graph based on data reported by Simonton (1991a).

for producing the least-publishable unit in the discipline, and a host of other factors (Simonton, 1997a). For example, some disciplines, such as mathematics, consist of a relatively finite inventory of highly abstract and well-defined concepts (e.g., "equation"), whereas other disciplines, such as the geosciences, are made up of a far larger collection of more concrete and not always well-delineated ideas (e.g., "mountain"). These contrasts affect both the rate at which ideational combinations can be created and the rate at which those ideas can be elaborated into creative products. At the same time, these two rates are somewhat independent of each other, allowing a great diversity of career trajectories. Therefore, the fit between Equation 3.1 and real data improves substantially when these two parameters are allowed to vary across disciplines (Simonton, 1997a). Moreover, the estimated ideation and elaboration rates are consistent with expectation (Simonton, 1989a). To illustrate, for mathematics $a = .032$ and $b = .044$, whereas for the geosciences $a = .026$ and $b = .034$ (using nonlinear estimation procedures to fit the curve to the data of Dennis, 1966). Because the rates are faster for mathematics than for the geosciences, the career landmarks should be proportionately sooner, in line with the empirical results illustrated in Figure 3.5.

Again, it must be underlined that all these predictions apply to achievements that are aggregated across large samples of scientists. Even then, the amount of variance explained is often only modest. Consequently, these patterns largely disappear when the focus returns to the career of an individual scientist, particularly when analyzed into annual units. However, this qualification has one minor exception. When the total output of a highly prolific scientist is aggregated into large units, it is possible for some features of the extended model to emerge. Because the output of a single individual can then surpass the total output of a hundred or more colleagues, the career course follows more closely what is observed in the aggregated data.

For instance, the age curve defined by Equation 3.3 and depicted in Figure 3.3 can describe fairly accurately the career trajectory of any sufficiently productive scientist or inventor. Thomas Edison provides a good illustration because he eventually held 1,093 patents, or an average output rate of 17 patents per year. This extensive output was tabulated into consecutive decades of his career, and the mean annual output per decade calculated (correcting for the abbreviated activity at the initial and final decades; Simonton, 1977). Using nonlinear estimation techniques (Simonton, 1989a), we can then estimate the parameters of Equation 3.4, thereby obtaining $C_{Edison}(t) = 2595(e^{-.044t} - e^{-.058t})$. According to this prediction formula, the correlation between theoretically predicted and empirically observed patent output is .74, a certainly nonrandom degree of correspondence. Yet this correlation shrinks to .58 when the same equation is applied to annual fluctuations in his patent output, showing that his yearly output is much less predictable (i.e., 55% versus 34% of the variance explained). For individuals less productive than Edison, both of these correlations would become appreciably smaller, indicating an even more random distribution across the career course. Given that creators like Edison are exceptions rather than the rule – as specified by Lotka's law – then the pattern of annual output must be random for the overwhelming majority of scientists.

It is for this reason that curvilinear age functions like that defined by Equation 3.4 have minimal explanatory power when applied to samples of scientists who are very heterogeneous in output (e.g., Bayer & Dutton, 1977; Levin & Stephan, 1989, 1991). Typically around 10% of the variance is explained. Even this percentage would become smaller if the most prolific scientists were removed from the samples studied. Hence, randomness predominates in the distribution of output across the career course. The age curve depicted in Figure 3.3 loses all applicability. Needless to say, its inapplicability becomes all the more conspicuous whenever the longitudinal tabulations include only high-impact work rather than total output. If the production of minor ideas is so unpredictable, the creation of major ideas is even more so.

Nonetheless, the extended, aggregate model represented by Equation 3.4 retains a consequential link with what takes place at the individual level – even in the case of a relatively unproductive scientist. The basis for this connection is m_i, which defines each researcher's creative potential. This individual-difference parameter corresponds directly to the distribution of creative products in annual units of a scientist's career. As already observed, these frequencies are accurately described by the Poisson distribution, a distribution that contains the single parameter μ. Yet this parameter varies appreciably across scientists. The larger the size of μ_i for individual i, the higher is the mean rate of output across his or her career course. According to the extended model, the parameter m_i determines the average output rate. This means the value of μ_i across a population of scientists is directly proportional to the corresponding value of m_i, thereby relating the aggregate model to events at the individual level. Equation 3.4 still leaves a trace on a scientist's career despite the fact that the curve depicted in Figure 3.3 is devoid of predictive utility.

OBJECTIONS

At the beginning of this chapter I proposed a relatively simple combinatorial model that explains the central results reviewed in Chapter 2. I then extended this model to account for additional features of the scientific career. Taken together, these explanations show that scientific creativity has precisely the empirical characteristics that would be expected if it resulted from some kind of chance process. So far, logic, genius, and zeitgeist play minimal roles, if any, in this theoretical account. Nevertheless, I must confess that the case for chance might not be totally convincing. Critics can easily raise objections to the interpretations I have offered. These objections can be grouped into two categories: (1) alternative explanations and (2) explanatory limitations.

Alternative Explanations

The first objection is that there already exist theoretical interpretations of the findings, explanations that have contrary theoretical implications. For example, the skewed distribution of total output can be explicated without recourse to a combinatorial model (Simonton, 1988b). First of all, the highly elitist distribution would result if scientific creativity were a multiplicative rather than additive product of several contributing variables, such as intelligence, motivation, imagination, and expertise (Burt, 1943; Rushton, 2000; Shockley, 1957; Simonton, 1999d). The distribution of the product of several normally distributed variables is also lognormal rather than normal. Such multiplicative models would endorse the genius perspective over the chance perspective supported by the combinatorial model.

A highly skewed productivity distribution can also be derived from a cumulative advantage process whereby the "rich get richer and the poor get poorer" (Simonton, 1999b). This is often expressed as the Matthew Effect based on the New Testament assertion "For unto every one that hath shall be given, and he shall have abundance: but from him that hath not shall be taken away even that which he hath" (Merton, 1968, p. 58). Cumulative-advantage models have undergone impressive theoretical development and empirical documentation (Allison, Long, & Krauze, 1982; Allison & Stewart, 1974). Not surprisingly, these models are favored by sociologists of science because they place the primary cause in the reward structure of the scientific community. Because the rejection rates for grant proposals and manuscript submissions are so high, it takes a certain amount of "luck" to succeed, but success itself improves the prospects for future success. In a sense, cumulative-advantage models integrate zeitgeist and chance perspectives in a rather unique fashion.

Notwithstanding the existence of these alternative explanations, the combinatorial account has advantages that render it superior from a scientific viewpoint. To begin with, neither the multiplicative nor the cumulative-advantage models can explain all the features of scientific careers, and the two rival models are completely incapable of explicating the various characteristics of multiples. Thus, they cannot be considered comprehensive interpretations. To accept either one would require us to provide piecemeal explanations for the remaining phenomena presented in Chapter 2. Even worse, the alternative models sometimes yield predictions that are flatly contradicted by the facts. Most strikingly, the cumulative-advantage model makes three predictions that are disproved by empirical data (Huber & Wagner-Döbler, 2001a, 2001b; Simonton, 1997a). First, the model makes an incorrect prediction about the relation between output in various career periods. In particular, the model implies that output in adjacent periods should be higher than output in nonadjacent periods, exhibiting a *simplex* structure rather than a single-factor structure. Second, the model predicts that contributions should be clustered toward the end of the career rather than randomly distributed throughout the career. Third and last, the cumulative-advantage model incorrectly predicts that the probability of success would be a direct result of research productivity. Hence, not only would the more prolific scientists have higher hit rates, but also the hit rates would increase over the course of the career – in defiance of the equal-odds rule.

Naturally, it is not inconceivable that the multiplicative and cumulative-advantage processes might still operate, but in conjunction with the combinatorial process and confined by that process. For example, the cumulative-advantage process could help account for why the distribution of citation rates across scientists tends to be so much more skewed than the distribution of publications (e.g., White & White, 1978). The Matthew Effect may function to exaggerate small differences in publication quality into huge differences in publication visibility.

Explanatory Limitations

The theoretical interpretation offered in this chapter is extremely abstract. Although the explanation was prefaced by the introspective reports of Helmholtz, Hadamard, Poincaré, and Faraday, its development beyond that point was essentially founded on an abstract probabilistic model. This model specifies nothing about the cognitive processes involved beyond what might be implied by those introspections. Neither does the explanation say much about the creative scientist. The only minor exception is the assumption that there exist individual differences in the capacity for acquiring the domain-specific phenomena, facts, concepts, variables, constants, techniques, theories, laws, questions, goals, and criteria. Finally, the combinatorial model completely ignores some critical features of the scientific enterprise. For instance, nothing was said about the nature of scientific research programs or the characteristics of peer review. At present, therefore, the theory seems somewhat sterile. However adequately it may account for publications and multiples, it remains a fleshless, bare bones account.

These deficiencies must be remedied. And they will. In the next chapter, I ground the conjectured process in the concrete characteristics of the scientific enterprise. This grounding includes not just research programs and peer review but also the disciplinary zeitgeist. The following chapter then concentrates on the creative scientist, showing that the proposed model falls right in line with what we know about those individuals who are most likely to have a high impact on their chosen disciplines. This chapter articulates how the chance and genius perspectives can be more closely integrated. Finally, Chapter 6 discusses the discovery process, with special focus on the experimental research on the subject. Besides indicating how the combinatorial model follows from that experimental literature, I delineate the role logic plays within the context of chance. By the time these three chapters are complete, the abstract model will become a finely differentiated and documented theory.

4

Scientific Activity

The statistical analyses that dominate the biological, behavioral, and social sciences tend to test the *null hypothesis* that the empirical results – whether they be mean differences or correlation coefficients – can be attributed to mere chance. By chance alone, it is possible to obtain sample means that look different, even when in the larger population the means are strictly identical. By mere chance, one can obtain correlation coefficients that appear much larger than zero, even when the correlations in the general population are exactly zero. In an analogous fashion, the theoretical interpretations provided in the previous chapter can be said to represent the null hypothesis that chance can account for all the central empirical features of two key behavioral phenomena – scientific productivity and multiple discovery. In this case, however, chance is not sampling error but rather some unspecified combinatorial processes operating within and among creative scientists. Beginning with the postulate that scientific creativity involves the virtually random combination of the phenomena, facts, concepts, variables, constants, techniques, theories, laws, questions, goals, and criteria that define a domain, a host of detailed features of scientific careers and communities can be explained and predicted. There is no need to hypothesize anything more mysterious, whether genius or zeitgeist. Even logic has no part in the explanation. According to Ockham's razor – the law of parsimony – scientists should not make explanations more complicated than required to fit the facts. By this standard, logic, genius, and zeitgeist appear mostly superfluous. Chance alone suffices to explicate the phenomena.

Yet it is definitely true that the creative product in science does not emerge out of some abstract combinatorial machine. On the contrary, scientific ideas originate in far more concrete circumstances. The Hollywood images portrayed in films such as *The Story of Louis Pasteur* in 1935 or *Madame Curie* in 1943 are perhaps closer to everyday scientific behavior. At least the scientists are shown working in laboratories, exchanging ideas with colleagues, and publishing their ideas before the world of science. These movies provide a much richer image of the scientific enterprise than is suggested by frequency distributions of publications or multiple grades. Hence, to make the theoretical explanation more plausible, it is necessary to embed the combinatorial model in the context of how scientific research is actually conducted and published.

That is the purpose of the current chapter. In particular, I scrutinize scientific creativity from three points of view: the individual, the field, and the domain. It should become apparent that this three-part discussion enriches the theoretical interpretation rather than contradicts it. Indeed, the analysis reveals some of the reasons why chance plays such a predominant role in scientific creativity.

INDIVIDUALS: RESEARCH PROGRAMS

Up to now, creative products have been examined in an entirely quantitative manner. In a sense, each scientific publication was interchangeable with any other because all we cared about was "bean counting." That is, we wanted to determine how the products were distributed across and within scientific careers. Even the discussion of the career landmarks was contingent on an underlying quantitative concept – namely, citations or impact. The only time we ventured into the qualitative aspects of creative products was when we treated multiple discovery and invention. Two or more creative ideas cannot be placed under the same label without making some decision about their qualitative content. Yet even here we tended to focus on quantitative features, such as temporal separation or degree of identity.

Hence, the overall picture suggested by this quantitative analysis is comparable to the mass production of homogeneous units, such as the manufacture of popular consumer products. This image is antithetical to the very concept of creativity. After all, a creative product must be an original product. To reproduce the same thing over and over cannot be considered creative activity. In addition, this depiction of scientific creativity tends to overlook the tremendous complexity of the process in the careers of real scientists. Creativity in science does not result from a static, repetitive, and well-delineated process as found in assembly-line manufacturing. Rather, creative output emerges out of a dynamic, incessantly changing, and ill-defined process. To appreciate this process, it is necessary to scrutinize the research programs of creative scientists.

Fortunately, these research programs have already been the focus of various lines of inquiry. The first and most indirect approach attempts to infer the characteristics of these programs by scrutinizing the bibliographies of highly successful scientists (Feist, 1997; Garvey & Tomita, 1972; Root-Bernstein, Bernstein, & Garnier, 1993; Simonton, 1992a). The specific aim is to discern how various research topics are distributed across the career course. A second and more direct approach entails the systematic analyses of manuscripts and notebooks, such as those left by Charles Darwin (Gruber, 1974) and Michael Faraday (Tweney, 1989). These analyses provide a much more detailed representation of what was going on "behind the scenes" of the overt publication record. A similar but less common strategy involves the analysis of tape recordings of the discussions that take place during actual laboratory meetings (Dunbar, 1995, 1997). Finally, active scientists sometimes become respondents to questionnaires or interviews that address their daily research activities and work habits (Hargens, 1978; Roe, 1953; Simon, 1974; Taylor, Locke, Lee, & Gist, 1984). Despite the diversity of these methods, the findings nonetheless converge on a coherent portrait of high-impact research programs (Simonton, 2003b).

In the first place, great scientists seldom make a name for themselves by focusing on one extremely narrow topic throughout the course of their career. Instead, they tend to display considerable scientific versatility by dealing with a variety of critical questions (Simon, 1974). For instance, one study of 2,260 scientists found a correlation of .24 between eminence and the number of distinct fields to which he or she made notable contributions (Sulloway, 1996). Newton's reputation depends on far more than just the *Principia*, his work on optics and mathematics being perhaps no less influential. In 1905 alone, Einstein published work that made significant contributions to four distinct areas: relativity theory, the photoelectric effect, statistical mechanics, and the size of molecules. So diverse were Einstein's creative products that his fame does not rest on any single line of inquiry. As Nobel laureate Max Born put it, Einstein "would be one of the greatest theoretical physicists of all times even if he had not written a single line on relativity" (Hoffman, 1972, p. 7). Supporting this seemingly exaggerated assertion is the fact that when Einstein received the Nobel Prize for Physics in 1921, the award citation explicitly mentioned just one contribution – namely, his work on the photoelectric effect.

A second generalization about high-impact careers is no less important than the first: highly creative scientists virtually never work on just one project at a time but rather they tend to pursue several independent inquiries simultaneously (Hargens, 1978; Simon, 1974). This *parallel processing* of research questions is certainly apparent in the career of Charles Darwin. Rather than devote fulltime to any one project, whether it be the *Origin of Species* or anything else, Darwin was constantly engaged in what has been styled a *network of enterprise* (Gruber, 1989). These are independent but interrelated inquiries that interact with each other in often complex and unpredictable ways. The best illustration is the circumstance that surrounded the creation of the *Origin*. Darwin first began compiling a notebook on the subject of the "transmutation of species" in 1837, the year after his return from his voyage on the *H.M.S. Beagle*. In 1859, the first edition of the *Origins* was published. Between 1837 and 1859, inclusively, Darwin was engaged on a great many other projects. These included

several studies on the geology of South America (1837–1846), coral formation (1837–1842), volcanic islands and mountain chains (1838–1844), and
geological formations in Scotland and Wales (1838–1842); preparation of
the volumes reporting the zoological findings of the *Beagle* voyage (five
volumes on fossil mammals, mammals, birds, fish, and reptiles worked
on from 1837–1845); extensive monographs on both fossil and modern
cirripedes (1847–1854); plus a host of miscellaneous papers, notes, and
reviews on topics as diverse as earthworms, mold, glacial action, erratic
boulders, volcanic rocks, a rock seen on an iceberg, dust falling on ships
in the Atlantic, the effects of salt water on seeds, seed vitality, the role of
bees in the fertilization of Papilionaceous flowers, Waterhouse's *Natural
History of the Mammalia*, and the species or genera *Rhea americana, Sagitta,
Planaria*, and *Arthrobalanus* (1837–1858). That is an impressive range of
topics, especially given that this period accounts for only about a quarter
of his entire career as a scientist! Obviously, Darwin had many different
things on his mind during the period when he conceived his theory of
evolution by natural selection.

It must be stressed that highly creative scientists are not mere dilet-
tantes who flit from topic to topic without rhyme or reason. On the contrary, usually permeating most of their work is a core set of themes, issues,
perspectives, or metaphors (Feist, 1997; Holton, 1982; Simonton, 1992a).
Hence, their research programs can be said to feature a certain "unity in
diversity." Their creative pursuits are both broad and deep. Equally important, the literature on research programs shows that the works in progress
vary on several other factors besides topic (Roe, 1972; Simon, 1974). In particular, each separate project varies tremendously regarding the following
six attributes:

1. *The likelihood of its successful completion* – Some works in progress
   are high-risk projects with a low expected probability of success,
   whereas other are relatively low-risk projects whose solution is virtually assured. Darwin's work on evolution was in the first category,
   particularly given his awareness of previous failed attempts to offer a

naturalistic explanation in opposition to the creationist position. In contrast, Darwin's work on cirripedes consisted of relatively straightforward if painstaking observations, and publication of the results would certainly generate no broad controversy.

2. *The intrinsic importance of the questions it addresses* – Some projects have the prospect of leading to major scientific breakthroughs, whereas others are much more mundane, merely consolidating what is already known (Sternberg, 1998). Although this dimension somewhat overlaps the first, they are not equivalent. For example, a scientist might tackle what at first seems to be a minor problem only to discover that its solution leads to a revolutionary innovation. Thus, when Max Planck attempted to solve the problem of blackbody radiation, he had no idea he would end up launching the quantum revolution. In contrast, sometimes a scientist considers ideas that have a low probability of success and at the same time a low probability of importance. For instance, Darwin's son Francis reported how his father "was willing to test what would seem to most people not at all worth testing. These rather wild trials he called 'fool's experiments,' and enjoyed extremely" (F. Darwin, 1892/1958, p. 101).

3. *The relevance of that project to other projects at the time* – Whereas some works in progress represent core questions in a scientist's research program, others are of more peripheral interest, pursued because they happened to provoke a scientist's curiosity. The psychologist B. F. Skinner (1959) once emphasized "a first principle not formally recognized by scientific methodologists: when you run onto something interesting, drop everything else and study it" (p. 363). And according to physiologist Claude Bernard, "Experimental ideas are often born by chance, with the help of some casual observation" (Horvitz, 2000, p. 22). Sometimes the impetus for such serendipitous inquiries comes without warning from external sources. For instance, Louis Pasteur interrupted his chemical research at the request of his former teacher, Jean Baptiste Dumas, who wanted Pasteur to solve the problem of a disease that was plaguing the French silkworm industry.

4. *The amount of progress that has so far been made on the project* – At one extreme are initial pilot studies that serve merely to explore new research territory, whereas at the other extreme are studies that have produced results ready to be written up for publication. Sometimes the time lapse between the initiation and completion phases occupies a decade or more. The gestation period for Darwin's *Origin* was about a dozen years, for Newton's *Principia* around two decades.

5. *The specific type of research involved* – Some projects may involve empirical studies, whether experimental or observational, others theoretical studies, such as mathematical models, and yet others reviews or critiques of the research literature. To be sure, some scientists concentrate on one particular type of research to the virtual exclusion of other types. Einstein was exclusively a theoretical rather than experimental physicist, for example. Even so, many great scientists display considerable diversity in the kinds of projects that are an integral part of their research programs. Newton was both a theoretical and an experimental physicist, besides doing work in pure mathematics. Darwin recorded systematic observations, conducted experimental studies, reviewed the literature, and developed theoretical interpretations.

6. *The degree of concentrated effort the investigator is devoting to the project at any given time* – A project that might first attract the scientist's primary efforts may encounter some obstacle to further progress, and thus be placed on the "back burner" while another project is elevated to the highest priority. Darwin's work on evolutionary theory illustrates this dynamic process well enough. Although he began his notebook on the subject in 1837, the degree of effort he devoted to his species theory waxed and waned up until the 1859 publication of the *Origin*. It was not until 1842 that he produced a pencil sketch of his theory, which he enlarged in 1844. But he did not begin collating his notes until 10 years later, and did not start writing in earnest until 1856 (at the urging of Charles Lyell). Even then, the project did not become the highest possible priority until after he received Wallace's

paper on evolutionary theory in 1858. He then dropped work on almost everything to get his *Origin* out in the following year. Even after the book's publication, Darwin would return to the *Origin* from time to time throughout his career as it went through several editions.

These features of high-impact research programs have major implications for understanding why scientific creativity appears to operate as a combinatorial process (Simonton, 2003b). Because the scientist has such a diversity of projects going on all at once, considerable *crosstalk* (or interference) can take place among the various works in progress (Miller, 2000). In effect, the ideas of one line of inquiry combine with the ideas of another line of inquiry. This crosstalk can sometimes result in unexpected solutions, progress on one project impinging on another project, even when the two are not viewed as being closely related. Poincaré (1921) provided an example in the following introspective report:

I turned my attention to the study of some arithmetical questions apparently without much success and without a suspicion of any connection with my preceding researches. Disgusted with my failure, I went to spend a few days at the seaside, and thought of something else. One morning, walking on the bluff, the idea came to me ... that the arithmetic transformations of indeterminate ternary quadratic forms were identical with those of non-Euclidean geometry. (p. 388)

Because the research programs consist of a dynamic mix of different projects, with unforeseen and unforeseeable interactions among the various projects, the output of these scientists should have the appearance of being generated by combinatorial processes. For instance, because of the probabilistic nature of the process, high-impact discoveries should be randomly distributed over the career course. As indicated in the Poincaré (1921) passage just quoted, sometimes the solution to an important problem must await the resolution of some other substantive question that is not even deemed relevant at the time. So chance has primacy over any other perspective simply because high-impact research programs are inadvertently designed to maximize the opportunities for serendipitous combinations of seemingly unrelated ideas.

FIELDS: PEER REVIEW

The chaotic flux of high-impact research programs is not the sole factor underlying the combinatorial nature of scientific creativity. Just as influential is the fact that the scientist is embedded in a field consisting of colleagues who are contributing to the same scientific enterprise. Because each scientist forms part of a field of scientists, he or she is exposed to various kinds of unanticipated events that have the net effect of undermining the expected flow of a research program. For instance, highly creative scientists often carry on a busy correspondence with colleagues, an informal activity that often makes them aware of new research results and efforts (Simonton, 1992b). This correspondence often involves the exchange of unpublished manuscripts and reprints that would not have been encountered otherwise. In addition, creativity in science is frequently connected with active participation in research conferences and conventions in which scientists are again exposed to unexpected ideas (Chambers, 1964). Finally, highly visible scientists are frequently asked to evaluate grant proposals submitted to funding agencies and manuscripts submitted to refereed journals. The ideas contained in these submissions can unexpectedly activate new trains of thought in their own research and thereby stimulate ideational combinations that might not occur otherwise. This stimulation is probably especially potent for those submitted proposals and manuscripts that concern research outside the reviewer's core research area.

Although such participation in peer review would clearly provide more or less random inputs into the scientists who serve as reviewers, the practice of peer review might also seem to cast doubt on the very validity of the equal-odds rule. After all, the assumption underlying peer review is that scientists have attained a consensus on what counts as quality research. In support of this assumption, studies have shown that scientists do indeed agree on the criteria by which research must be judged (Sternberg &

Gordeeva, 1996; Wolff, 1970). These include theoretical significance, practical significance, substantive interest, methodological competence, quality of the presentation, the adequacy of the literature review, objectivity in reporting results, and value for future research. Moreover, to avoid any doubts about the assessment of submitted proposals and manuscripts, editors frequently provide referees with a specified set of criteria (Gottfredson, 1978; Wolff, 1973). These judgments often are expressed in terms of explicit rating scales. Thus, the very existence of these criteria implies that scientists are fully capable of discriminating good from bad research.

If so, how can quality be a probabilistic consequence of quantity? From the very start of the career, and throughout its course, each scientist receives constant feedback from colleagues about the quality of his or her work. Hence, over time, each scientist should internalize those criteria, and eventually be able to augment the ratio of hits to total attempts. Not only would the quality ratio increase over the career course, but also the most prolific scientists – those who have passed through the peer-review cycle most frequently – should have higher overall hit rates than their less productive colleagues.

This apparent paradox can be resolved without compromising the thesis that scientific creativity involves a huge dose of chance. The resolution is based on recognizing that the peer-review process does not provide the feedback required for scientists to bypass the equal-odds rule. This ineffectiveness is apparent when we consider the following three complications:

1. If editors and reviewers exhibit such a strong consensus on the properties of a high-impact article, then that agreement should take the form of impressive interjudge reliabilities in separate assessments of manuscripts submitted for publication. This expectation runs counter to the accumulated evidence (Cicchetti, 1991; Weller, 2001). For instance, one investigation calculated the following reliability coefficients for referee evaluations of submitted manuscripts: probable reader interest in problem, .07; importance of present contribution, .28; attention to relevant literature, .37; design and analysis, .19;

style and organization, .25; succinctness, .31; and recommendation to accept or reject, .26 (Scott, 1974; cf. Marsh & Ball, 1989; McReynolds, 1971; Scarr & Weber, 1978). Needless to say, if a submitted manuscript reported that its measures had reliabilities this low, it (probably) would be rejected for publication on methodological grounds! So poor is the consensus among referees that their recommendations to accept a paper agree only about one-fifth of the time (Weller, 2001). As a consequence, most published articles should suffer rejection if resubmitted for publication. This bizarre outcome has been empirically demonstrated (Peters & Ceci, 1982). Indeed, the evaluation process that underlies all peer-reviewed journals has been generally shown to be "a little better than a dice roll" (Lindsey, 1988, p. 75). Luck has more impact than logic in the final editorial decision. Furthermore, the same minimal concordance confronts peer review when it is applied to research proposals submitted to major funding agencies (Cole, 1983). The main predictor of whether a project gets funded is the total number of grant proposals submitted, as would be expected from the operation of the equal-odds rule alone (Cole, Cole, & G. Simon, 1981).

2. The judgmental criteria by which manuscripts are actually evaluated do not always operate as implicitly claimed by the evaluators. In the first place, the assessment of a manuscript's quality is often influenced by extraneous factors such as the prestige of the institutions with which the authors are affiliated, the existence of a special relationship between the authors and the editor or reviewers, the authors' gender, the professional status of the referees, and even the length of the submitted manuscript and the number of references it contains (Crane, 1967; Petty, Fleming, & Fabrigar, 1999; Stewart, 1983). Although the unfortunate effects of these contaminating factors can be ameliorated somewhat by implementation of a blind review process (Bowen, Perloff, & Jacoby, 1972), those factors can intervene elsewhere as well, such as the decision to cite someone's

work once it is published (see, e.g., Ferber, 1986; Greenwald & Schuh, 1994). Second, even when a criterion is used, it is too often used in the wrong way. For instance, the quality of an investigation must be judged by both the importance of its research topic and the methodological rigor by which the topic is investigated. Yet the evidence indicates that methodological flaws are more likely to be overlooked if the topic is considered a highly significant one (Wilson et al., 1993). That bias can even lead to the recommendation that methodologically weak papers be accepted for publication.

3. Given the low reliability of reviewer assessments, plus the introduction of various contaminating factors, it would seem rather difficult for the peer evaluations to have much connection with a publication's actual impact on the discipline. And, in fact, such ratings tend to have poor predictive validity (Cole, 1983; Gottfredson, 1978). At most, a mere 10% of the variance is shared. For example, one study found that articles that were granted "best paper" awards did not have appreciably more citations than those failing to receive this honor (Lee et al., 2003). Another investigation obtained a correlation of .18 between peer-rated quality and citation counts (Shadish, 1989). Even worse, the publication attributes that predicted subjective quality evaluations were seldom the same as those that predicted objective citation measures. Moreover, it was much easier to predict the quality ratings than the citation counts. On the one hand, about 50% of the variance in the subjective quality assessment could be predicted through a combination of predictors (although these predictors were themselves subjective and therefore shared method variance with the criterion). On the other hand, only 10% of the variance in the objective citation counts could be similarly predicted. Significantly, the same low predictive power of peer evaluations applies to grant proposals as well. That is, the priority scores given research proposals fail to predict the later impact of either funded or unfunded projects (Cole, 1983). Despite the supposedly objective nature of science,

the ultimate influence of a scientific publication is not more readily predicted than that of a literary, artistic, or musical composition (see, e.g., Martindale et al., 1988; Simonton, 1980c, 1980d).

Why is peer review so unreliable as a gauge of the creativity of scientific products? There are several confounding factors (cf. Weller, 2001). First of all, the scientists who constitute a given specialty are not completely homogeneous with respect to the phenomena, facts, concepts, variables, constants, techniques, theories, laws, questions, goals, and criteria that represent their domain-specific expertise (see Figure 3.1). Because the samples are overlapping but not equivalent, each scientist applies certain criteria in an idiosyncratic manner (e.g., contribution to knowledge, topic selection, or literature review). To be sure, if a submitted manuscript or grant proposal were evaluated by a large representative sample of disciplinary colleagues, the reliability of the composite evaluation would be much higher. To illustrate, if there were 30 referees, and if the correlations among the separate referee assessments averaged around .20, the reliability of the summary judgment would still be .88, a highly impressive coefficient. Unfortunately, it is rare for peer review to depend on more than a half dozen evaluators, and the more typical number is less than half that size. As an example, with just three reviewers the reliability of the final decision is just .43, which fails to satisfy research standards.

Furthermore, many of the criteria require highly subjective judgments about which there must be a diversity of opinions anyway. For instance, who can objectively judge whether a journal's readers will find a particular problem interesting? Just as problematic are the criteria that require the evaluator to become a prophet. A case in point is the judgment about whether a study has important implications for future research. One reason why this criterion often has low predictive validity is that a new scientific idea can be *premature* (Hook, 2002) – that is, the idea's "implications cannot be connected by a series of simple logical steps to canonical, or generally accepted, knowledge" (Stent, 1972, p. 84). Examples include Gregor Mendel's quantitative analysis of genetic inheritance and Barbara

McClintock's research on genetic transformation ("jumping genes"). Premature discoveries are often produced by lone wolves whose domain samples depart significantly from the norm (e.g., scientist 1 in Figure 3.1). In such cases, it is expecting too much to have referees distinguish premature but significant ideas from those that are merely unimportant, and permanently so.

Aggravating matters all the more is the unwieldy number of relevant criteria, often running into the dozens (Gottfredson, 1978; Shadish, 1989; Sternberg & Gordeeva, 1996). Hence, evaluators are left with a bewildering array of standards for judging the merits of any potential contribution. This multidimensionality also implies that the attributes of a publication operate in a statistical rather than deterministic fashion to influence its final success. The correlation of any one characteristic with a work's impact must be necessarily reduced as the number of participating factors increases. Finally, it is very likely that the attributes that contribute to the impact of any product operate in a complex configurational manner (Simonton, 1999c). That is, interaction effects and curvilinear functions may dominate the determination (see, e.g., Simonton, 1980d, 1990). What might be the best method to adopt for one substantive problem may be the worst for another; what might be an ideal way to organize one discussion might be horribly ineffective for another; 20 manuscript pages might be just right for treating one topic, but too long for another and too short for a third; and so forth. To assess a manuscript's scientific worth may thus require a subtle, probabilistic manipulation of multiple dimensions interlinked in complex relationships.

The last problem would be not be so devastating if the human cognitive apparatus were supremely sophisticated in its information-processing capacities. Yet the human mind is not by any means an ideal processor of raw data (see, e.g., Faust 1984; Fiske & Taylor 1991; Kahneman, Slovic, & Tversky 1982). Instead, the human intellect is subject to many varieties of inaccuracies, constraints, and biases in perception, memory, thinking, and problem solving. Of special interest is the demonstrated human incapacity in the reliable inference of probabilistic, multidimensional, and configurational relationships among phenomena. It also must be emphasized that these constraints, biases, and inaccuracies apply to everyone, including those who submit their manuscripts for publication. Authors are not necessarily any better at judging their own work than are journal referees, and sometimes authors may be even less adequate because of self-serving biases and other intellectual contaminants. Indeed, we know from the historical record that even the greatest scientists can get it very wrong. Mendel believed the theoretical significance of his research concerned evolution rather than inheritance. Specifically, his studies of peas were to shed light on the process of hybridization. The mathematical modeling of the inheritance process was only a secondary aspect of his classic studies. Hence, it could be argued that Mendel himself was not truly a "Mendelian" geneticist (cf. Brannigan, 1981; Olby, 1979). He no more appreciated the real impact of his work than did his contemporaries. It works the other way, too, of course. All too often scientists have an overly high opinion of their own work and thus find themselves cut down to size by those asked to serve as journal referees.

All told, the evaluations investigators receive from peer review have minimal informational value. Indeed, if the feedback is practically random, it could serve largely to enhance the combinatorial nature of the creative process. The evaluations add just another source of chance to the serendipitous influx of other factors, such as the crosstalk among concomitant projects and the unanticipated impact of outside reading. Thus, the current peer-review process in all likelihood makes a positive contribution to scientific creativity. Scientists are thereby exposed to contrasting points of view, an exposure that often would stimulate the creative process. Indeed, those journal editors who deliberately solicit divergent reviews are probably enhancing the amount of creativity eventually seen. In contrast, if peer review were highly reliable, it would most likely exert a stifling influence on the discipline. Scientists would then quickly learn how to ensure the acceptance of their submitted manuscripts, with the result that published articles would become ever more homogeneous, conventional, and unoriginal – in a word, uncreative.

DOMAINS: DISCIPLINARY ZEITGEIST

The previous two sections have dealt mainly with scientific careers. It is now time to look again at scientific communities – specifically at multiple discovery. According to the theoretical account sketched in Chapter 3, all the key features of this phenomenon can be explained without having to posit some mysterious form of sociocultural determinism. Instead, multiples can be explicated as an essentially chance event. The zeitgeist has been reduced to just three supporting roles. First, the sociocultural system in large part determines the available means of communication and therefore influences the rate at which scientific ideas can be disseminated (Brannigan & Wanner, 1983b; Simonton, 1987). Second, the spirit of the times can be conceived as the collection of phenomena, facts, concepts, variables, constants, techniques, theories, laws, questions, goals, and criteria that enter the disciplinary pool from which creators draw their unique samples of ideas for their combinatory activities. Third, the zeitgeist, whether sociocultural or disciplinary, can influence which problems attract the most effort at a particular point in time, because of either practical urgency or theoretical significance. By chance alone, increasing the size of the field devoted to a specific set of ideas must enhance the odds of generating the best ideational combinations.

Too often advocates of the zeitgeist viewpoint believe the third provision suffices to ensure the inevitability of specific discoveries and inventions (e.g., Merton, 1961b). Yet that conclusion does not follow from the second provision. The repository of ideas that constitute a domain supplies the necessary (but not sufficient) conditions for all discoveries made in a specific period of a discipline's history. Hence, if a prerequisite idea is missing from the given zeitgeist, the corresponding ideational combination cannot emerge. This is true no matter how many scientists are working on the problem. For example, because a true calculus probably cannot appear without an analytic geometry having first appeared, Newton's mathematical achievements presuppose those of Descartes. Ironically, this very necessity augments even more the probabilistic nature of scientific creativity. A scientist may try to solve a problem for which the prerequisite elements are not yet in place and thus be doomed to failure without any awareness that a piece of the puzzle is missing. Many astronomers attempted to explain a certain irregularity in Mercury's orbit without knowing that an explanation was impossible from the perspective of Newtonian mechanics. In a sense, the probability of a solution was zero until the advent of Einstein's general relativity theory. Because it is virtually impossible to predict whether an essential component is missing from the domain, scientific creativity becomes necessarily capricious. Computer simulations have shown that the assignment of a priori orderings to scientific ideas has the repercussion of increasing the indeterminacy of the process (Simonton, 1986b). The number of trials needed for a solution may increase by a factor of 100 or more. Hence, the scientific enterprise wastes an immense amount of time spinning its wheels trying to solve problems for which the prerequisites have not entered the domain. Throwing more scientists at such unsolvable problems just adds to the wasted effort.

But what about those instances in which the necessary conditions have been met? Do the corresponding discoveries or inventions then become inevitable? Again, the proper answer is negative. The repository of domain-specific ideas provides the necessary, but not sufficient, basis for the combinations that lead to contributions (Simonton, 1986c, 1987). Just because the prerequisite ideas are in place for a particular discovery, it by no means guarantees that the discovery will be made right away, or even appear at all. As a consequence, many discoveries consist of ideas that have been in existence for decades, if not centuries, the delay reflecting the combinatorial process by which the ideational combinations are generated. An example is paper chromatography, which earned Martin and Synge a Nobel Prize even though Martin himself admitted "all the ideas are simple and had peoples' minds been directed that way the method would have flourished perhaps a century earlier" (Daintith, Mitchell, & Tootill, 1981, p. 531). The same inference of unpredictability can be drawn from rediscoveries in which one multiple is separated from the other by decades or more. Because Mendel's findings were independently rediscovered 35 years later, had he not carried out his experiments, genetics would have been discovered for the first time in 1900 rather than 1865.

Of course, a zeitgeist proponent can argue that it ultimately does not matter whether a given contribution is inevitable with respect to its specific date. Inevitability would still remain with respect to the contribution itself. Indeed, this is often seen as something that sets scientific creativity apart from other forms of creativity. As one historian of science expressed it, "if Michelangelo and Beethoven had not existed, their works would have been replaced by quite different contributions. If Copernicus or Fermi had never existed, essentially the same contributions would have had to come from other people" (Price, 1963, p. 69). However, even here the zeitgeist doctrine of inevitability is suspect. The crux of the matter is the phrase "essentially the same contributions." As pointed out in Chapter 2, the assertion of identity is overly dependent on the implementation of excessively generic categories. The separate contributions that compose a hypothetical multiple are seldom duplicates and are very often extremely different. This variation in the degree of identity means that it is not irrelevant which contribution happened to see the light of day. The history of science would have been irrevocably different.

The molecular biologist Gunther Stent (1972) made this very point with respect to Watson and Crick's formulation of the structure of deoxyribonucleic acid (DNA):

If Watson and Crick had not existed, the insights they provided in one single package would have come out much more gradually over a period of many months or years. Dr. B might have seen that DNA is a double-strand helix, and Dr. C might later have recognized the hydrogen bonding between the strands. Dr. D later yet might have proposed a complementary purine-pyrimidine bonding, with Dr. E in a subsequent paper proposing the specific adenine-thymine and guanine-cytosine replication mechanism of DNA based on the complementary nature of the two strands. All the while Drs. H, I, J, K & L would have been confusing the issue by publishing incorrect structures and proposals. (p. 90)

Similar counterfactual scenarios might be generated regarding other famous breakthroughs of science, from Copernicus to the present day. Generic eventuality is not equivalent to specific inevitability.

Actually, in the case of the calculus it is possible to provide more than a hypothetical illustration. Despite its status as a grade-two multiple, Newton's conception was radically different from that of Leibniz. For instance, Newton's notation is more awkward than Leibniz's, so much so that it is Leibniz's that largely prevails today. Even more fundamentally, Newton placed primary emphasis on differentiation, giving integration a subordinate role, so much so that he failed to provide it with an explicit treatment or symbolic representation. In contrast, Leibniz assigned immense importance to integration, devising the integration symbol currently used and emphasizing its inverse relation with differentiation. Some of these contrasts come from the fact that Newton and Leibniz possessed overlapping but not identical samples from the domain of contemporary mathematics. For example, Newton's sample was partly shaped by his teacher Isaac Barrow, whereas Leibniz's was greatly influenced by Blaise Pascal. In addition, whereas Newton was preoccupied with practical problems in mechanics, Leibniz was more obsessed with the theoretical development of a universal language in which integration played a major part (the *summa omnium*). In any case, the subsequent history of mathematics was to prove that these differences were not trivial. While British mathematicians patriotically developed Newtonian fluxions, mathematicians on the continent of Europe built upon Leibniz's calculus. It was the Leibnizian tradition that turned out to be far more fruitful, inspiring such great mathematicians as Jakob and Johann Bernoulli, G. F. A. de l'Hospital, Leonhard Euler, and Jean Le Rond d'Alembert. Indeed, the Newtonian tradition may have exerted a stifling effect on British mathematics.

94

Finally, it cannot be overstated that the ultimate agent of scientific creativity is the individual and not the discipline or the sociocultural system. The zeitgeist cannot generate ideational combinations in the absence of those individuals. Although creative scientists depend on the ideas that define the domain, those same scientists are responsible for transforming that domain. Each time a scientist successfully creates and communicates a new combination of these disciplinary ideas, that combination enters the ideational pool from which future discoveries or inventions can be made. Once Newton used gravitational mechanics to explain the orbits of the known planets, subsequent scientists could use the same laws to predict the existence of a previously unknown planet (namely, Neptune). Furthermore, these additions to the repository vary greatly in their capacity to stimulate new scientific discoveries (Sternberg, 1998). On the one hand, some investigations merely replicate or slightly extend previous work within a given paradigm. Probably a significant proportion of uncited scientific publications are of this nature. On the other hand, other investigations report discoveries that are anomalous with respect to the scientific paradigms of the day and can play a powerful role in stimulating future scientific revolutions (Kuhn, 1970). Thus, research on blackbody radiation had this catalytic role in the advent of Planck's quantum theory, which led to the quantum revolution.

Nonetheless, we do not want to commit the error of placing too much emphasis on the individual. Although the domain is defined by the contributions made by creative scientists, we cannot conclude that the genius perspective has won out over the zeitgeist perspective. Both perspectives must yield explanatory ground to the chance perspective. This was apparent in the earlier discussions of research programs and peer review. The creative scientist is just as much at the whim of the dice throw as is the disciplinary zeitgeist. It is no more inevitable that a given scientist will make particular discovery than it is inevitable that the same discovery will emerge in a given time and place.

The last statement is reinforced by an interesting convergence between what has been learned about scientific creativity at the individual level and that occurring at the community level. In the former case, the Poisson distribution describes the number of discoveries in a given year, whereas in the latter case, Poisson distribution describes the frequencies of various multiple grades. Furthermore, these two Poisson distributions have very similar parameters (i.e., $\mu \approx 1$). The convergence not only confirms that Poincaré's (1921) "good combinations" constitute low-probability events but also implies that the estimated probability would be about the same for individuals and communities. At the level of the individual scientist, it takes many combinatorial trials to get one hit, whereas at the community level it takes many individuals recombining the same set of ideas to obtain a single success. Rarely does the typical scientist have more than one good idea in any given year, and just as rarely do two or more scientists operating within the same field come up with the same good idea. The odds are comparably low in either case. Both genius and zeitgeist are contingent on chance.

TWO IMPLICATIONS

The discussion of individual, field, and domain has provided a substantive basis for the theoretical explanation outlined in Chapter 3. The combinatorial nature of scientific creativity has been shown to be consistent with what is known about high-impact research programs, the operation of peer review, and the effects of the disciplinary zeitgeist. So far, nothing appears to impose any substantial constraint on the conclusion that scientific creativity functions like a chance combinatorial process. Indeed, this chapter has helped document some of the reasons why discovery and invention fail to operate as a straightforward, step-by-step, logical process. Research programs are far too unsystematic, the feedback from peers too unreliable, and the disciplinary zeitgeist too passive. This substantive documentation is expanded in the next two chapters where the theoretical account is grounded in what we know about creative scientists and scientific discovery. But before I do so, I first wish to discuss two intriguing implications that ensue from considering the individual, field, and domain all at once.

As said earlier, any given domain consists of the contributions of individual scientists. Sometimes these contributions involve replacement according to the principle of "out with the old and in with the new." Thus Lavoisier's oxygen theory replaced Stahl's outdated phlogiston chemistry. In such cases, the domain may change its composition without necessarily growing. More often, however, new discoveries and inventions are added to the domain so that the repository becomes richer and more complex. As the cumulative body of scientific ideas increases, the number of potential ideational combinations expands dramatically, generating an "information explosion" in science. Yet, this is not the only growth that is taking place. Paralleling the expansion of the domain is the growth in the number of scientists who define the corresponding field. In most disciplines this growth has been approximately exponential, so much so that most of the scientists who have ever lived are still living (Price, 1963).

The two upward trends in the number of ideas and the number of scientists taken together imply that the production of new discoveries should become highly accelerated. There exists ample evidence that this is the case (Fowler, 1987; Lehman, 1947; Price, 1963; Rainoff, 1929). In fact, this accelerated growth of scientific ideas has been successfully explicated via a combinatorial model. This model explicitly assumes "the rate of growth in the number of ideas is proportional jointly to the number of ideas in hand and the number of minds to consider them" (Fowler, 1987, p. 18). In particular, the model assumes, in a manner clearly consistent with Poincaré's (1921) introspective report, that discovery requires a "random creative collision process" in which ideas are "the result of a 'collision' between minds and ideas" (Fowler, 1987, p. 15). The differential equation describing this process may be given as

$$dI/dt = \gamma IN$$

where I is the number of ideas making up a discipline (i.e., the size of the domain), N is the number of minds working with those ideas (i.e., the size of the field), and γ is a constant that likely varies across disciplines. Stated in words, the rate at which ideas are added to the domain is proportional to the product of the size of the domain and the size of the field. The hypothesized process has been shown to provide an excellent fit to the rate that discoveries have been accumulating in physics (Fowler, 1987).

What is perhaps more fascinating is the second implication that the creativity of individual scientists has become amplified almost as much as the creativity of the entire scientific community (Price, 1963; Simonton, 1992b). The larger the scientific community in which an individual is embedded, and the richer the cumulative body of scientific knowledge, the more impressive the creativity that can be displayed by the most prolific scientist in a given field. This effect is implicit in Price's law, which claims that if N represents the number of scientists active in a field, the square root of this number ($N^{1/2}$) represents the number of scientists who are responsible for half of all contributions to the discipline (Price, 1963; cf. Allison et al., 1976). According to this law, as the number of scientists increases, a smaller proportion of scientists will account for half the work (cf. Zhao, 1984). In a sense, the discipline becomes more and more elitist as the field recruits more active participants. If genius is defined as someone belonging to the prolific elite, then the expansion of the field has the ironic effect of accentuating the impact of the individual. In a doubly ironic sense, the expanded field augments the productivity of the most prolific contributors by exposing them to a more massive influx of serendipitous events. With more colleagues having more diverse samples from the increasingly rich pool of ideas, the top scientists can benefit even more from the disordered bombardment. Genius is accentuated by chance – where that chance is bolstered by the disciplinary zeitgeist.

5

Creative Scientists

As observed in Chapters 1 and 2, the psychology of science is not a homogeneous research area. On one side of the disciplinary divide are psychologists who conduct laboratory experiments on problem solving to tease out the logic of discovery. On the other side are psychologists who subject active scientists to psychometric assessment techniques to discern the personal attributes associated with scientific creativity and genius. Of these two divergent traditions, the second is the oldest. Francis Galton's (1874) survey of Fellows of the Royal Society of London represents the first bona fide psychological study of distinguished scientists. Since then, a vast literature has accumulated on the characteristics and backgrounds of creative scientists (Feist, 1998; Mansfield & Busse, 1981; Simonton, 1988b). This body of knowledge belongs to a more inclusive literature on the personal attributes of creative individuals of all kinds (Martindale, 1989; Simonton, 1999a).

The last fact raises a critical issue: to what extent is scientific creativity separate from other forms of creativity? Is the psychology of the creative scientist really no different from that of the creative artist? Or are there some fundamental contrasts? From the logic perspective, it would seem that scientific creativity must differ from artistic creativity at least insofar as science depends more heavily on logical analysis, especially mathematics and statistics. The zeitgeist perspective also suggests a fundamental discrepancy. As pointed out in Chapter 4, the creative products of Beethoven or Michelangelo seem to have a unique status that renders them irreplaceable, whereas the ideas of Copernicus or Fermi would have appeared in some other guise had neither scientist ever existed. On the other hand, the genius perspective would seem to argue that creativity in the sciences does not differ in any substantial way from creativity in the arts. For instance, Samuel Johnson (1781), the author of the first English-language dictionary, held "the true Genius is a mind of large general powers, accidentally determined to some particular direction" (p. 5). In this view, Albert Einstein might just as well have become Pablo Picasso or Igor Stravinsky had the circumstances of his birth or training been different.

The chance perspective, in contrast, has a different take on this issue. As argued in the preceding two chapters, creativity functions as if it were a random combinatorial process. Nonetheless, not every type of creativity is equally probabilistic. That is, the various domains differ in the extent to which that process must be constrained. These constraints include restrictions on (1) the ideas that enter the combinatorial process, (2) the degree to which the combinatorial process is fully random, and (3) the criteria that are applied to determine what constitutes a good combination resulting from that process (Simonton, 1999c). In general, scientific creativity is far more constrained by such standards than is artistic creativity. For example, where artistic creators often include ideas from everyday life – especially in literature and the visual arts – scientific creators must restrict their ideational samples to a more specialized domain. Picasso can easily introduce an apple, a guitar, or a clown into any of his paintings, but it is more difficult to imagine a legitimate way that Einstein might incorporate any of these same commonplace objects into one of his scientific papers. Another constraint difference between science and art is even more obvious: the role of logic. Artistic creators often rely heavily on incongruity, implausibility, ambiguity, suggestion, and allusion, whereas scientific creators must depend on consistency, plausibility, clarity, implication, and explicitness. An artist may resort to "poetic license" with impunity, but for the scientist to introduce something comparable is condemned as a non sequitur.

Yet, it must also be recognized that differences regarding the magnitude of constraint exist within the sciences as well as the arts. In the latter case, for example, formal and academic styles tend to be much more constrained than surrealist and expressionist styles (Ludwig, 1998). In addition, as an artistic style develops over time, the combinatorial process tends to become ever more free, and eventually even the constraints imposed by artistic conventions tend to break down (Martindale, 1990). Nearly parallel contrasts are apparent in the sciences.

First, disciplines vary greatly in the theoretical, methodological, and substantive restrictions that are imposed on scientific creativity. This variation in constraints may largely reflect disciplinary contrasts in a domain's paradigmatic structure or coherence (Kuhn, 1970; Thagard, 1992). According to Kuhn (1970), a paradigm signifies "some accepted examples of actual scientific practice – examples which include law, theory, application, and instrumentation together – provide models from which spring particular coherent traditions of scientific research" (p. 10). Scientists "whose research is based on shared paradigms are committed to the same rules and standards for scientific practice" (p. 11). Clearly, some sciences, such as physics, are highly paradigmatic, whereas other sciences, such as sociology, are much less so, if they can be said to have paradigms at all. These contrasts in disciplinary constraints correspond roughly to the hierarchy of the sciences proposed by Auguste Comte (1839–1842/1855). Furthermore, empirical research has demonstrated the objective reality of these distinctions (Simonton, 2002, 2004). For instance, highly paradigmatic disciplines exhibit (1) greater consensus in the peer evaluation of research problems and findings, (2) faster rates of research impact and obsolescence, and (3) higher ratios of laws to theories in their cumulative body of knowledge.

Second, within paradigmatic disciplines, the degree of constraint varies across time. In some periods, scientists practice what Kuhn (1970) termed *normal science*. These practitioners are engaged in *puzzle-solving* research that is highly constrained by an established and widely accepted paradigm. Thus, physicists in the 18th and 19th centuries were largely confined to the range of ideas permitted by Newtonian mechanics and, later, Maxwell's equations. In contrast, during certain periods scientists revolutionize their disciplines by offering an entirely new paradigm that operates under fewer constraints. In fact, a significant feature of a revolutionary paradigm is that it eventually replaces the old restrictions with entirely new constraints on what counts as normal science (Kuhn, 1970). Relativity and quantum theories were of this nature, redefining how physicists answered questions – and even what questions physicists asked.

The foregoing considerations lead to three empirical predictions. First, creative individuals should display characteristics that allow them to engage in the hypothesized combinatorial process. Second, although these attributes set creative persons apart from noncreative persons, scientific creators do not exhibit these characteristics in so pronounced a degree as do artistic creators. Creative scientists should fall somewhere between creative artists and otherwise comparable noncreative persons. Third, under two circumstances scientific creators exhibit characteristics closer to (but still separate from) those of artistic creators: (1) all scientists working in less paradigmatic disciplines, and (2) revolutionary scientists working in more paradigmatic disciplines.

What evidence is there for these three predictions? To provide an answer, I discuss creative scientists in two sections. In the first section, I examine the intellectual and personality traits associated with creativity in science. In the second section, I review the developmental correlates of scientific creativity. Before doing so, I must make it explicit that I focus on those features that address the two predictions derived from the chance perspective. Characteristics that are not pertinent to that question are ignored. For instance, there is no doubt that creative scientists are highly motivated, goal-oriented individuals who have the drive, energy, and persistence necessary to achieve distinction in their chosen field (Busse & Mansfield, 1984; Chambers, 1964; Roe, 1953). Even so, this motivation is not unique to scientific creators or even to exceptional creators in general (Cox, 1926; Galton, 1869; Simonton, 1994). This same attribute figures prominently in all forms of outstanding achievement, whether by creators, leaders, performers, or athletes. Yet, it is clear that some of these achievement domains probably do not entail any chance combinatorial process. Certainly such a process plays a minimal role if any in the performance of a virtuoso violinist or champion golfer. Hence, this particular factor has no immediate relevance to the question at hand. Creative scientists are highly motivated, but they are not *creative* because they are so highly motivated.

DISPOSITION

Below I examine five individual factors that may provide the foundations of scientific creativity. These are intelligence, associative richness, openness to experience, psychopathology, and janusian thinking. Taken together, these factors enable us to understand how cognition and personality support the combinatorial process.

Intelligence

Creative scientists are highly intelligent. For instance, one historiometric study estimated IQ scores based on biographical information about precocious accomplishments (Cox, 1926). Representative scores include the following: Leibniz, 195; Pascal, 190; Harvey, 170; Descartes, 165; Huygens, 160; Galileo, 160; Kepler, 155; Charles Darwin, 155; Linnaeus, 155; Newton, 150; Lavoisier, 150; Faraday, 135; and Copernicus, 135 (using corrected IQs for ages 0–16). These retrospective estimates may be a little on the high side because psychometric studies obtain somewhat lower, but still impressive, IQ scores (cf. Roe, 1953). For example, one study found that creative mathematicians averaged a 135 IQ on the Wechsler Adult Intelligence Scale or WAIS (Helson & Crutchfield, 1970), while another found that creative research scientists averaged WAIS IQ scores of 133 (MacKinnon & Hall, 1972). In general, the mean IQ is about two standard deviations above the population average.

However, the implications of these results must be tempered by two additional findings. First, the variation in the IQ scores received is so large that many distinguished scientists exhibit a psychometric intelligence no higher than that of the average college graduate (e.g., around IQ 120). Thus, according to one investigation, creative research scientists had IQs that ranged from 121 to 142, albeit nearly three-fourths had WAIS IQs greater than or equal to 130 (MacKinnon & Hall, 1972). Second, the range is so great that the IQ distributions for eminent scientists differ very little from those of their less eminent colleagues. For example, in the study just cited the mean WAIS IQ scores for a comparison group of scientists was only one point lower (i.e., 133 versus 132), a negligible difference (MacKinnon & Hall, 1972). In fact, when IQ scores are correlated with some valid criterion of scientific distinction, the correlations are nearly zero. For instance, one study of 499 academic researchers in the physical, biological, and social sciences found that IQ correlated .05 with the number of published papers and .06 with the number of citations (Cole & Cole, 1973). Another study of research scientists actually found a slightly negative correlation ($r = -.05$) between intelligence and a citation measure of scientific achievement (Bayer & Folger, 1966). The same near-zero correlations appear if a different criterion of scientific accomplishment is used, such as peer and supervisor ratings (e.g., $r = -.05$, in Gough, 1976; see also Cole & Cole, 1973; Feist & Barron, 2003; Taylor, 1963).

These findings suggest that a minimum amount of intelligence is probably required to become a creative scientist. That threshold level is probably equivalent to an IQ of around 120 (cf. Barron & Harrington, 1981). That figure represents the minimum intellect required to master the basic knowledge and techniques that constitute an individual's sample from the population of phenomena, facts, concepts, variables, constants, techniques, theories, laws, questions, goals, and criteria that define the domain. However, something more is required besides the acquisition of domain-specific expertise. The scientist also must be able to engage in the requisite combinatorial process. This second requirement implies that the intellect must be organized in a manner that allows that process to take place (Simonton, 1980a).

Associative Richness

More than a century ago physicist Ernst Mach (1896) pinpointed a critical contrast between two cognitive capacities. On the one hand, he observed that a scientist must have "a powerfully developed *mechanical* memory, which recalls vividly and faithfully old situations, [which] is sufficient for avoiding definite particular dangers, or for taking advantage of definite particular opportunities" (p. 167, italics in original). This capacity seems to belong to the set of intellectual abilities gauged by IQ tests. On the other hand, Mach also stressed that "more is required for the development of *inventions*. More extensive chains of images are necessary here, the excitation by mutual contact of widely different trains of ideas, a more powerful, more manifold, and richer connection of the contents of memory, a more powerful and impressionable psychical life, heightened by use" (p. 167; italics in original). It is from this associative richness that Poincaré's good combinations are most likely to emerge. In Mach's own words, "from the teeming, swelling host of fancies which a free and high-flown imagination calls forth, suddenly that particular form arises to the light which harmonises perfectly with the ruling idea, mood, or design" (p. 174). Cognitive order emerges from the associative chaos.

Hierarchies. Mach's associationist account may be framed in terms of a well-known psychological theory of creativity (Mednick, 1962). According to this theory, creativity involves the ability to make remote associations between distinct ideas. Highly creative individuals are said to have a flat hierarchy of associations in comparison to the steep hierarchy of associations of those with low creativity. The contrast between the two conditions is shown in Figure 5.1. Figure 5.2 then indicates the repercussions of this contrast for the expected networks of associations. For persons with a steep association hierarchy, as depicted in the upper part of the figure, ideas are connected by just a few high-probability associations.

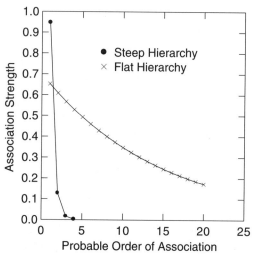

FIGURE 5.1. Steep versus flat association hierarchies according to Mednick's (1962) theory of creativity. Graph adapted from Simonton (1999c).

This means that any given idea will normally be linked to just one or two closely related ideas. As a result, many ideas will be associatively isolated from other ideas in the network, rendering their combination extremely unlikely. For example, the ideas forming the cluster FKLP are disconnected from the ideas constituting cluster UVKW. Indeed, idea X is isolated from all the rest. This compartmentalization of information differs greatly from the network expected from a flat association hierarchy, as shown in the lower part of Figure 5.2. Although the associations are generally weaker, the number of associations is much larger, so that every idea is connected either directly or indirectly with very other idea. In fact, unlike the case for steep association hierarchies, most ideas can be associatively connected with other ideas by multiple paths. This multiplicity implies a superior ability to combine a diversity of ideas. More available connections means more possible combinations.

Besides capturing Mach's (1896) conception of what is required for invention in science, the flat association hierarchies graphed in Figures 5.1 and 5.2 imply that the creative process will be highly "chancy." This

Steep Association Hierarchy

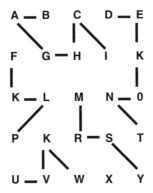

Flat Association Hierarchy

FIGURE 5.2. Contrasting association networks generated by the steep versus flat association hierarchies in Figure 5.1. Letters A to Y indicate ideas taken from the domain, and lines indicate associations connecting those ideas, with the thickness of the lines signifying the strength of the association.

chanciness is apparent in the following three considerations (Eysenck, 1995; Simonton, 2003b):

First, a flat association hierarchy indicates that for any given stimulus, the creative person has many associations available, all with roughly equal probabilities of retrieval. Persons who are very low in creativity, by comparison, have steep association hierarchies in which any given stimulus elicits just one or two responses in a highly predictable fashion. Clearly, the thought processes of individuals with flat association hierarchies should be more unpredictable than the more stereotyped thinking linked with steep hierarchies. Where the latter will respond in the same way to the same stimulus time after time, the former will respond more variably because the most probable response at any one moment is largely decided by the psychological equivalent of a coin flip.

Second, besides the more nearly equiprobable nature of the associations, flat association hierarchies are necessarily more susceptible to relatively minor priming effects (Simonton, 1999c). That is, an unexpected input of an external stimulus or an internal train of thought can easily change the relative probabilities of the associations making up the hierarchy. Hence, for highly creative persons, the most probable sequence of associations will be highly unstable over time, making their behavior more unpredictable relative to those who are less creative.

Third, not all associations making up a given hierarchy are equally likely to evoke that remote connection that provides the solution to a given problem. Rather, the vast majority of associations lead to cul-de-sacs during the incubation phase of the creative process. Given that successful association linkages are so rare, the odds of chancing upon the most fruitful association sequence become quite unpredictable. Sometimes the correct association arrives early, sometimes a bit later, and yet other times even later still. Essentially, the incubation period behaves like a game of craps in which a winning throw has the same chance of appearing no matter how long the gambler has been playing the game.

These three points together imply that scientific creativity should operate very much like a Poisson process. That is, the flat association hierarchy will, in effect, yield a large number of trials, each having a very low probability of producing a successful outcome.

Constraints. Nevertheless, it must be recognized that the process of generating remote associations is not completely unrestrained. Because scientific creativity tends to operate under more logical and substantive constraints, the associative process must be correspondingly more re-stricted. There is already sufficient evidence to indicate that this is the case. For example, consider the following six empirical findings:

1. Although creative scientists generate more unusual word associations than noncreative scientists (Gough, 1976; Mullins, 1963), extremely rare associations are not associated with creativity in science (Gough, 1976). Thus, the relation between scientific creativity and associative originality is described by an inverted-U curve indicating that exis-tence of an optimum level of associative richness. The peak appears when the associations are those given between 1% and 10% of the time (Gough, 1976).

2. Whereas creative scientists display a great deal of cognitive complex-ity when talking about their research, they display no such com-plexity when discussing a topic unrelated to their research – namely, teaching (Feist, 1994). Because cognitive complexity is positively cor-related with creativity (Charlton & Bakan, 1988–1989; Suedfeld & Coren, 1992), it is apparent that the creativity of scientists may not necessarily extend beyond their research activity.

3. Although conspicuous primary-process (primordial) imagery is posi-tively associated with creativity in the arts (Martindale, 1990; Simon-ton, 1989c), it is negatively associated with creativity in the sciences (Simonton, 1992a). Such imagery is characterized by abundant emo-tional, sensory, concrete, and subjective ideas and hence tends to support more associative richness than does secondary-process (con-ceptual) imagery that is abstract, logical, and objective (Ochse, 1989; Suler, 1980).

4. Creativity in science is more strongly associated with exceptional intelligence than is creativity in the arts (Cox, 1926). Although it could be the case that creative artists are actually less intelligent than creative scientists, a more likely explanation is that the scientific cre-ativity requires more the kind of analytical intelligence assessed in standard psychometric instruments (Gardner, 1983, 1993; Sternberg,

2004). This intelligence presumably imposes more constraints on the combinatorial process than would be desirable in the arts (see also Hudson, 1966).

5. The ability to generate remote associations is intimately connected with the capacity to engage in divergent thinking. Divergent thought is the process of generating lots of distinct and original ideas in response to a given stimulus (Guilford, 1967). Research suggests that divergent thinking is more strongly connected with behavioral creativity if the assessment or training is domain specific rather than generic (Baer, 1993, 1994, 1996; Han, 2003; Mumford et al., 1998). Similarly, the measurement of associative richness is more predictive of scientific creativity when the stimulus words come from the scientific domain (Gough, 1976).

6. Achieved eminence is positively associated with versatility – that is, with the ability and interest to make contributions to multiple domains (Raskin, 1936; Simonton, 1976a; Sulloway, 1996). Obvious examples are people like da Vinci, who was a painter, sculptor, architect, engineer, and scientist, and Goethe, who was a poet, dramatist, novelist, and scientist. Even so, eminent creators in the sciences tend to be appreciably less versatile than their counterparts in literature and philosophy (Cassandro, 2001). This lowered versatility implies a more severe restriction on the range of ideas to which scientists apply their combinatorial processes.

These six empirical findings, however indirectly, converge on a single conclusion: Although the creative scientist displays the associative richness suggested by Mach (1896), that richness is more limited in content and extent than is the case for the creative artist. Furthermore, there is reason to believe that the same contrasts that separate artistic from scientific creativity also differentiate various forms of scientific creativity. For example, eminent psychologists who favor a more natural science orientation display lower levels of cognitive complexity than do equally eminent psychologists who favor a more human science orientation (Suedfeld, 1985).

Presumably the creative process in the natural sciences operates under more constraint than in the human sciences. A similar argument could help explain why IQ scores are higher for scientists in paradigmatic sciences than for those in the nonparadigmatic sciences (Gibson & Light, 1967). Although no evidence yet exists on this point, I predict that within paradigmatic sciences, a parallel set of variables will distinguish the practitioners of normal science from the proponents of revolutionary science.

Openness to Experience

Apart from the cognitive capacity for rich associations, highly creative individuals feature certain personality traits that render their thoughts less predictable and hence more supportive of chance combinations (Simonton, 1999c). Most significantly and consistently, creativity is positively associated with *openness to experience* (King et al., 1996; McCrae, 1987). This trait concerns "the breadth, depth, and permeability of consciousness, and . . . the recurrent need to enlarge and examine experience" (McCrae & Costa, 1997, p. 826). Corresponding with this propensity is a diversity of interests and hobbies, a preference for complexity and novelty, and a tolerance of ambiguity (Barron, 1963; Davis, 1975; Gough, 1979). This inclination is also related to the creative person's capacity for *defocused attention*. This is the capacity that enables the mind to encompass simultaneously two or more unrelated stimuli or associations, thus enabling the mind to conceive ideational combinations impossible under more focused attention (Dewing & Battye, 1971; Gabora, 2002; Kasof, 1997; Mendelsohn, 1976; Mendelsohn & Griswold, 1966). Defocused attention is diametrically opposed to the concentrated and directed attention more characteristic of the analytical thinking required when individuals are engaged in deductive reasoning (Ansburg & Hill, 2003). In short, the intellect of the creator is an open system with respect to events available in the external world.

A necessary repercussion of this characteristic openness is that the intellect of a highly creative individual is more frequently exposed to a tremendous variety of extraneous influences. Such diverse input can often deflect the associative process toward unanticipated directions. Chains of thought will accordingly crosscut in unanticipated ways and thereby bring otherwise unrelated ideas into consciousness so as to form novel combinations. Such priming effects become all the more unpredictable when coupled with the flat association hierarchies mentioned earlier (Simonton, 2003b). If a large number of associates have nearly equal probabilities, then experiential openness destabilizes the relative order of those associates from one moment to the next. The overall effect is that of a highly unpredictable combinatorial process.

Although the above research on openness to experience did not specifically concentrate on scientific creativity, sufficient reason exists to conclude that science operates no differently (Feist & Barron, 2003). For instance, creative scientists, relative to their less creative colleagues, are much more likely to have diverse hobbies, such as painting, art collecting, drawing, poetry, photography, crafts, and music (Helson, 1980; Helson & Crutchfield, 1970; Root-Bernstein, Bernstein, & Garnier, 1995). Although these outside interests serve largely a recreational function, they also expose the hobbyist to diverse and unexpected experiences that can leave an impression on the scientist's thought processes during the incubation period. This consequence is evident in the frequent anecdotes of how scientists have made great discoveries while engaged in some favorite avocation.

Perhaps this positive consequence is most apparent with respect to recreational reading. Achieved eminence is generally correlated with voracious and omnivorous reading (Simonton, 1984c), and attained distinction in science is no exception. Notable scientists tend to read widely (Blackburn, Behymer, & Hall, 1978; Smith et al., 1961; Van Zelst & Kerr, 1951), including extensive reading in areas outside their main discipline (Dennis & Girden, 1954; Manis, 1951; Simon, 1974). Such interdisciplinary exposure increases the odds they might chance upon facts or concepts that turn out to be surprisingly relevant to one of their current projects. A classic example is how Charles Darwin's casual reading of Thomas Malthus's

Essay on the Principle of Population inspired the crucial concept of the struggle for existence. In his own words,

In October 1838, that is, fifteen months after I had begun my systematic enquiry [on evolution], I happened to read for amusement Malthus on *Population*, and being well prepared to appreciate the struggle for existence which everywhere goes on from long-continued observation of the habits of animals and plants, it at once struck me that under these circumstances favourable variations would tend to be preserved and unfavourable ones to be destroyed. The result of this would be the formation of new species. Here, then, I had at last got a theory by which to work. (F. Darwin, 1892/1958, p. 43)

An extradisciplinary influence may even come from well beyond science, albeit its impact may be less profound than witnessed in the Darwin example. Thus, theoretical physicist Murray Gell-Mann named the "Eight-Fold Way" after Buddhist philosophy and coined the term "quark" after a phrase in James Joyce's *Finnegans Wake*.

It should be noted that the associative richness discussed in the previous section bears a direct relation with the openness discussed here. In particular, individuals with flat association hierarchies are more likely to pick up on peripheral cues during problem solving (Ansburg & Hill, 2003). Hence, both can be considered as two manifestations of the same underlying characteristics. Creative intellects are open both to remote associations taking place within the mind and to irrelevant stimuli occurring outside the mind.

Psychopathology

Another apparent trait of highly creative individuals operates in a more complicated manner: creative persons often display symptoms of psychopathology (Juda, 1949; Ludwig, 1995; Post, 1994). This propensity is revealed by higher than average scores on the clinical scales of the nbsp;Minnesota Multiphasic Personality Inventory (Barron, 1969) as well as elevated scores on the Psychoticism Scale of the Eysenck Personality Questionnaire (Eysenck, 1993, 1995; Rushton, 1990). Those low on the latter dimension are socialized, conventional, and conformist, whereas those high on this dimension are impulsive, egocentric, antisocial, impersonal, hostile, and aggressive, and, at the higher extremities, they display tendencies toward psychopathic, affective, and schizophrenic disorders. These empirical results may partly reflect the creator's need for independence or autonomy to avoid the constraints of conventional views. Yet another portion of these findings may be more directly connected to the cognitive process behind creativity. Eysenck (1994) has shown, for example, that psychoticism is positively correlated with the capacity for unusual associations and with appreciation for highly complex stimuli. Both of these outcomes would have the consequence of making the thought process more unpredictable and hence more random than systematic.

Interestingly, Eysenck (1993, 1995) has also shown that psychoticism is positively associated with a relative inability to filter out extraneous information. More specifically, high scores on psychoticism are correlated with weakened *negative priming* and, especially, less effective *latent inhibition*. The latter involves a preconscious process by which the mind ignores stimuli that have been previously determined to be irrelevant in a given situation. Because of this attention failure, the creative mind is more likely to be bombarded by stimuli that influence the outcome in unexpected ways (see also Stravridou & Furnham, 1996; Wuthrich & Bates, 2001). The upshot would be ideational combinations that would not occur otherwise. Not surprisingly, reduced latent inhibition also has a positive association with openness to experience (Peterson & Carson, 2000; Peterson, Smith, & Carson, 2002) and to creativity assessed by both psychometric measures and behavioral measures based on actual creative achievements (Carson, Peterson, & Higgins, 2003). Naturally, these aspects of psychoticism can be taken to dysfunctional levels, such as the allusive and overinclusive thinking processes of psychotics (Eysenck, 1995). Hence, creativity is associated with middling placement along a continuum with normality at one end and insanity at the other (see also Barron, 1969; Ghadirian, Gregoire, & Kosmidis, 2001).

Although these findings appear supportive of the hypothesized combinatorial process, the personalities of creative individuals are not identical no matter what the domain may be (Feist, 1998). Instead, the individual-difference variables that are most clearly implicated in supporting the combinatorial process should vary according to the ideal mix of chance and constraint. In line with this expectation, scientific creators should exhibit lower levels of psychopathology than artistic creators. So far, the empirical literature endorses this theoretical expectation (Ludwig, 1992; Miles & Wolfe, 1936; Post, 1994; Raskin, 1936). To illustrate, one inquiry found that eminent natural scientists had a 28% rate of exhibiting some mental disorder during their lifetime, which is significantly lower than the 73% rate for eminent artists and the 87% rate for eminent poets (Ludwig, 1995). Yet 28% exceeds the rate in the general population. In addition, there is some evidence on behalf of the expectation that scientists in less paradigmatic disciplines display higher rates than those in more paradigmatic disciplines: 51% of eminent social scientists exhibited some kind of mental disorder, a rate almost double that for the natural scientists (Ludwig, 1995). Another investigation found that social scientists are more "Bohemian, introverted, unconventional, imaginative and creative in thinking and behavior" than natural scientists (Chambers, 1964, p. 17; see also Cattell & Drevdahl, 1955). So even without an overt mental disorder, creativity in the social sciences appears to be noticeably less constrained than creativity in the natural sciences. At the same time, social scientists are more conventional and less imaginative than are artistic creators (Rubinstein, 1999).

Of course, the theory would also predict parallel contrasts between revolutionary and normal scientists, the former displaying higher rates of psychopathology than the latter (Simonton, 1999c). Although no direct evidence exists concerning this prediction, empirical research does support the analogous expectation with respect to artistic creativity. In particular, artists who create in highly formal and academic styles tend to have lower levels of psychopathology than artists who create in surrealist and expressionist styles (Ludwig, 1998). This result raises the likelihood that the parallel outcome would appear among creative scientists. Certainly, anecdotal evidence provides some backing for this difference. For example, several revolutionary scientists suffered from clear mental or emotional disorders, including Copernicus, Charles Darwin, Descartes, Einstein, Faraday, Sigmund Freud, Kepler, Newton, and Pascal.

Janusian Thinking

The final dispositional trait provides a link between the discussion of psychopathology and the earlier discussion of remote association. Although associative richness is useful in obtaining original combinations of ideas, it is not the only associative process that can obtain such ideational combinations. It is also conceivable that highly creative individuals are unusual with respect to "the first thing that comes to mind." If the first association to a given stimulus departs from the norm in a significant manner, then that association alone can elicit original associative pathways. Of course, should the first association be too bizarre, this associative inclination might be more strongly linked to psychopathology. If extremely rare associations seldom contribute to scientific creativity, then certainly rather uncommon first associations are not going make a superior contribution. Nevertheless, certain types of unusual associations could be especially conducive to the creative process.

This possibility is illustrated by an empirical inquiry into *janusian thinking* (Rothenberg, 1983). This process involves "actively conceiving two or more opposites or antitheses simultaneously" (p. 938). The term comes from the Roman god who had two faces simultaneously looking at opposite directions. This mode of thinking was assessed with a word association test. Janusian thought was specifically revealed when the first response was an opposite of the stimulus word. Both the proportion of opposites and the time taken to generate the response were then measured, where faster reaction times indicate an even greater janusian inclination. The research participants consisted of 12 creative scientists,

18 patients hospitalized for psychiatric disorders, and 113 college students divided into high and low creative groups according to their achievements and interests.

In comparison to all other groups, the creative scientists gave the highest proportion of opposite responses, and they did so at the fastest rate. The psychiatric patients, in contrast, gave the lowest proportion of opposite responses and also had the slowest rate of responding. The highly creative students were more similar to the creative scientists, both giving opposite responses at a much quicker rate than when giving more commonplace (nonopposite) responses. The students who were low in creativity, in contrast, exhibited associative behavior that fell roughly between that of the patients and that of the two high creativity groups. Hence, associative opposites are characteristic of creativity rather than psychopathology. They may be unusual, but they are not outlandish. The association of "hot" to "cold" is more constrained than the association of "dog" to "cold."

It is especially significant that the creative scientists exhibited such a strong tendency. After all, these scientists were labeled creative by the highest possible standard: Every one had received the Nobel Prize in one of the three natural science categories. In particular, the research participants were Luis W. Alvarez, David Baltimore, Owen Chamberlain, Allan M. Cormack, Max Delbrück, Donald A. Glaser, Arthur Kornberg, Joshua Lederberg, Edwin M. McMillan, Edward M. Purcell, Emilio Segrè, and Glenn T. Seaborg. Furthermore, subsequent research has shown that janusian thinking was evident in the mental processes that Einstein and Bohr used in making their major contributions (Rothenberg, 1987; see also Rothenberg, 1996). Thus, Einstein's general theory of relativity emerged after he realized that an observer who jumped off a house roof would not, in his immediate vicinity, find any evidence of a gravitational field. This apparent absence arises even though gravitation causes the observer's accelerating plunge. Similarly, Bohr's principle of complementarity made the janusian claim that light is both a particle and a wave rather than just one or the other.

Perhaps no scientist illustrated janusian thinking better than did Bohr. Once, after Wolfgang Pauli presented a new theory of elementary particles, a critical discussion arose among the members of the audience. Bohr summarized the debate by telling Pauli "we are all agreed that your theory is crazy. The question which divides us is whether it is crazy enough to have a chance of being correct. My own feeling is that it is not crazy enough" (Cropper, 1970, p. 57). Years later one of Bohr's sons made a more general observation regarding his father's preferred modus operandi. "One of the favorite maxims of my father was the distinction between the two sorts of truths, profound truths recognized by the fact that the opposite is also a profound truth, in contrast to trivialities where opposites are obviously absurd" (Bohr, 1967, p. 328). Bohr's janusian propensities might seem more akin to someone who was suffering serious mental illness. Yet this cognitive process enabled him to make scientific contributions of the highest order.

These examples imply a curious relation between the genius and logic perspectives. Because janusian thought appears to be more illogical than more ordinary ways of thinking, genius seems to consist in no small part of the capacity to suspend logic whenever necessary. This reinforces the conjecture first proposed in Chapter 1.

DEVELOPMENT

I have just shown that the intellect and personality of creative scientists are compatible with the theoretical interpretation presented in Chapter 3. But this demonstration raises a critical question: How does a person acquire the necessary disposition? One potential response is that scientific creativity is contingent on genetic endowment. "Genius must be born, and never can be taught," said John Dryden (1693/1885, p. 60), the English dramatist. This was the position taken by Galton (1869) when he constructed extensive family pedigrees for eminent scientists in his book *Hereditary Genius* (see also Bramwell, 1948; Brimhall, 1922, 1923a, 1923b; Galton, 1874). In addition, modern behavior genetics has shown that some of the intellectual and personality traits associated with creativity have substantial heritability coefficients (Eysenck, 1995; Simonton, 1999c). This is certainly true for psychoticism, for example. Genetics may even partially account for why some creators go into the sciences, whereas others go into the arts. For instance, although creative individuals tend to come from family lines that exhibit higher than average rates of psychopathology, those rates are higher for artistic pedigrees than for scientific pedigrees (Juda, 1949; Karlson, 1970). This difference even suggests that a portion of the contrast between revolutionary and normal scientists may have a genetic foundation (Sulloway, 1996).

Nonetheless, behavior genetics cannot tell the whole story. A significant part of creative development depends on environmental factors. In other words, scientific creativity may be a function of both nature and nurture, a possibility first suggested by Galton (1874) as well. Of these nongenetic influences, three may stand out as the most important: family experiences, education and training, and the sociocultural context (Simonton, 1988b, 2002).

Family Experiences

Although behavior geneticists devote considerable time to understanding the genetic foundation of individual differences, they also dedicate much effort to assessing the contributions of the family environment. These environmental experiences typically are divided into two categories: shared and nonshared.

Shared Environment. In this category are those experiences shared by all children growing up in the same family. In this case, a considerable body of research indicates that high achievers come from different family backgrounds than low achievers. In particular, individuals who attain a high degree of eminence in almost any field tend to have atypical family experiences. That is, they are somewhat less prone to grow up in stable, intact, majority-culture families. With respect to ethnicity, for example, empirical studies have documented the edge enjoyed by recent immigrants (Bowerman, 1947). As Galton (1892/1972) observed, "it is very remarkable how a large proportion of the eminent men of all countries bear foreign names" (p. 413). Thus, one study of 20th century eminent personalities found that nearly one-fifth were either first- or second-generation immigrants (Goertzel, Goertzel, & Goertzel, 1978). Comparable figures are found for scientific creators. In one sample of highly eminent scientists, 25% were second-generation immigrants (Eiduson, 1964). Among distinguished mathematicians, 32% were foreign born (Visher, 1947), and 52% were either foreign born or second-generation Americans (Helson & Crutchfield, 1970). One recent investigation scrutinized the origins of the most influential figures in the physical and life sciences in the United States (Levin & Stephan, 1999). Judging from citation impact and membership in the National Academy of Sciences, "individuals making exceptional contributions ... are disproportionately drawn from the foreign born" and "are also disproportionately foreign educated, both at the undergraduate and graduate level" (p. 1213).

Family background may also be atypical with respect to religious affiliation. This was first demonstrated in Galton's (1874) study of Fellows of the Royal Society of London. Rather than coming from families belonging to the Church of England, their backgrounds tended to represent a "strange variety of small and unfashionable religious sects" (p. 123). This religious unconventionality is apparent in the 20th century as well (Lehman & Witty, 1931; Roe, 1953). The more widespread the religious beliefs held by families, the lower is their expected output of future scientists, on a per capita basis. Thus, Unitarians and Quakers are far more supportive of creative development in science than are Roman Catholics and Baptists. In this context should be placed the consistent finding that distinguished scientists are more likely to emerge from Jewish families (Berry, 1981; Cole & Cole, 1973; Feist, 1993; Helson & Crutchfield, 1970; Roe, 1953). Indeed, Jews have received a disproportionate share of the Nobel Prizes in the sciences (Berry, 1999; Zuckerman, 1977).

Even if the family is not unusual with respect to ethnicity or religion, the childhood and adolescence of eminent achievers may depart from the norm in other ways. For instance, highly eminent persons frequently suffer from serious illnesses or physical disabilities (Ellis, 1926; Goertzel & Goertzel, 1962), a tendency that may hold for highly distinguished scientists as well (Roe, 1953). Less than trouble-free developmental experiences can arise from other causes, such as family economic difficulties, including periods of outright poverty (Berry, 1981; Goertzel & Goertzel, 1962; Raskin, 1936). An even more dramatic example is the high incidence of partial or complete orphanhood (i.e., the loss of one or both parents prior to attaining majority). Several studies have suggested that orphanhood rates are especially high among eminent personalities, with rates ranging around 25–50% (Albert, 1971; Eisenstadt, 1978; Illingworth & Illingworth, 1969; Walberg, Rasher, & Parkerson, 1980). Some evidence also exists that parental loss is to be found at elevated frequencies among distinguished scientists (Eiduson, 1964; Silverman, 1974). For instance, a study of 64 eminent scientists concluded "one of the first things that stands out is the frequency with which these subjects report the death of a parent during their childhood" (Roe, 1953, p. 84). Another inquiry that looked at famous scientists from earlier historical periods – figures like Copernicus, Descartes, Pascal, Newton, Leibniz, Quételet, and Maxwell – found that they typically lost their mother around age 4 or their father around age 7 (Silverman, 1974). Among 32 famous mathematicians, moreover, one-quarter lost a parent before age 10 and almost one-third suffered parental loss before the age 14 (Bell, 1937). However, it has been argued that when the figures are compared against the most appropriate baselines, the supposed orphanhood effect disappears (Woodward, 1974).

To put these conflicting results in proper perspective, it is necessary to return to the basic thesis that creativity involves an ability to engage in an approximately random combinatorial process. Given this assumption, creative development requires acquisition of the capacity to see the things in unconventional ways, to go against traditional ways of viewing the world. In other words, the person must learn how to relax the logical or zeitgeist constraints on the thought process to imagine the impossible or uncustomary. In this context, the events and circumstances just presented can be considered to provide the experiences necessary to break the boundaries imposed by a highly conventional and predictable upbringing (Simonton, 1999c). The greater the number and severity of these childhood events and circumstances, the more divergent the developmental track and hence the greater the cognitive freedom the individual will enjoy as an adult. Stated more boldly, the ability to generate unpredictable or unconventional ideas is nurtured by development within an unpredictable or unconventional environment.

The argument here closely parallels what was said earlier regarding psychopathology. Just as tendencies toward mental disorder can disrupt the cognitive processes in a manner supportive of combinatorial creativity, so can a dysfunctional or divergent childhood stimulate the same capacity. Yet by offering this comparison, we are implicitly making a corresponding prediction. Because different forms of creativity require distinct levels of constraint, tendencies toward psychopathology were not expected to be uniform across the various creative domains. By the same token, the theory of combinatorial creativity should lead us to predict a similar pattern for these deviating developmental experiences. In particular, creative artists should come from more diverse and chaotic family backgrounds than do creative scientists.

There is ample empirical evidence that this is the case (Simonton, 1999c). Unconventional and divergent childhood experiences are much more common among artistic creators than among scientific creators (Post, 1994; Simonton, 1986a). This contrast holds across different specific sources, such as poverty and orphanhood (Berry, 1981; Brown, 1968; Eiduson, 1964; Raskin, 1936). For example, those writers who receive the Nobel Prize for literature are far more likely than laureates in the sciences to have "either lost at least one parent through death or desertion or experienced the father's bankruptcy or impoverishment" (Berry, 1981, p. 387). Furthermore, the diversity can operate via more subtle means. In comparison to artistic creators, scientific creators are most likely to come from professional homes with stable families and to have parents who were native born and who were more similar to each other with respect to geographical, religious, and ethnic origins (Raskin, 1936; Schaefer & Anastasi, 1968; Terman, 1954). In brief, artistic creators tend to come from more unconventional, heterogeneous, and unpredictable home environments than do scientific creators.

Yet this argument can be taken a step further. Earlier it was suggested that any proclivity toward psychopathology should be greater for revolutionary than for normal scientists. Although no evidence could be marshaled on behalf of this suggestion, I did note that an analogous pattern held within the arts. The greater the degree of constraint imposed on the creative process for a specific artistic style, the less conspicuous are any psychopathological tendencies (Ludwig, 1998). Also consistent with expectation was the finding that eminent scientists in more paradigmatic disciplines displayed lower rates of mental disorder than those in less paradigmatic disciplines (Ludwig, 1995). Moreover, empirical inquiries have suggested that disciplinary contrasts in paradigmatic constraints correspond with a scientist's family environment (Chambers, 1964; Roe, 1953). More specifically, scientists in the natural sciences are more likely to come from stable and conventional homes than scientists in the social sciences. For instance, social scientists are more prone to come from divorced families and to have been more rebellious against their parents. Natural scientists, by comparison, are more likely to have come from the homes of parents who had professional occupations.

So at this point it seems reasonable to ask whether scientists who overthrow the disciplinary paradigms come from different family backgrounds than do scientists who accept and develop those paradigms by engaging in "puzzle-solving" research. To be more specific, do the home experiences of revolutionary scientists fall somewhere between those of normal scientists and those of artistic creators? Although no researcher has directly addressed this issue, Sulloway (1996) published some relevant findings in his systematic scrutiny of 28 scientific revolutions. According to his quantitative analysis, revolutionaries, in contrast to their more conventional colleagues, are more likely (1) to have experienced pronounced parent–offspring conflict, (2) to have suffered early parental loss (at least for laterborns), and (3) to claim minority status with respect to either ethnicity or gender. This certainly falls right in line with what would be expected according to the theoretical interpretation. Fortunately, this interpretation framework receives support from another aspect of family background.

Nonshared Environment. So far the discussion has been confined to comparisons across families. Even so, children from the same homes do not necessarily have identical environments. On the contrary, siblings may develop along distinct trajectories owing to the impact of a particular child's ordinal position or birth order (Adler, 1938; Zajonc, 1976). Moreover, the firstborn child in the family is more likely to undergo a more conventional and orderly development relative to the laterborns in the same family (Sulloway, 1996). This differential is reflected in empirical findings such as the disproportionate representation of firstborns among college graduates and among members of the professions (Altus, 1966; Schachter, 1963). More particularly, creative scientists are more likely to be firstborns, whereas artistic creators are more likely to be laterborns (Bliss, 1970; Clark & Rice, 1982; Eisenman, 1964; Galton, 1874; Roe, 1953). There are two exceptions to this tendency, but both can be considered "exceptions that prove the rule."

First, firstborns predominate among classical composers (Schubert, Wagner, & Schubert, 1977). Yet classical music represents perhaps the most formal, constrained, and conventional of all types of artistic expression. This feature is evident in the highly abstract form of its notation as well as the mathematics-like nature of music theory (e.g., harmony and counterpoint). In a sense, the composition of classical music can be considered a kind of artistic creativity not too far removed from mathematical creativity.

Second, and most significantly, laterborns predominate among revolutionary scientists, in contrast to those who practice normal science (Sulloway, 1996). This predominance can be seen in major scientific revolutions such as the Copernican heliocentric system, Harvey's theory of blood circulation, Newton's celestial mechanics, Lavoisier's new chemistry, Hutton's theory of the earth, Darwin's theory of evolution by natural selection, and Einstein's theory of special relativity. In the case of evolutionary theory, for instance, the proponents included laterborn scientists such as T. H. Huxley, Charles Lyell, Joseph Dalton Hooker, Alfred Russell Wallace, Ernst Haeckel, and, of course, Charles Darwin. In contrast, the opponents who insisted on retaining the traditional creationist theory of life's origins included firstborn scientists such as Adam Sedgwick, Louis Agassiz, and Pierre Flourens.

No doubt more research needs to be done on the family backgrounds of scientific creators. Even so, what has been reviewed so far supports the inference that the degree of constraint imposed on the creative process is positively associated with the extent to which a creator's childhood experiences were conventional, orderly, and predictable. Highly probabilistic creativity, by comparison, is more prone to emerge in homes where developmental experiences are more unconventional, disorderly, and unpredictable. This distinction separates not only scientific and artistic creators, but also normal scientists from their more revolutionary colleagues.

Education and Training

Many creative scientists have voiced rather negative attitudes toward education. Albert Einstein provides a concrete illustration of this discontent. For instance, he once remarked that

it is, in fact, nothing short of a miracle that the modern methods of instruction have not yet entirely strangled the holy curiosity of inquiry; for this delicate little plant, aside from stimulation, stands mostly in the need of freedom; without this it goes to wreck and ruin without fail. It is a very grave mistake to think that the enjoyment of seeing and searching can be promoted by means of coercion and a sense of duty. (Schlipp, 1951, p. 17).

His opinions were especially negative about the procedures most commonly used to test the student's mastery of the material: "One had to cram

125

all this stuff into one's mind for the examinations, whether one liked it or not. This coercion had such a deterring effect on me that, after I passed the final examination, I found the consideration of any scientific problems distasteful to me for an entire year" (Hoffman, 1972, p. 31). Given Einstein's bad attitude, it comes as no surprise that his teachers were not very impressed with him. For example, one of his university professors, Hermann Minkowski, admitted that Einstein's later scientific achievements "came as a tremendous surprise . . . for in his student days Einstein had been a lazy dog. He never bothered about mathematics at all" (Seelig, 1958, p. 28). Another exasperated professor, Heinrich Weber, told Einstein directly, after years of frustration: "You're a clever fellow! But you have one fault. You won't let anyone tell you a thing. You won't let anyone tell you a thing" (Hoffman, 1972, p. 32).

These reactions are not atypical. Among the eminent scientists who responded to Galton's (1874, p. 237) question about their educational experiences, 11% complained about "want of system and bad teaching," while another 37% expressed dissatisfaction with the "narrow education" they had received. All told, 57% had some kind of complaint. Of the remaining minority, many praised experiences somewhat peripheral to their formal training, such as "home teaching and encouragement." Merely 10 of 87 survey responses could be placed in the category "education praised throughout, or nearly so." Moreover, those with more positive experiences came from institutions that provided what Einstein considered most basic to a good education. Typical praise in this vein are "Freedom to follow my own inclinations, and to choose my own subjects of study, or the reverse," "The great proportion of time left free to do as I liked, unwatched and uncontrolled," and "Unusual degree of freedom" (p. 254).

Notwithstanding these negative attitudes, education has some part to play in a scientist's creative development. After all, no one can expect to make contributions without first acquiring the phenomena, facts, concepts, variables, constants, techniques, theories, laws, questions, goals, and criteria that define their chosen domain. At least some portion of each scientist's sample comes from the curriculum provided by schools, colleges, and universities. At the same time, such formal education can hamper creative development insofar as it restricts freedom of thought, making the scientist adhere too closely to traditional ways of viewing phenomena. So somehow scientific talent must pull off a balancing act between mastering a domain and being mastered by a domain. Kuhn (1977) referred to this as an "essential tension" in scientific creativity because "the successful scientist must simultaneously display the characteristics of the traditionalist and of the iconoclast" (p. 343).

To understand better how this essential tension works, we need to make two comparisons: (1) creative scientists versus creative artists and (2) creative scientists versus noncreative scientists.

Creative Scientists versus Creative Artists. One way to probe the optimal tradeoff between these two antagonistic forces is to compare creators in the sciences with those in the arts. According to what we have repeatedly argued, scientific creativity should require more tradition, artistic creativity more iconoclasm. Hence, a corresponding differential should appear in the training of scientific and artistic creators. The following three findings show that this seems to be the case:

1. Scientific creativity requires much more formal training than does artistic creativity (Simonton, 1986a; Terman, 1954). For example, eminent scientists are more likely to have university training than comparably eminent writers (Raskin, 1936; Simonton, 1986a). Indeed, some studies have found a curvilinear inverted-U relation between artistic creativity and formal education level so that those with higher degrees are at a relative disadvantage (Simonton, 1976a, 1983, 1984d). In contrast, highly productive scientists are more likely to have progressed farther in formal training, typically obtaining doctoral degrees (Simonton, 1983, 1992a; Van Zelst & Kerr, 1951).
2. Scientists tend to be much better students than artists, as indicated by the grades they receive in school and college (Schaefer & Anastasi, 1968). Thus, the contrast in academic performance between scientists

and artists appears to reflect the comparative degree of constraint that must be imposed on the creative process in the sciences versus the arts.

3. The influence of mentors differs between the two forms of creativity. Although the creative development is enhanced by working under notable creators in the same domain, artistic talent is best nurtured by studying under a diversity of artists while scientific talent is better nourished by studying under just one (Simonton, 1984a, 1992a, 1992b). Hence, the impact of mentors is more heterogeneous in the arts than in the sciences. The same conclusion may hold for role models in general.

Thus, the educational experiences and achievements of artistic creators can be distinguished from those of scientific creators, the distinction following the pattern expected according to theory.

Creative Scientists versus Noncreative Scientists. Do highly creative scientists exhibit the same differential when compared to their less creative colleagues? Here the research results are more ambiguous. On the one hand, Fellows of the Royal Society of London were found to have generally unimpressive undergraduate records, records that were certainly no better than scientists who failed to be so honored (Hudson, 1958). On the other hand, some studies have shown that indicators of undergraduate and graduate performance display modest but positive correlations with a scientist's productivity, citation rate, and eventual eminence (Chambers, 1964; Rodgers & Maranto, 1989; Segal, Busse, & Mansfield, 1980; Taylor, 1963). In particular, the more distinguished researchers in the physical, biological, and behavioral sciences tend to boast higher grade point averages, win more honors and prizes, and receive more scholarships and fellowships. This might suggest that traditionalism has much more weight than iconoclasm in the determination of scientific creativity. However, this conclusion must be qualified by the following two considerations.

128

First, the training of highly creative scientists is not confined to formal instruction. On the contrary, a significant proportion of their expertise is acquired through some form of self-education. One particular form that this independent learning may take is the early cultivation of domain-relevant hobbies and extracurricular activities (Roe, 1953). For instance, one study of 335 biologists found that both publication and citation counts were positively correlated with the amount of free time spent on extra science projects or building radio sets (Segal, Busse, & Mansfeld, 1980). Although these interests sometimes interfere with schoolwork, they also can provide the basis for later discoveries. Helmholtz (1891/1971) provides an illustration of this possibility:

I must confess that many times while the class was reading Cicero or Virgil, both of whom I found very tedious, I was calculating under the desk the path of light rays in a telescope. Even at that time I discovered some optical laws, not ordinarily found in textbooks, but which I afterward found useful in constructing the ophthalmoscope. (p. 469)

Another form of self-education is early, voracious, and omnivorous reading, a behavior strongly associated with the attainment of eminence in a diversity of domains, scientific or otherwise (McCurdy, 1960; Simonton, 1984d). For instance, Roe's (1953) 64 illustrious scientists reported that they began to do a great deal of reading when very young. As pointed out early in this chapter, this reading habit continues throughout the life of creative scientists, becoming a continual source of intellectual growth and diversification.

Second, frequently the training creative scientists receive is peripheral to the discipline in which they later make their contributions. This may be particularly the case for scientific revolutionaries. Kuhn (1970) observed "almost always the men who achieve these fundamental inventions of a new paradigm have been either very young or very new to the field whose paradigm they change" (p. 90). This is the case, because "obviously these are the men who, being little committed by prior practice to the traditional rules of normal science, are particularly likely to see that these rules no longer define a playable game and to conceive another set that can replace them" (p. 90). Helmholtz (1891/1971) again provides an example:

I must, however, say that I attribute my success in great measure to the fact that, possessing some geometric understanding and equipped with a knowledge of physics, I had the good fortune to be thrown into medicine, where I found in physiology a virgin territory of great fertility. Furthermore, I was led by my knowledge of vital processes to questions and points of view which are usually foreign to pure mathematicians and physicists. (pp. 472–473)

Although there is some evidence supporting the importance of professional marginality as a development factor in scientific innovation (Hudson & Jacot, 1986; Simonton, 1984d; cf. Gieryn & Hirsh, 1983), much more research needs to be done on this subject.

The last point must also be amplified with respect to the whole question of formal education. Investigators have not yet investigated how revolutionary scientists differ from normal scientists regarding level of education, scholastic performance, and self-instruction. If the theoretical interpretation is correct, scientific revolutionaries should fall somewhere between normal scientists and artistic creators.

Sociocultural Context

Creative scientists are not evenly distributed across nations or historical periods (Candolle, 1873; Berry, 1999; Kroeber, 1944; Schneider, 1937; Yuasa, 1974; Zhao & Jiang, 1985). Instead, scientific creativity tends cluster into specific times and periods. Expressed differently, the center of scientific activity tends to jump from one nation to another across the course of the history of science. This shifting is illustrated in a study of science from 1501 to 1950 where the scientific center was defined "as a period in which the percentage of scientific achievements of a country exceeds 25% of that in the entire world in the same period" (Yuasa, 1974, p. 81). According to this definition, the centers of scientific creativity appeared in the following order: Italy, 1540–1610; Great Britain, 1660–1730; France,

1770–1830; Germany, 1810–1920; and the United States, 1920 to the present. These changes indicate that scientific creativity does not take place in isolation from the larger milieu. Instead, diverse political, cultural, social, and economic events impinge on the creative scientist and the scientific community, deflecting creativity in one direction or another – and even stifling discovery and invention altogether.

To document these effects, I first look at general factors that determine creativity activity and then turn to those factors that uniquely support scientific creativity.

Creative Epochs. Empirical research has shown that international war has a generally negative impact on creativity activity (Simonton, 1994). More specifically, warfare has adverse consequences for the frequency of discovery and invention (Fernberger, 1946; Price, 1978; Simonton, 1980b). This is not to say that certain kinds of creativity might be enhanced by concurrent warfare – the development of the atomic bomb and radar during World War II providing famous examples. Yet the net effect is negative. Scientific and technological creativity becomes channeled into excessively narrow, highly practical topics that are most unmistakably germane to the war effort. Pure research, or applied research not immediately connected with the national emergency, will be diminished if not entirely curtailed, as happened to the development of television during World War II.

The powerful adverse impact of war notwithstanding, its influence is relatively short term. So long as the conflict is not unusually devastating, the nation's scientific activity can quickly return to its prewar level. Yet other conditions exert more durable effects. For instance, scientific creativity tends to be fostered by philosophical systems that stress empiricism, materialism, individualism, and determinism (Simonton, 1976b), by nations that are predominantly Protestant rather than Roman Catholic (Berry, 1999), and by political and educational institutions that are secular rather than religious (Candolle, 1873). Because ideologies and organizations display considerable inertia over any historical period, these effects normally last generations rather than just a few years, as is the case for military conflict. Somewhere between these short- and long-term effects are sociocultural circumstances that affect creative development. That is, certain events or environments are conductive to the acquisition of creative potential in childhood and adolescence, whereas other events or environments function in a more antagonistic manner, in either case determining the magnitude of creativity displayed by a whole generation. This is the case for some political events, for example. Thus, on the one hand, growing up in times of political instability tends to be antithetical to creative development (Simonton, 1975, 1976c). In particular, the amount of creativity evident in a given generation is a negative function of the level of assassinations, coups d'état, and military mutinies that existed 20 years earlier, when the potential creators were teenagers and young adults. On the other hand, growing up when a civilization is fragmented in a large number of peacefully coexisting independent states tends to be conducive to the development of creative potential (Simonton, 1975). Political fragmentation also favors the emergence of ideological diversity in which thinkers represent a variety of philosophical positions and schools. In fact, nationalistic revolts against the oppressive rule of empire states tends to have a positive consequence for the amount of creativity in the following generations (Kroeber, 1944; Simonton, 1975; Sorokin, 1947/1969). Many nations have experienced Golden Ages after winning independence from foreign domination, ancient Greece providing a classic example.

The rationale for the last-mentioned consequence may be that nationalistic rebellion encourages cultural heterogeneity rather than homogeneity (Simonton, 1994). Rather than everyone having to speak the same language, read the same books, follow the same laws, hold the same beliefs, and so on, individuals are left with more options. This suggests that cultural diversity may facilitate creativity, and there is evidence that this is the case. Creative activity in a civilization tends to increase after it has opened itself to extensive alien influences, whether through immigration, travel abroad, or studying under foreign teachers (Simonton, 1997b). By enriching the cultural environment, the ground may be laid for new creative syntheses. As Sorokin (1947/1969) noted, the creativity of individuals or groups are enhanced when they reside

at the point of intersection of cross-currents of various appropriate or relevant systems of meanings and values. Since any new system of meanings is a blend of two or more existing systems, such a union occurs more naturally amidst several crosscurrents of different ideas, beliefs, and patterns. Such a milieu contains richer material for a new synthesis or creative combination than a cultural milieu of monotonous stereotypes. The point of junction of various cultural streams supplies a larger number of the elements necessary for a new creation. (p. 542)

This finding is consistent with the creativity-augmenting effects of ethnic marginality, which was mentioned when we discussed family background. The result is compatible with other empirical results as well, such as the positive effects of bilingualism on individual creativity (Carringer, 1974; Lambert, Tucker, & d'Anglejan, 1973; Lopez, Esquivel, & Houtz, 1993). Also supportive is the finding that almost all Nobel laureates in the sciences "have carried out study courses abroad, either as students, research workers, or professors" (Moulin, 1955, p. 261). In general, cultural heterogeneity associates with creativity, whereas homogeneity correlates with stagnation.

Scientific Epochs. Most of the foregoing conditions demarcate the political and cultural zeitgeist that favors the emergence of creative genius in almost any domain. However, if scientific creativity tends to be more highly constrained than artistic creativity, then we might expect creative scientists to grow up in more stable and homogeneous settings than do creative artists. Unfortunately, not very much research is relevant to this theoretical expectation. Even so, what little research is available appears to support this inference. For instance, political instability has no effect on creative development in the visual arts; a negative effect holds in the sciences (Simonton, 1975). In addition, there is tentative evidence that cultural cross-fertilization has a stronger and more consistent impact on the development of artistic creativity than the development of scientific creativity (Simonton, 1997b). This is another question that deserves more empirical inquiry.

Before leaving the subject of creative development in science, I should discuss a common misconception about the impact of the sociocultural context. Too often the influence of the political, social, and cultural milieu is taken as proving the superiority of the zeitgeist perspective over the genius perspective. Galileo became a great scientist only because he had the fortune of being born in Italy during the time when it became the center of scientific creativity. Similarly, Newton's creative genius could appear only because he lived in Great Britain when the center had shifted there from Italy. If Galileo and Newton had switched birth years without changing national origins, then neither would have secured a place in the annals of science. To a certain extent, this argument is just a continuation of the supposed impact of the disciplinary zeitgeist in our earlier discussions of the multiples phenomenon. The external zeitgeist merely replaces the internal zeitgeist as the primary agent in the emergence of scientific creativity.

As plausible as this argument may sound on first hearing, it suffers from a substantial limitation: the sociocultural context can explain differences in creativity only when the scientists grew up in distinct times or places. Hence, it can account merely for why British scientists active 1660–1730 were superior to Italian scientists during the same period. On the other hand, the explanation cannot explicate contrasts in creativity among those scientists who developed under the same sociocultural circumstances. Why did Galileo surpass Guidubaldo dal Monte or Pietro Antonio Cataldi? Or, why did Newton attain more acclaim than Edmund Halley or Isaac Barrow? To address these matters, it may be necessary to turn to those developmental factors that make each person unique despite their living in the same historical period and geographical location. These individualizing factors include each scientist's genetic endowment as well as his or her home environment, education, and training.

CONCLUSION

To a very large extent, this chapter can be said to elaborate the genius perspective on creativity. The chapter began by indicating how creative scientists share a set of intellectual and personal characteristics. It then documented these differences even more by treating the home environment, education and training, and sociocultural context that most strongly supports creative development of scientific talent. The main impact of these dispositional and developmental variables is to help reduce the constraints that convention and tradition impose on creative thought. Furthermore, it was constantly stressed that creative genius in science departs significantly from creative genius in the arts. Because adherence to a scientific paradigm imposes a high degree of constraint on creativity, the creative scientist is less divergent in either disposition or development than is the creative artist. Two important qualifications must be imposed on this statement, however. First, scientists in highly paradigmatic sciences operate under more severe constraints than do those in less paradigmatic sciences. The latter therefore display dispositional traits and developmental experiences closer to artistic creators. Second, scientific revolutionaries, whose creativity is less restricted than that of normal scientists in paradigmatic disciplines, exhibit characteristics that also fall somewhere between the typical scientific creator and the typical artistic creator.

Although the genius perspective seems to acquire some degree of reinforcement, the other perspectives still participate in scientific creativity. First, and most obviously, the dispositional and developmental variables are precisely those that would be anticipated from the combinatorial interpretation offered in Chapters 3 and 4. In effect, creative persons have inherited and acquired the capacity for chance. Second, the zeitgeist perspective still plays a role in the guise of the sociocultural context. Certain political, social, cultural, and economic environments are most conducive to creative development. Third, the logic perspective retains some importance in providing some of the constraints that necessarily govern scientific creativity. For example, a large part of a scientist's education and training entails learning what can and cannot be considered to be a logically coherent derivation or inference. Creative artists, in contrast, are granted more latitude to conceive artworks that seemed totally incoherent to many of their contemporaries. Examples include Picasso's *Les Demoiselles d'Avignon* and Stravinsky's *The Rite of Spring*. Einstein did not have that option. However revolutionary his ideas, they could contain no errors of logic or factual contradictions. As a consequence, his first paper on relativity theory can be considered an exemplary piece of scientific writing, his deductions and their implications following inevitably from his initial assumptions. The relevance of the logic perspective will become better appreciated in the next chapter.

6

Scientific Discovery

I t is now necessary to look at the rival tradition in the psychology of science – the tradition that stresses the *logic* of scientific discovery. In contrast to the psychologists who apply correlational methods to study the disposition and development of creative scientists, these psychologists conduct laboratory experiments and computer simulations to study problem solving. Fittingly, the proponents of this experimental tradition are largely researchers in the cognitive sciences, most particularly cognitive psychologists and computer scientists. These investigators tend to be completely unsympathetic with, if not totally hostile toward, the genius perspective on creativity, scientific or otherwise. For instance, one advocate gave a book the provocative title *Creativity: Beyond the Myth of Genius* (Weisberg, 1992). Here the author flatly denies that creative individuals differ from noncreative individuals on any important cognitive or personality variable. In addition, he argues that creative thinking involves the same kinds of thought processes that everyone uses to solve everyday problems. Thus, no fundamental difference separates Einstein's thinking from that of his far less influential contemporary, Friedrich Hasenöhrl. Each applied deliberate, systematic, conscious, and logical processes to the domain knowledge he possessed.

Clearly, these assertions contradict not just the genius perspective but the chance perspective besides. This contradiction is made most explicit in the discovery programs that purport to simulate scientific creativity by a straightforward, step-by-step analysis of empirical data (Langley et al., 1987; Shrager & Langley, 1990; Wagman, 2000). Such computer simulations seem to include no provision for the introduction of chance. Hence, if this second tradition is correct, creativity in science is best understood from the logic perspective. Einstein and other creative scientists make their discoveries by exploiting ordinary human rationality, not by engaging in the chance combinations theorized in Chapter 3.

I believe the antagonism between this second psychological tradition and the genius and chance perspectives is ill founded. In the first place, Chapter 5 already provided sufficient reason for questioning the categorical dismissal of individual differences. The inventory of dispositional and developmental correlates cannot be ignored by anyone who pretends to approach the subject with scientific objectivity. Indeed, because the effect sizes revealed by meta-analyses of the extensive literature are of the same magnitude as the effect sizes found in other research topics in psychology, a psychologist – even an experimental psychologist – cannot reject these findings without also denying that psychology is a science (Feist, 1998). By the same token, there is ample rationale for accepting the fundamental thesis that creativity involves chance combinations. It is the goal of the current chapter to present the relevant arguments. The evidence comes from two quarters. First, I show that the logical processes cited by the experimental tradition actually operate in a highly probabilistic fashion. Second, I review some central findings of the experimental literature that do not fit so well with the notion that scientific creativity requires a linear, deterministic logic. In fact, laboratory experiments and computer simulations actually provide some of the best support for the chance perspective.

LOGICAL PROCESSES

The experimental tradition regarding scientific creativity is actually represented by two successive historical developments. The first occurred with the advent of Gestalt psychology. The Gestalt psychologists were primarily interested in insightful problem solving (Köhler, 1925; Wertheimer, 1945/1982). The second development came upon the advent of cognitive psychology about a half century later. The cognitive psychologists incorporated many of the central findings of the Gestalt school by casting them in terms of computer metaphors and computational models. Of special significance in the emergence of this more recent development was Newell and Simon's (1972) *Human Problem Solving*. This classic established much of the terminology and theoretical concepts that were to become the basis for subsequent experimental studies and computer models. For instance, according to this seminal work, a problem consists

of an initial state, a goal state, and a set of permissible transformations from one state to another (called "operators") that, when executed in a correct sequence, result in a solution path from the initial state to the goal state, via a series of intermediate states and subgoals. Operators have constraints that must be satisfied before they can be applied. The set of states, operators, goals, and constraints is called a "problem space," and the problem-solving process can be conceptualized as a search for a path that links the initial state to the goal state. (Klahr, 2000, p. 23)

This may seem like highly technical jargon, but the basic concepts are simple. In a nutshell, problem solving entails finding the path that gets you from where you are to where you want to be using solely the means that are permitted. This may be illustrated via an elementary algebra problem: Find the values of x that solve the equation $x^3 - x^2 = 6x$. The equation defines the initial state, and the goal state is defined by all the numbers that retain the equality when substituted into the equation as values of x (the equation's solutions or roots). The set of permissible transformations, or operators, are the standard algebraic manipulations. For instance, we can divide both sides of the equation by equal quantities without changing the equality. However, this particular operator has a constraint – namely that division by zero is not permitted. When one of these algebraic transformations is applied to the equation, we obtain a possible intermediate state in route to a solution. For example, subtracting $6x$ from both sides yields the new equation $x^3 - x^2 - 6x = 0$. Although the application of various operators will generate a great variety of such intermediate states, we are interested only in that subset that can establish a direct path from the initial state to the goal state. It turns out that the new equation gets us partway there. All we need to do is to factor the cubic expression to produce $x(x - 3)(x + 2) = 0$. Because the left side of the equation equals zero when each of the factors equals zero, we obtain the solution, or goal state – namely, $x = 0, 3$, and -2.

Clearly, the first step in problem solving is to construct the problem space. This construction presumes that the problem solver has acquired a sufficient amount of domain-relevant knowledge and skill. Successful acquisition means the individual has become an *expert* rather than a *novice* in a particular discipline (Ericsson, 1996). So far, this domain mastery does not seem to depart significantly from what was hypothesized in Chapter 3, where it was assumed that each scientist acquires a sample of phenomena, facts, concepts, variables, constants, techniques, theories, laws, questions, goals, and criteria (Assumption 1 in Chapter 3). Yet according to the Newell-Simon tradition, the acquired expertise invariably includes specialized techniques that enable many problems to be solved in a more or less algorithmic fashion. That is, these techniques indicate the most suitable series of operators to apply to trace an efficient path from the initial state to the goal state. The expert needs merely to identify the class of problems in which a given problem belongs and then apply the appropriate algorithm for its successful solution. These problem-solving techniques are so powerful that they have been termed *strong methods* (Klahr, 2000). A basic example of strong methods is the algebraic techniques that allow the cubic equation given earlier to be solved in the blink of an eye.

Given the acquisition of these strong methods, it would appear that scientific creativity cannot function according to some chance combination process as outlined in Chapter 3. Moreover, this acquisition seems incompatible with the empirical results reported in Chapter 3. For instance, algorithmic problem solving seems inconsistent with the equal-odds rule. Once a scientist acquires the problem-solving techniques appropriate to his or her discipline, then solution should follow solution in an almost inevitable progression. If any longitudinal trend occurs at all, it should be pointed in the direction of increased success rates with enhanced experience. In addition, it seems reasonable to infer that those scientists who have produced the largest output should enjoy higher hit rates than those whose low output provided them with much less practice in the application of the disciplinary algorithms. Applying the algorithmic solutions is like doing problem sets over and over until "practice makes perfect." Finally, nothing in the application of such strong methods would lead to the expectation that creative ideas should be Poisson distributed and randomly scattered over the course of the career.

However, this argument overlooks a very significant fact: the kinds of problems that are most amenable to algorithmic or strong methods tend not to fall in the class of problems that would be considered highly creative. On the contrary, such techniques are most applicable to routine problem solving within a particular discipline. In contrast, scientific creativity is associated with problems in which one or more of the components of the problem space are *ill-defined* (Klahr & Simon, 1999). Thus, the initial state may be poorly specified, the operators multiple and diverse, the constraints vague and unstable, the goal states ambiguous – and any combination of these possibilities. For example, the goal might be something vague and unspecific like "find a cure for cancer" or "build a better mousetrap." On the other hand, the goal might be quite explicit, and yet the rest of the problem space be inadequately defined. For instance, Johannes Gutenberg knew exactly what he was aiming at – namely, the mass production of inexpensive *Bibles*. It was not immediately obvious, however, that the problem space would come to include components as disparate as Chinese playing cards and wine presses. Problem spaces become especially ill defined in periods of scientific history when a discipline is ripe for a paradigmatic revolution. Anomalies such as blackbody radiation, the orbit of Mercury, and the null result of the Michelson–Morley interferometer experiment could not readily be solved by using problem spaces defined by classical physics. Certainly no strong methods existed that could provide satisfactory solutions. Indeed, eventually the solutions came from the construction of problem spaces that required totally new paradigms – quantum and relativity theories.

So what happens when strong methods do not work? According to this experimental tradition, scientists must rely on an assortment of heuristics or *weak methods* (Klahr, 2000). These heuristics provide general "rules of thumb" for tackling the problem. Examples include the use of analogy, hill climbing, means-end analysis, and just plain trial and error. It is at this point that the problem-solving process becomes, in effect, tantamount to a chance-combinatorial model. This conclusion is evident in the following two considerations:

First, the heuristics operate mostly in a highly probabilistic manner. That is, they can neither guarantee a solution nor ensure that a solution, even when possible, will be the optimal solution or will be encountered sooner rather than later. This chanciness is most apparent in the trial-and-error heuristic, but it holds for most of the others as well. A case in point is hill climbing. This involves a version of trial and error in which the problem solver repeatedly applies operators that seem to find an intermediate state that is closer to the goal state. One problem with this heuristic, unfortunately, is that there is no assurance that the "hill" one is ascending represents a global rather than local maximum. Hence, the solution that is arrived at may be far from optimal, yielding a low-quality idea. Therefore, sometimes the individual must "go downhill" before an optimal solution is reached. Yet it is impossible to know in advance when it is necessary for "things to get worse before they get better." Thus, the application of these heuristics introduces an immense amount of uncertainty and unpredictability into the creative process. This unreliability would also generate the requisite unevenness in the quality of the ideas that result.

Second, for problems that are not only ill defined but also quite novel, it will not be clear which heuristic will work best. Indeed, the more ill defined and novel is the problem space, the larger the number of potential heuristics and the lower the a priori probability of a solution by any given heuristic (Simonton, 1999c). In fact, just as we distinguished between steep and flat association gradients in Chapter 5, so may we distinguish steep and flat hierarchies with respect to available heuristic methods. The problems that are most likely to elicit solutions that are deemed genuinely creative are those with flat hierarchies in which a large number of heuristic techniques are available, each with approximately equal a priori odds of success. As a consequence, the discovery of the most appropriate heuristic may require a *meta-heuristic* – namely, trial and error in the application of heuristics. Heuristics might be applied in various combinations, this time using analogy first and hill climbing second, next time some the other way around, all the time not knowing which strategy is most likely to lead to an acceptable solution. Thus, once again, a large dose of chance is introduced into scientific creativity. The more ill defined and original the problem, the greater the injection of chance.

In Chapter 4 it was observed that creative scientists tend to work on several projects simultaneously. Some of these projects are rather routine and others far more risky, perhaps even impossible. In light of the above two considerations, the merits of this research strategy should be apparent. Although the routine problems can be readily solved by algorithmic methods, these problems are far less likely to be judged creative by colleagues. The solution of high-risk problems, in contrast, will contribute far more to the scientist's reputation as a creative contributor to the field. Yet the solutions of the latter problems are more iffy because they rely on weak and uncertain heuristics. By pursuing a mixture of problems having diverse probabilities of successful solution, a scientist can be confident that at least something of value will emerge. At the same time, it seems likely that really good ideas will be relatively rare, particularly insofar as many solutions will be incomplete (e.g., represent local rather than global maxima). As a result, high-impact ideas will most likely be randomly distributed across the career, and quality will correlate with quantity in line with the equal-odds rule. In addition, because the number of trials will normally be very large and the probability of success per trial extremely small, the output of good combinations in any given career period should be Poisson distributed. In brief, the behavioral consequences of these problem-solving strategies would be the key features of scientific careers documented in Chapter 2.

CHANCE PROCESSES

The inquiries inspired by Newell and Simon (1972) do not represent the only experimental research relevant to understanding scientific creativity. On the contrary, the latter phenomenon has been studied from a variety of theoretical and substantive approaches. Moreover, this alternative research literature lends additional support to the impact of chance processes. This implication will become evident when I discuss the findings regarding (1) insight problems, (2) creative production, (3) computer problem solving, and (4) group creativity.

Insight Problems

Not all problem-solving tasks are the same. Besides distinctions such as those between well-defined and ill-defined problems, problems can be distinguished according to whether they are *reasonable* or *unreasonable* (Perkins, 2000). Reasonable problems are of the kind that can be solved in a step-by-step manner. A crossword puzzle is of this nature. Given a sufficient vocabulary, the empty spaces can be filled in one by one. Unreasonable problems, in contrast, cannot be treated this way because the task contains some "trick" or "catch" that must be understood before someone can arrive at a solution. This feature derails any step-by-step process that proceeds without the realization "things aren't what they seem." Hence, successful problem solving in these cases requires that the person acquire an *insight* into the nature of the trick. Riddles provide commonplace instances of such insight problems, such as the classic riddle that the Sphinx posed to Oedipus.

Needless to say, most scientific breakthroughs are precisely of this nature as well. An example is Newton's revolutionary insight that universal gravitation could provide the basis for integrating celestial and terrestrial mechanics. Via this "trick" Newton could prove that Kepler's Third Law follows immediately from Galilean ballistics – that planets rotate around the sun according to the same principles that govern a canonball's trajectory on the earth. Once Newtonian celestial mechanics became established, it could be extended in a more reasonable, step-by-step fashion to other problems. For example, both J. C. Adams and Leverrier were independently able to calculate the orbit of a new planet, Neptune, based on perturbations in the orbit of Uranus – calculations that were soon confirmed by direct observation. Yet when Leverrier attempted to apply the same gravitational principles to an aberrancy in the orbit of Mercury, he failed miserably, the predicted new planet (Vulcan) never receiving observational confirmation. This was an unreasonable problem whose solution had to await the dramatically different insight underlying Einstein's general relativity theory, an insight in which gravitation became defined by mass-induced curvatures in space–time.

Fortunately, a rather large experimental literature has grown around the subject of insightful problem solving (Sternberg & Davidson, 1995). Of special relevance to the thesis argued in this book is the research on the *incubation* period of the creative process (Wallas, 1926). This period occurs when the problem cannot be immediately solved but ends up being "placed in the back of the mind" or "put on the back burner." The scientist then turns to other problems that seem more amendable to solution. Although experimental psychologists do not completely agree on what exactly is happening during this phase of the creative process, one fact is undeniable: during the incubation period the scientist's mind undergoes extensive exposure to a host of diverse experiences that may or may not be relevant to a successful solution. These experiences are of two kinds. First, the thinking process may be affected by external events in the outside world, including everyday events that normally would not be considered germane. In fact, some experimental research indicates that this external stimulation is more effective to the extent that it is extraneous to the given problem (Mandler, 1995). Second, the process may be influenced by internal mental events, some involving everyday thoughts and some involving thoughts about other projects on which the scientist is actively working. This influx of internal and external ideas can then prime associative pathways that diverge dramatically from more controlled and constrained thinking. This priming occurs via a process that is often called *spreading activation* (Martindale, 1995). The initial stimulation evokes responses in various pathways in the associative network (Gruszka & Necka, 2002). One of these pathways may eventually lead to the key concept that solves the problem that has been "put on hold," but not forgotten. Hence, the incubation period can be said to entail an *opportunistic assimilation* of serendipitous experiences that sets the associative process on a more fruitful track (Seifert et al., 1995).

This abstract account can be illustrated with an oft-told tale from the history of scientific creativity. The king of Syracuse had just had a new crown made but suspected the goldsmith had replaced some of the gold he was given with silver, a lighter and cheaper metal. When Archimedes was asked to verify the crown's purity, he was at first perplexed – notwithstanding his status as the greatest scientist and mathematician of his time. Because the crown was of highly irregular shape, it seemed impossible to determine its volume, and therefore he could not measure whether the crown weighed as much as an equal volume of pure gold. In short, it was an unreasonable problem. So he entered into an incubation period. The solution came when he took a bath, and noticed that the tub overflowed to the degree that his body displaced the water. In the same way, a submersed crown would displace a volume of water equal to its volume. According to the legend, Archimedes ran down the street naked, screaming "Eureka!" (Greek for "I have found it"). In this case, an external event set his mind along an unexpected path, enabling him to go from the initial state to the goal state. Yet it is apparent that a modest change in this scenario would convert the external event into an internal event. Perhaps during the incubation period Archimedes realized that he needed a bath. On the way to the baths he recalled the last time he did so, when he had spilled water all over the floor upon sitting in the tub. Suddenly he turns around and runs home, but this time with his clothes on.

This interpretation of the insight process implies that the length of the incubation period will be determined largely by pure "luck" (Perkins, 2000; Simonton, 1988b). After all, the experiential input is not directed by the problem itself but rather by other problems or general life experiences. Sometimes the precipitating input will arrive within hours, and other times it may take weeks, even years – without the scientist being able to either control or anticipate the course of events (Simonton, 1995). Archimedes certainly had no a priori reason to believe taking a bath would lead to the solution of his problem. Moreover, should the scientist attempt to take deliberate conscious control over the incubation process, the consequence would most likely be a restriction in the necessary openness to "irrelevant" influences, thereby undermining the effectiveness of the search for a solution. Trying to solve unreasonable problems by reasonable approaches will be an exercise in futility. So, again, scientific genius requires the capacity to know when it is time to dispense with logic – and even when to forego conscious deliberation of the problem.

In fact, experimental research has shown that insight problems are much more easily solved intuitively than by applying explicitly conscious logical inference (Schooler & Melcher, 1995; Simonton, 1980a). One reason for this effect is that conscious processing tends to narrow greatly the range and variety of associations stimulated by the problem (Mandler, 1995). In contrast, unconscious processing activates a richer array of associations, while at the same time rendering the mind more open to peripheral cues in the environment (Ansburg & Hill, 2003). Furthermore, these intuitive processes are far more likely to take advantage of tacit knowledge that might lead the associative process toward more productive directions (Reber, 1993). Einstein was quoted in Chapter 1 as maintaining that intuition was more important than logic in scientific discovery, but he also explained that this intuition is "supported by being sympathetically in touch with experience" (Holton, 1971–72, p. 97). In other words, creative scientists must acquire a tremendous wealth of domain-specific tacit knowledge via an intensive immersion in a particular phenomenon. This immersion that gives them a strong intuitive sense – a "gut feeling" or "hunch" – of how that phenomenon may operate (cf. Platt & Baker, 1931). It is likely that this immersion provides the associative richness discussed in Chapter 5, with many of these rich interconnections taking place at an unconscious level (Simonton, 1980a). Without this domain-specific but tacit knowledge, intuitive thought cannot be effective, producing error rather than insight (Bowers, Farvolden, & Mermigis, 1995). Intuition is no "magic bullet" but rather a hard-earned cognitive, even if unconscious, capacity.

In any case, it should now be manifest that insightful problem solving operates in such a way as to render scientific creativity highly unpredictable, as expected from the chance perspective. Certainly the operation is consistent with the critical findings described in Chapter 2. For instance, given the probabilistic variation in the length of the incubation period, creative ideas should be randomly distributed across consecutive years of a scientist's career.

Creative Production

One major objection that can be raised against experimental research on insight problems concerns the nature of the task. The participants in these experiments are presented with problems with known solutions. Successful solution requires that the research participant converge on a single, predetermined "correct answer." Genuine creative behavior never works this way, in science or otherwise. Instead, creativity is applied to open-ended problems in which the answer is unknown. Indeed, nobody may know for sure whether an answer even exists. Therefore, to understand better how creativity works in real-life settings, experimental inquiry must turn to the generation of creative products. That is, participants can be asked to produce original ideas under various experimental conditions, and the creativity of those ideas can then be evaluated (Amabile, 1982). Investigations using this approach have demonstrated that creativity is enhanced when research participants are exposed to random, novel, complex, or incongruous stimuli (Finke, Ward, & Smith 1992; Proctor, 1993; Rothenberg,

1986; Sobel & Rothenberg, 1980; Wan & Chiu, 2002). For instance, one experiment was able to stimulate creativity in both writers and artists by exposing them to photographs that superimposed two unrelated images (Rothenberg, 1986; Sobel & Rothenberg, 1980). This process of superimposition can be said to simulate those episodes of scientific creativity in which incongruous visualizations are similarly united (Rothenberg, 1987). An example is the wave-particle duality in which particles are seen as having wave properties and waves are seen as having particle properties.

More directly related to scientific discovery is the experimental research on the Geneplore model of creativity (Finke, Ward, & Smith, 1992). According to this model, creativity entails the process of two steps: (1) the generation of combinations and (2) the exploration of their possibilities. To test this model, research participants are given shapes or forms – lines, circles, triangles, letters, spheres, cubes, rings, hooks, etc. – from which they must create objects with recognizable functions (e.g., furniture, appliances, tools and utensils, weapons, or toys). Judges then rated the creativity of the products that resulted from this inventive activity. Some of the inventions arrived at were truly ingenious, including a hip exerciser, a shoestring unlacer, and a hamburger maker. More interesting still was how the imaginativeness of the inventions depended on the experimental conditions. In some conditions the participants themselves could select the shapes for the imaginative constructions, whereas in other conditions the participants were simply given a random selection of forms. In yet another experimental manipulation participants could choose the category of object they had to invent or the category was selected randomly by the experimenter. The researchers showed that participants arrived at the most innovative solutions when *both* the object parts they had to work with *and* the category of object they had to invent were randomly selected from the larger pool of possibilities. The best creativity tends to be serendipitous rather than deliberate. One could hardly obtain a more probabilistic basis for launching the combinatory process. By beginning with the totally unexpected, the participants in these experiments were forced to stretch their creativity to the highest degree.

In conclusion, laboratory experiments in which problem solvers must tackle open-ended problems show the importance of infusing the creative process with the illogical and unpredictable. This infusion helps break the constraints imposed by logic and convention. The outcome is a creative product that scores higher in creativity according to independent assessments.

Computer Problem Solving

I have just shown that the experimental literature on insight problems and creative production all support the thesis that creativity in science cannot be founded on a deterministic logic. This generalization is further endorsed by the characteristics of computer programs that successfully simulate human creativity (Boden, 1991, 1995; Johnson-Laird, 1993). Thus, one comprehensive review of the available programs observed "a convincing computer model of creativity would need some capacity for making random associations and/or transformations," a necessity that is often simply accomplished "by reference to lists of random numbers" (Boden, 1991, p. 226). To be sure, many of these programs were designed to simulate artistic rather than scientific creativity. As argued in the previous chapter, artistic creators normally operate under fewer constraints than do scientific creators, thereby maximizing the significance of chance. Even so, computer programs that make genuine scientific contributions also function via a chance combinatorial process.

This fact is best illustrated by the programs that operate according to evolutionary principles (Simonton, 1999c). Biological evolution takes place by the generation of random variations – genetic recombination and mutation – and the subsequent selection of the variations that are most adaptive. By the same token, computer programs can incorporate a random procedure to generate combinatorial variations that can be tested for fitness against some criterion. In both cases, the surviving combinations are recycled through variation-selection process until fitness is maximized. This generic procedure has been implemented in programs known as *genetic algorithms* (Goldberg, 1989; Holland, 1975, 1992). Such programs start with a population of randomly generated strings of ones and zeroes, such as 011010. These binary strings function the same way as a genetic code. That is, the strings define the traits of some entity or system, in this case a potential solution to a given problem. The trial solutions represented by this random collection of binary strings can then be tested to determine which come closest to solving the problem. The least successful strings are then deleted, while the most successful are allowed to reproduce. This reproduction occurs sexually. Specifically, each strand pairs off with another strand, and then each pair exchange portions of their strands with their mates (the exact point of crossover itself being randomly determined). For example, suppose 001001 and 110100 represent two strands that survived the first round of selection. They may mate by splitting after the fourth bit, the first part of one strand joining with the second part of the other strand. The outcome would be 001000 and 110101. Furthermore, randomly changing one or two bits on a subset of strands can introduce genetic mutations. Once this new generation is produced, the corresponding trial solutions can be tested again against the criterion. The whole evolutionary process may repeat, cycle after cycle, until the criterion of success is fully attained.

Despite the utterly random procedures for producing combinations, genetic algorithms have proven to be quite effective problem solvers. They already can solve real-world problems, such as planning fiber-optic telecommunication networks, designing gas and stream turbines, enhancing the efficiency of jet engines, making forecasts in currency trading, and improving oil exploration and mining operations (Holland, 1992). Moreover, the basic approach could be taken a step further to generate a much more complex problem solving systems – namely, those named *genetic programming* (Koza, 1992). In this technique, a whole population of computer programs is subjected to blind variation, and thus the evolutionary process operates at a higher level of structure. This approach has worked well in problems such as the designing of electrical circuits, the solution of algebraic equations, the determination of animal foraging behavior, and optimal game-playing strategies (Koza, 1994; Koza et al., 1999). Even more to the point, these evolutionary programs can make scientific rediscoveries. For example, genetic programming also managed to arrive at Kepler's Third Law of Planetary Motion (Koza, 1992). Interestingly, during the course of the evolution of a solution, the program first came across a less accurate statement of the relationship between planetary distance and time of revolution. It just so happens that this solution was the same as that Kepler himself had published a decade before arriving at the more precise law. In other words, both Kepler and the computer chanced upon the same local maximum before arriving at the global maximum!

Given these computational achievements, a strong prima facie case has been made on behalf of the thesis that scientific creativity involves chance combinations. The fact that these evolutionary programs have also rediscovered Kepler's Third Law – as well as making bona fide contributions of their own – provides a potent counterargument to the so-called "discovery programs" mentioned in Chapter 1 (Langley et al., 1987; Shrager & Langley, 1990; Wagman, 2000). Although the latter programs also make rediscoveries, and operate according to the principles set down by the pro-logic Newell-Simon tradition, they are vulnerable to several powerful criticisms (Gooding, 1996; Simonton, 1999c; Sternberg 1989; Tweney, 1990). Perhaps the most crucial objection concerns the rather rigid manner in which these programs process data. These rule-driven programs solve problems by applying a predetermined set of heuristic principles to the given data. Assigning an a priori ordering to the operations that will be applied minimizes trial-and-error procedures. When BACON rediscovered Kepler's Third Law, for example, it began with the linear relationship between the two variables involved. Because that failed the criterion of a proportional relationship, one of the variables was squared and the empirical test was again applied. This iterative process continued until the cube of one variable was found to be proportional to the square of the other, as the law specifies.

Although in a certain sense this sequence of transformations and tests involved some trial-and-error, there was too much wisdom underlying the procedure to make it count as truly blind. Rather than randomly try out all possible mathematical relationships, the hypothesized functions proceed from the simple to the complex by successive powers. The rigidity of this information-processing procedure becomes all the more problematic when we recognize that the hierarchical ordering of the data manipulations was installed after the fact. One must therefore wonder whether the programs were specifically tailored to fit the problems in a post hoc manner. In other words, the programs might actually be tautological rather than creative. Indeed, the same heuristics that enabled BACON to discover Kepler's Third Law may be totally inadequate to make other kinds of rediscoveries (e.g., the Balmer formula for the hydrogen spectrum). In contrast, problem-solving programs built upon evolutionary principles can make their discoveries from scratch, without imposing some preconceived method of analysis. It is probably for this reason that genetic algorithms and genetic programming techniques have actually made original discoveries and inventions rather than confining themselves to creating what has already been created.

The evolutionary programs have another advantage over the discovery programs: their operation is more compatible with other empirical findings and theoretical arguments presented in this book. The evolutionary programs are contingent on chance, whereas the discovery programs are dictated by logic. Yet from what we have seen so far, chance rather than logic most likely provides the foundation of creativity in science.

Group Creativity

All the above discussion suffers from a major liability: an invariable concentration on the individual. This focus held whether the research concerned insight problems, creative production, or computer problem solving. Yet this individualistic perspective overlooks a major feature of modern scientific creativity: scientific discoveries most often emerge largely from collaborative groups, particularly in research laboratories located in either academic or industrial settings. For example, a typical scientific laboratory at a research university might consist of the principal investigator, various co-investigators, postdoctoral and doctoral students, laboratory technicians, and perhaps even advanced undergraduates. Therefore, to understand more fully the creative process in science requires a better appreciation for how creative ideas might emerge from interactions among group members.

Unfortunately, most laboratory experiments on this subject have two drawbacks. First, the studies tend to use unrepresentative research participants, most often college students taking lower-division psychology courses. This is a far cry from studying scientific research labs. Second, the participants typically are presented with unrepresentative problem-solving tasks. Not only are they not asked to make major discoveries, but, even worse, they are usually given tasks that require no division of labor or special expertise. Given these two drawbacks, it is difficult to generalize the results to real-world problem-solving groups, such as those that dominate the scientific enterprise.

Even so, two experimental findings are of special value in the current context:

1. Group brainstorming involves the process of individuals generating lots of ideas in a group environment. Because this is the laboratory analog of the periodic lab meeting that is so characteristic of modern science, it is valuable to know the factors that operate during the brainstorming process. Research on this question has divulged how idea sharing among group members can result in the cognitive stimulation of each member (Dugosh et al., 2000). In other words, by exchanging ideas each group member can be stimulated in an unexpected manner and thereby provide another source of external serendipitous influence on the train of thought of a participating individual (see also Brown & Paulus, 2002).

2. Other studies have looked at the effectiveness of group problem solving, including how that effectiveness is determined by group membership. Of the many investigations in this vein, probably the most

pertinent here, are those that show that group creativity is enhanced when the members are exposed to divergent points of view (Nemeth & Kwan, 1985, 1987; Nemeth & Wachtler, 1983). Specifically, members exposed to ideological or behavioral dissent tend to discover solutions to problems that were given by neither the majority nor the majority working separately. Furthermore, despite the novelty of these solutions, the solutions would tend to be more likely correct rather than incorrect.

These experimental findings combined suggest that a research team whose membership is more heterogeneous with respect to expertise, experience, and status may prove more creative than one that is far more homogeneous. Because the information exchanged during lab meetings and at the bench has a stimulatory function, communication among separate members functions in a manner similar to what happens within a single scientist who is simultaneously engaged on several distinct projects. Just as work on one project can lead to serendipitous priming of other products undergoing the incubation phase, so may the thoughts of one scientist have unexpected effects on the thoughts of his or her colleagues. The more diverse are the collaborator backgrounds and expertise, the greater the level of mutual stimulation. The upshot is group problem solving that is more creative.

Another way of expressing this argument is to think in terms of each scientist's disciplinary sample. If each collaborator in a research laboratory possesses an identical sample of ideas from the same scientific domain, then the number of potential ideational combinations for the group could hardly surpass that for each individual working alone. This expectation is in line with brainstorming experiments that find that the productivity of a certain number of individuals working together seldom exceeds the productivity of the same number of individuals working alone (Diehl & Stroebe, 1987). On the other hand, if the research laboratory consists of members who have domain samples that only partially overlap, the total number of ideas available for entering the combinatorial process will be much greater, at least after the collaborators begin to exchange ideas. The creativity of the whole will be greater than the creativity of the parts.

This implication was confirmed in a comprehensive empirical study of 1,222 research units in six European countries (Andrews, 1979). There were two criteria of group-level creativity: objective productivity and subjectively rated effectiveness. Then each research unit was assessed on several indicators of group diversity. These included heterogeneity with respect to each member's scientific discipline, specialty area, source of funding, professional role, and research projects. Both criteria of group creativity correlated positively with the measures of group heterogeneity. This result received corroboration in Dunbar's (1995) more recent studies of research laboratories. Based on his objective and comprehensive observations – including tape recordings of lab meetings – he offered several recommendations about how to increase the probability that a particular group will make major scientific discoveries. One of these recommendations was that "members of a research group should have different but overlapping research backgrounds" (p. 391), again underlining the positive repercussions of heterogeneity. The domain samples of the scientists should converge just enough that they agree on nomenclature, goals, methods, and other components essential to effective collaboration.

Yet for the research group to benefit from the heterogeneity, it is also necessary for the members to experience the interpersonal intellectual stimulation indicated by the brainstorming experiments. In line with this expectation, Dunbar (1995) advised that "opportunities should be provided for the members of the research group to interact and discuss their research, by having overlapping research projects and breaking the laboratory into smaller groups working on similar problems" (p. 392). The latter part of this stipulation supports the earlier conjecture that this free exchange among scientists can function in much the same way as the interproject crosstalk occurring within the mind of individual scientists. In a sense, information processing is distributed among collaborators rather than being concentrated in the simultaneous lines of inquiry taking place within a single scientist. It is telling, therefore, that Dunbar (1995) also recommended that laboratory activities adopt some of the same practices we have associated with high-impact research. For instance, he advised that "researchers should be encouraged to engage in combinations of high-risk and low-risk projects" and that "surprising results should be noted" (p. 391). In short, highly creative laboratories should exhibit more member heterogeneity, information exchange among research collaborators, project diversity, and openness to serendipitous results.

Although Dunbar (1995) did not specifically examine the distribution of creative output over time, research groups satisfying these specifications must not be just more creative but also more unpredictable. The rationale for this inference is the same for what justified the same inference with respect to individual scientists. Accordingly, this research implies that (1) discoveries should be randomly distributed across time, (2) the output of discoveries in a given unit of time should be Poisson distributed, and (3) notable discoveries should be mixed with lesser discoveries in a manner consistent with the equal-odds rule. In brief, the output of highly creative laboratories should display the characteristics expected by the chance perspective.

CONCLUSION

This chapter opened with a discussion of the experimental side of the psychology of science. Unlike their counterparts in correlational and psychometric psychology, experimental psychologists tend to emphasize the logic of discovery. This emphasis is most explicit in the research tradition that emerged from Newell and Simon's (1972) *Human Problem Solving*. At first glance, the Newell–Simon tradition seems totally at odds with the chance perspective. Even so, this antagonism disappeared when the central principles of this tradition were subjected to detailed scrutiny. Only well-defined problems can be solved with algorithmic certainty. Yet the solutions to these types of problems are least likely to be deemed creative. In contrast, true creativity is more likely to be ascribed to solutions to ill-defined problems. These latter solutions require that the scientist resort

157

to an inventory of heuristic tools. And at this point the role of chance expands into view. Besides the fact that many heuristics are inherently probabilistic in operation, the selection of the most effective heuristic itself evokes a probabilistic decision. In effect, the application of heuristics requires the introduction of a higher-level process of trial and error.

The discussion then went a step farther by showing that not all experimental research can be subordinated to the Newell–Simon tradition. Perhaps it should not be too surprising that investigations conducted outside this tradition tend to lend more support to chance than to logic. First, investigations into insight problems revealed the unpredictability injected by the opportunistic assimilation of internal and external stimuli during the incubation period. Second, experiments on creative production showed how creativity can be stimulated by illogical, novel, or random stimuli. Third, research on computer problem solving has found that machines best simulate human creativity after first introducing a random mechanism. Fourth and last, studies of group problem solving have indicated how much creativity depends on the unexpected consequences of the free exchange of ideas among collaborators who are heterogeneous in background and experience. When these findings are combined with the preceding analysis, the conclusion is clear: scientific discovery cannot be explicated in terms of a linear and deterministic logic. Too many uncertainties and chaotic influences enter the creative process.

This last conclusion draws even more support when the central findings of this chapter are integrated with the main results in the previous chapter. That is, if what we know about scientific discovery is combined with what we know about the creative scientist, scientific creativity appears all the more like a process governed by dice throws than by decision trees or if-then statements. May a single example suffice to suggest the implications. When I discussed the incubation process, I noted that the associative process becomes susceptible to the influx of both internal and external events. Yet Chapter 5 included several attributes of highly creative scientists that would certainly affect the magnitude of this haphazard influence. For instance, the greater a scientist's associative richness, the more associations that are elicited by any given stimulus, and hence the more impressive is the quantity and diversity of associations that might impinge on the intellect during the incubation period. At the same time, because creative scientists are not as adept at filtering out supposedly extraneous information, they constitute an open system that will react more strongly to the variety of stimuli that are present in the external world. This reactivity is accentuated by their openness to experience, including an unusual range of interests, hobbies, and activities.

In the final analysis, the mind of a highly creative scientist will be a virtual cauldron of chance, a boiling infusion in which Poincaré's "hooked atoms of Epicurus" bounce and collide. From that bubbling broth emerge scientific discoveries of the first order.

7

Consolidation: Creativity in Science

S cientific creativity has now been examined from a multitude of view-points. Chapter 2 began the survey by looking at how creative products emerge from scientific careers and scientific communities. In particular, I described the distributions of publications across and within careers and the distinctive features of multiple discoveries. This chapter provided the critical behavioral data that inspired the theoretical interpretation provided in Chapter 3. The next three chapters then extended the explanatory thesis to other aspects of creativity in science. In Chapter 4, the focus was on scientific activity, which entailed the threefold scrutiny of the individual (research programs), the field (peer review), and the domain (disciplinary zeitgeist). Chapter 5 then turned to the dispositional characteristics and developmental factors associated with individual differences in scientific creativity. Finally, Chapter 6 presented the experimental literature on discovery processes, with special attention on the research regarding insight problems, creative production, computer problem solving, and group creativity.

The time has thus arrived to consolidate all these results and explanations. This consolidation begins by providing a synthesis of the four central perspectives on scientific creativity. It ends by discussing the larger implications of the theoretical and empirical findings.

INTEGRATION

As stressed in the opening chapter, scientific creativity may be viewed from four distinct perspectives: logic, genius, chance, and zeitgeist. In light of what has been shown in subsequent chapters, however, their order of treatment should be changed slightly here. Chance should be treated first, followed by logic, zeitgeist, and, lastly, genius. This sequence does not always indicate relative importance, but rather this progression permits a more coherent integration.

Chance

"Chance is the only source of true novelty," said Francis Crick, co-discoverer of DNA's structure (Kaplan, 2001, p. 224). This assertion is endorsed by the central thesis of this book – namely, that chance must be considered the primary basis for scientific creativity. This necessity first became apparent in Chapter 2. To begin with, the distribution of creative output within and across scientific careers has certain telltale features of a probabilistic process. These features include the equal-odds rule that describes the relation between quantity and quality of products, the random distribution of products across annual units of the career, and the Poisson distribution of the number of products generated per year. In addition, the phenomenon of multiple discovery and invention betrays the impact of chance to an even more surprising degree. This impact is witnessed in the distinctive distributions of multiple grades, degrees of simultaneity, and magnitudes of duplicate identity, as well as the consequences that a scientist's productivity and choice of research topic have for the likelihood of multiple participation. Whether we look at scientific careers or scientific communities, the big events that define the history of science appear to result from some kind of combinatorial process or set of processes.

This appearance was accentuated in Chapter 3 where I offered a model of scientific creativity based on chance combinations. The model was introduced by quoting what distinguished scientists have said about the creative process. These introspective reports, most notably those of Poincaré (1921), unequivocally affirm that creativity requires something that closely approximates a random combinatorial process. This concept was then formally expressed in terms of six basic assumptions about the individual, the field, and the domain that determine creativity within a scientific discipline. With these assumptions, the central findings of Chapter 2 could be given satisfactory interpretations. The explanatory framework was then extended to account for new phenomena that emerge when creative output is aggregated across individuals and within time units larger than single years. Specifically, the extended model accounted for expected career trajectories in creative productivity, including how these trajectories vary according to individual differences and interdisciplinary contrasts. The chapter concluded with a discussion of some possible objections. In response, I maintained that no alternative explanation elucidates the range of phenomena explicated using a chance-based model.

This reply received additional endorsement in the following three chapters. Chapter 4 dealt with scientific activity, Chapter 5 with creative scientists, and Chapter 6 with scientific discovery. The significance of chance emerged no matter what we examined, including research programs, peer review, disciplinary zeitgeist, the disposition and development of creative scientists, and the results of laboratory experiments on insight problems, creative production, computer problem solving, and group creativity. Hence, the impact of chance goes well beyond the circumscribed phenomenon of serendipity, the event traditionally associated with chance in scientific creativity.

To be sure, it may seem strange to identify chance as a *cause* of scientific creativity. After all, chance is not a specific variable or factor, unlike what can be claimed in the case of logic, genius, or zeitgeist. Indeed, many would argue that chance per se does not really exist, at least at the level of psychological phenomena. Even so, the operation of chance is not inconsistent with the most exhaustive determinism. Chance is a mere coverall term for the situation in which there are so many unknown – and perhaps unknowable – causes that it is impossible to make anything more than probabilistic assertions. In this sense, the chance account accommodates more fully the immense complexity of scientific creativity. This richer accommodation differs greatly from the causally simpler logic, genius, and zeitgeist perspectives. According to the chance perspective, the creative process is contingent on so many complex and interacting factors that it necessarily behaves *as if* it operated via a random combinatorial mechanism.

Although chance thus appears as the most proximate cause of scientific creativity, it is by no means the only valid perspective. To argue otherwise means to sacrifice truth for parsimony. Instead, probabilistic processes are joined by other factors, albeit factors that operate mostly as distal causes – causes a step or two removed from the proximate cause. That is, these additional factors impinge upon, intensify, modify, qualify, or in some other manner adjust the operation of chance. The added factors are logic, zeitgeist, and genius.

Logic

I have argued – as logically as possible – that logic plays a secondary role in the generation of highly creative ideas. Problems that most lend themselves to straightforward logical analyses tend to require mere algorithmic solutions and hence tend to be more routine than original. These do not normally represent the kinds of ideas that win any scientist a Nobel Prize. Truly original, even revolutionary ideas, in contrast, are far less susceptible to step-by-step, predetermined modes of solution. Even heuristics have a strong probabilistic component in both the application of specific heuristics and the selection of the most appropriate heuristics. Moreover, because original problems are frequently unreasonable in the sense that they cannot be solved without first noticing the "catch" or "trick," scientific discovery becomes all the more resistant to a purely logical analysis. In fact, the process begins to appear much more probabilistic, in a manner fitting the chance perspective. In short, the more original, even "earthshaking" the discovery, the less likely it is that logic played the primary causal role in the event. At least this inverse association holds on the average.

The Role of Logic. Nevertheless, the preceding claim is not equivalent to maintaining that logical processes have no place whatsoever in science. Most obviously, scientific contributions display considerable variation in the amount of originality they require. At one extreme are journal articles that report unexpected breakthroughs, such as Einstein's 1905 papers on special relativity, the photoelectric effect, and Brownian motion. At the other extreme are scholarly research summaries such as those that dominate the chapters in edited volumes. Between these two extremes are reports of puzzle-solving research that closely adhere to widely accepted paradigms. The less originality demanded by a given publication, the more logical processes will prevail over those that are more probabilistic.

Even in the case of contributions that presuppose substantial originality it is advisable to distinguish between the *context of discovery* and the *context of justification* (Reichenbach, 1938; see also Popper, 1959). To comprehend discovery requires a grasp of the psychological processes responsible for that event. To understand justification demands an appreciation of the arguments by which the truth of that discovery is established before the community of scientists. Arguments that justify a discovery must be logical at their very heart. Pleading and haranguing do not suffice. Nonetheless, it also must be recognized that the discovery process unavoidably occurs before the justification process. Logical justification requires something to justify. In addition, the two processes must be considered largely independent and distinct.

The primacy, independence, and distinctiveness of discovery relative to justification are evident in Einstein's description of his own creative process. "Taken from a psychological viewpoint ... combinatory play seems to be the essential feature in productive thought – before there is any connection with logical construction in words or other kinds of signs which can be communicated to others" (Hadamard, 1945, p. 142). Consequently, "conventional words or other signs have to be sought for laboriously only

164

in a secondary stage, when the mentioned associative play is sufficiently established and can be reproduced at will" (p. 143). The crucial distinction could not be affirmed more explicitly. First the scientist freely plays around with ideas, the logic participating only after the associative process has converged on a good combination.

Even when attention is restricted to the context of discovery, a combinatorial model of scientific creativity cannot be said to exclude logic. On the contrary, logic imposes some formidable constraints on the creative process in science (Simonton, 2003a). These constraints are of three main kinds:

1. Logic often limits what ideas enter the combinatorial operation. Not all phenomena, facts, concepts, variables, constants, techniques, theories, laws, questions, goals, and criteria can participate, but rather only those that have some rational connection to potential solutions. The most manifest instances of these limitations are those ideas that violate the basic tenets of science. Scientific explanations of phenomena cannot include God, spirits, "little green creatures," or similar unverifiable causes. Miracles and perpetual motion machines are ruled out of court. In general, the participating ideas must belong to a legitimate scientific domain.

2. Logic usually determines the degree of randomness in the combinatorial process. Many ideas are intimately connected with certain other ideas because they form part of a coherent theoretical system or paradigm. Thus, some ideas more properly belong to relativity theory and others to quantum theory (e.g., the differential status of gravitation). That means ideas cannot always be mixed together in any combination whatsoever. These restrictions are analogous to those imposed on genetic recombination, a more obvious combinatorial process. Genes located close together on the same chromosome cannot display complete independent assortment but rather are subject to chromosomal linkage, reducing the freedom of genetic

recombination. The closer two genes lie on the chromosome, the more severe the constraint.

3. Logic largely decides the criteria that are applied to determine what constitutes a good combination resulting from the combinatorial process. It sometimes happens that what at first appears to constitute a sensible solution fails to survive logical scrutiny. The combination may turn out to be logically inconsistent with an established theory or incontrovertible fact. For instance, an idea may contradict the law of energy conservation. As noted elsewhere in this book, these false hunches or intuitions are actually quite common. One of the problems that repeatedly confronted Einstein in the development of his unified field theory is that the successive versions were constantly yielding implications that were flatly contradicted by well-known phenomena.

The Limits on Logic. These three logical constraints notwithstanding, it must be acknowledged that their operation is far from perfect or inevitable. Scientists may not notice the logical problems inherent in an apparent good combination. As a result, they may have to wait for colleagues to point out the faults, whether during peer review or after publication. A notorious illustration of the latter possibility occurred when Gottlob Frege, having spent many years developing a complete mathematical logic, received a letter from Bertrand Russell that pinpointed a logical contradiction that undermined the entire enterprise. If a specialist in logic can make such a spectacular error, it seems unlikely that most creative scientists can do much better.

Indeed, even unquestioned scientific geniuses can commit truly inexcusable mistakes. A prime instance occurred during the series of debates between Einstein and Bohr in which the former tried to undermine the latter's Copenhagen interpretation of quantum theory. In 1930, Einstein offered a critical analysis of the Heisenberg indeterminacy principle. At first, Bohr could identify absolutely no flaw in Einstein's argument, but he finally spotted a fatal error in the most unlikely place: the critique failed to take into consideration the principle of equivalence that constitutes the conceptual core of Einstein's own general theory of relativity! One would think Einstein to be the last scientist in the world to make such a disastrous blunder.

One of the reasons why slips like this can take place is that the constraints of logic always have to compete with other criteria that have a totally distinct origin and thus may not necessarily be compatible with logical standards. A recurrent example is the constraints founded on aesthetic criteria (Wechsler, 1978). Many creative scientists have stressed the importance of elegance, beauty, and even emotional sensibility when judging new scientific ideas (Planck, 1949; Poincaré, 1921). Although vaguely defined, such criteria may influence the creative process in ways that run counter to logic. Poincaré (1921) observed how sometimes "a sudden illumination seizes upon the mind of the mathematician ... that ... does not stand the test of verification," but explained this intrusion by saying "we almost always notice that this false idea, had it been true, would have gratified our natural feeling for mathematical elegance" (p. 392).

In some cases, moreover, aesthetic criteria may prove more indicative of scientific value than do logical criteria. According to Paul Dirac (1963), Erwin Schrödinger failed to publish a relativistic wave equation because it yielded predictions inconsistent with experimental results. Yet Dirac was able to do so by ignoring the facts and aiming toward mathematical elegance, thereby earning his own Nobel Prize. Dirac's final inference was "it is more important to have beauty in one's equations than to have them fit experiment" and "that if one is working from the point of view of getting beauty in one's equations, and if one has really a sound insight, one is on a sure line of progress" (p. 47).

Needless to say, because aesthetic criteria are so subjective, they tend to be highly idiosyncratic to particular scientists. Beauty is in the eye of the beholder, whether in the sciences or the arts. As a consequence, disagreements about the value of new scientific ideas may center on differences in taste rather than debates about logic. The history of quantum theory provides another illustration. In the mid-1920s two contrasting quantum

167

mechanics appeared. The first, by Heisenberg, was based on discrete and discontinuous quantities, conceived in terms of particles, and expressed mathematically in terms of matrix algebra. The second, by Schrödinger, was predicated on continuous quantities, conceived in terms of waves, and stated mathematically in terms of differential equations. Heisenberg admitted "the more I ponder about ... Schrödinger's theory the more disgusting it appears to me," an adverse reaction that Schrödinger reciprocated when he said "I was discouraged, if not repelled, by what appeared to me a rather difficult method of transcendental algebra, defying any visualization" (Cropper, 1970, p. 90). The ironic part of this story is that the two alternative mechanics turned out to be mathematically equivalent. Not only is each logically coherent, but a one-to-one correspondence can be constructed between them. So the choice of one over the other could not be based on logical grounds. The selection must be founded on what a scientist personally considers to represent beauty or elegance in science.

All in all, logic has a substantial but circumscribed part to play in scientific creativity. With respect to the context of discovery, it stands at the periphery relative to the processes associated with chance. And although logic has a critical function with respect to the context of justification, even here it must compete with rival standards, such as aesthetic criteria.

Zeitgeist

The previous section did not include another fundamental restriction on the impact of logic on scientific discovery: what is considered rational or irrational is to some undetermined extent contingent on the disciplinary zeitgeist. Specifically, each domain is defined by a set of ideas about what constitute legitimate ideational combinations and what must be rejected on a priori grounds. In highly paradigmatic sciences, these criteria have the force of law. Indeed, such standards are often viewed as common sense. The difficulty, of course, is that the criteria can often be extremely arbitrary. They may be riddled with unjustified assumptions, cognitive biases, and cultural preconceptions. As Einstein expressed it, "common sense is nothing more than a deposit of prejudices laid down in the mind before you reach eighteen" (Bell, 1951, p. 42). So, these unscientific impositions can pass undetected until some scientist offers a new, revolutionary paradigm. Then often quite suddenly, the impossible becomes permissible and the essential becomes superfluous. There were periods in the history of science in which all heavenly bodies had to have circular orbits, heavy objects necessarily fell faster than light bodies, the vacuum could not exist, action-at-a-distance was impossible, and species never evolved – ideas all rendered obsolete by Kepler, Galileo, Pascal, Newton, and Darwin, respectively.

Perhaps the most dramatic example is the quantum revolution, which dispensed with some basic logical principles that have governed science for centuries. A case in point is the concept of superposition that permits a quantum object to be two opposite things simultaneously (e.g., a photon can be in two totally different places at the same time). As a consequence, a decisive aspect of creativity in science is for the scientist to discern when it is time to think the unthinkable. In the absence of this step, science majors today would still be studying Ptolemaic astronomy, Aristotelian physics, medieval alchemy, and creationist biology.

The above point raises the broader issue of the place of zeitgeist in scientific creativity. To address this question properly, it is necessary to distinguish two manifestations of zeitgeist: disciplinary and sociocultural.

Disciplinary Zeitgeist. The first is defined by the ideas – the phenomena, facts, concepts, variables, constants, techniques, theories, laws, questions, goals, and criteria – that make up the domain of a scientific discipline at a particular point in time. This collection of ideas provides the necessary but not sufficient basis for all discoveries and inventions that can be made at that moment in disciplinary history. Naturally, this repository is dynamic rather than static. Each discovery or invention, once successfully communicated and disseminated, becomes an integral part of this body of accumulated theory, knowledge, and technique. One consequence of this accumulation is the accelerated pace at which scientific creativity takes place – a pace speeded up all the more by the increase in the number of scientists making up any given field.

On the other hand, contrary to the traditional interpretation of the multiples phenomenon, the disciplinary zeitgeist does not operate in a deterministic manner. Because the location of a good combination must ultimately depend on a chance combinatorial process, zeitgeist can only sit back and wait for a potential discovery or invention to become an actual discovery or invention. The disciplinary zeitgeist lacks direct causal efficacy. The best that can be done is to enhance the chances by encouraging more trials. This encouragement can be accomplished when the scientists making up a field designate some problem as sufficiently "hot" or "urgent" to justify awards and recognition for those lucky enough to find a solution. A celebrated example was David Hilbert's 1900 address on the "Problems of Mathematics" before the International Mathematical Congress in which he enumerated 23 central issues that were to preoccupy mathematicians for generations.

Sociocultural Zeitgeist. This consists of the political, economic, social, and cultural circumstances that impinge on the scientific enterprise from the outside. These external factors are important in determining both the quantity and the quality of scientific creativity in a given historical period. With respect to quantity, some sociocultural conditions are conducive to scientific activity, encouraging young talent to become scientists. Other conditions discourage individuals from entering science, or at least undermine the creativity of those who still manage to become scientists. These positive and negative conditions together largely explain why scientific genius tends to cluster in specific times and places rather than being randomly distributed geographically and historically. With respect to quality, the sociocultural zeitgeist partially determines what disciplines will be most widely encouraged and even the topics within each discipline that will receive the greatest emphasis. A clear-cut instance of this impact is the fashion in which war channels scientific creativity into areas most relevant to national survival. Finally, it must be acknowledged that the sociocultural zeitgeist provides much of the infrastructure of scientific activity. This foundation includes the libraries and electronic databases that store scientific knowledge and the communication systems by which that knowledge is spread. As pointed out in Chapter 3, the accelerated communication of new findings has consequences for the occurrence of multiples, lowering their grade and shrinking their temporal separation.

Nevertheless, the sociocultural zeitgeist, like the disciplinary zeitgeist, is far from omnipotent. Indeed, in the final analysis the power of the sociocultural zeitgeist is contingent on the disciplinary zeitgeist. A nation may decide to provide an immense amount of funds to support research in strategically critical areas, but that investment will be wasted if the necessary conditions have not been satisfied. This disciplinary constraint on sociocultural influence is illustrated by the fate of nuclear fusion. Despite strong governmental support for developing a "cheap, clean, and inexhaustible" source of energy, the knowledge base was just not there. The world is accordingly not much closer to building nuclear fusion power plants than it was decades ago. This stands in stark contrast to the rapid development of power plants based on nuclear fission. In the latter case all the essential ideas were already in place when the "peaceful use of atomic energy" was first championed.

Genius

The foregoing presentations of the chance, logic, and zeitgeist perspectives have definite implications for the genius perspective. Thus, according to what has been learned about zeitgeist, it is clear that the scientific genius does not operate in isolation from the disciplinary and sociocultural milieu. Certainly no scientist, no matter how creative, can generate ideas from nothing. Instead, as the chance perspective suggests, creative ideas necessarily emerge when the combinatorial process is applied to the ideas that define each scientist's sample from a given domain – the disciplinary zeitgeist. In addition, the creative scientist must have a somewhat flexible attitude toward logic. Although analytical thinking is absolutely mandatory when scientists must justify their discoveries to their colleagues, its place in the creative process must be more restricted. The combinatorial process functions in relative freedom from a priori constraints. Only in the case of routine problems that can be solved algorithmically does logical analysis participate at the onset. Yet solutions to such problems are less likely to represent major scientific breakthroughs.

High versus Low Creativity. At the same time, it has been made manifest that highly creative scientists differ from their less creative colleagues on several parameters. According to the documentation provided in Chapters 4 and 5, these differences are threefold.

1. The magnitude of creativity displayed by a scientist is correlated with specific dispositional traits, both intellectual and personal. On the intellectual side is the capacity to generate numerous and diverse associations in response to a given stimulus situation. On the more personal side is a trait like openness to experience, including defocused attention and receptiveness to novelty, variety, complexity, and even ambiguity. The only qualification for these dispositional attributes is that the optimal magnitude depends on the type of creativity being displayed. Scientists engaged in extremely constrained problem solving, such as that practiced in normal science in highly paradigmatic disciplines, should exhibit these characteristics to a lesser degree than scientists immersed in less constrained activity, such as that witnessed in revolutionary science or in less paradigmatic disciplines. Yet even revolutionary scientists or scientists in more unconstrained domains will be less extreme on these intellectual and personal traits than tends to hold among artistic creators.

2. Individual differences in scientific creativity are correlated with specific developmental experiences. Some of these experiences are associated with the home environment, whereas others are linked with education and training. Whatever their specific origins, these experiences facilitate the acquisition of creative potential by stimulating the

development of the intellectual and personal qualities mentioned in the preceding paragraph. The more rich, unusual, and various these developmental experiences, the more impressive is the scientist's capacity to overcome the constraints of tradition and to play the iconoclast. Naturally, because scientific creativity requires an optimal tradeoff between iconoclasm and traditionalism, these developmental experiences are not so extreme as those seen in artistic creativity. Even so, the development of revolutionary scientists is less structured and conventional than the development of normal scientists. A comparable gap separates scientists in highly paradigmatic disciplines from those disciplines that are less paradigmatic.

3. A scientist's creativity is associated with distinctive behavioral activities. Three activities are particularly significant. First, creative scientists work simultaneously on a diversity of research activities. That is, at any one time they may be working on projects that are high versus low risk, original versus routine, empirical versus theoretical, core versus peripheral, and so forth. Second, creative scientists manifest heavy involvement in a variety of professional activities, such as peer review, journal reading, correspondence, professional meetings, and the like. Third and last, creative scientists actively participate in various recreational activities. These include omnivorous reading, keeping up on results in other disciplines, and intellectual or creative hobbies. Needless to say, these behavioral features of the creative scientist largely reflect their distinctive dispositional characteristics and developmental experiences. For instance, a great deal of this divergent and complex behavioral activity can be attributed to experiential openness, a characteristic that itself is at least partly attributable to early developmental factors.

Chance and Creativity. Taken together, these dispositional, developmental, and behavioral characteristics delineate the profile of the scientific genius. Hence, their identification may be adopted as support for the genius perspective. Even so, the same traits also provide the psychological foundation for the chance perspective, as was indicated in Chapters 4 and 5. Stated more provocatively, to the extent that scientists feature this threefold profile, the chance and genius perspectives converge.

Figure 7.1 helps illustrate the nature of this convergence. The figure provides a schematic representation of the behavioral activity of highly creative scientists. First and foremost is the activity that is directly involved in the scientist's research. The involvement in a diversity of research projects is depicted by a sequence of vertical arrows. The length of each arrow represents the duration of the project, the arrowhead indicating when a project has been completed (i.e., the results published). The thickness of these arrows conveys the fact that the projects vary appreciably on several parameters, such as the their relative degree of originality or likely impact. Finally, two other vertical arrows are presented in the figure, using dotted lines rather than the solid lines used to indicate separate research projects. The first vertical arrow represents the scientist's professional activities (attending conferences, evaluating submitted manuscripts or grant proposals, correspondence, etc.), and the second represents his or her recreational activities (casual reading, hobbies, entertainment, vacations, etc.). Of course, scientists with teaching responsibilities would add a third dotted verticle arrow, but this is ignored.

Now comes the critical aspect of the graph: the horizontal arrows. Each arrow represents an occasion in which the activity indicated by one vertical arrow exerted an influence on the activity indicated by another vertical arrow. These horizontal arrows fall into two broad groups.

First are those arrows with dashed-line shafts that connect solid-line vertical arrows. These symbolize crosstalk among separate research projects – thereby forming the network of enterprise. Notably, the research projects vary considerably regarding the frequency with which they affect work on other projects. Core projects have implications for many other ongoing efforts, whereas peripheral projects seldom make such contributions. An instance of a core project is Darwin's long-term work on evolution, an endeavor that intermittently informed nearly everything else he was doing at the same time. His lengthy and laborious work on

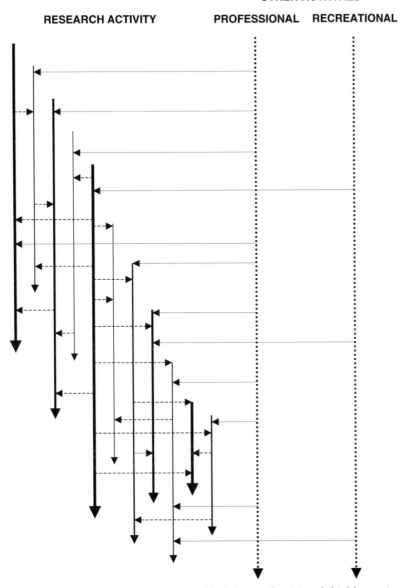

FIGURE 7.1. Schematic representation of the behavioral activity of a highly creative scientist. Vertical arrows show the course of research, professional, and recreational activities, while horizontal arrows depict the crosstalk within and among these activities.

175

cirripedes, by comparison, did not generate the same wealth of interproject influences.

Second are those horizontal arrows with solid-line shafts that connect the dotted-line vertical arrows with the solid-line vertical arrows. These symbolize the impact of various professional and recreational activities on a scientist's works in progress. Because professional activities are more likely to produce relevant inputs into the creative process, horizontal lines leading from this vertical arrow are more common than those leading from that representing recreational activities. Nevertheless, this disparity in quantity is partly compensated by a contrasting inequality in impact. The influences coming from recreational activities may have a higher likelihood of yielding breakthrough results by the very fact that these influences are most likely to be considered irrelevant. Darwin's reading of Malthus is an example.

Lastly, it must be noted that the specific consequence of these effects is highly variable. Sometimes the consequence is to initiate a new research project (namely, those instances in which a horizontal arrow touches on the beginning of a vertical arrow). On other occasions, the impact takes place late in the work devoted to a particular project and may even represent episodes in which the "missing piece of the puzzle" is finally provided by an outside source. The remaining horizontal arrows strike various places between these extremes on the vertical arrows. These represent adventitious influences that neither initiate nor solve a problem, but nonetheless facilitate its later solution by helping the scientist overcome an obstacle in an intermediate step.

How does Figure 7.1 illustrate the convergence of genius and chance? With respect to the genius perspective, it is already clear that highly creative scientists are more likely to work on several diverse projects simultaneously and to engage in varied professional and recreational behaviors. Just as important, because scientific creativity is correlated with associative richness and openness to experience, highly creative scientists are more receptive to the cross-connections. For example, they are more likely to notice when something they are reading for pleasure turns out to have some bearing on a current research problem. In the case of the chance perspective, it should be apparent that, for the most part, these cross-influences represent serendipitous effects. That is, the scientist most often did not anticipate that a contribution to solving some problem would come from work on another problem or even from some outside professional or recreational activity. Hence, the frequent occurrence of these cross-influences augments the unpredictability of the creative process.

This inherent unpredictability then leads to the kinds of phenomena that were documented earlier in this book. For instance, because the initiation and solution of a given research problem is contingent on unexpected influences from seemingly irrelevant activities, the specific location and length of the several vertical arrows representing research projects will be highly unpredictable as well. Any given project might just as likely start earlier or later and terminate earlier or later. Because the projects vary greatly in creative significance, high-impact works are randomly mixed with low-impact works. The upshot is the equal-odds rule that says quality is a probabilistic function of quantity. Furthermore, because the resolution of many research projects requires the influx of serendipitous events, and because those events themselves may have a generally low probability of occurrence, the solution of any given problem has a correspondingly low likelihood of success. Hence, the distribution of contributions across annual units of a scientist's career should be random and Poisson distributed within units.

The probabilistic consequences of the process displayed in Figure 7.1 concentrate on creative behavior. Yet it should be equally obvious that the underlying thought processes should exhibit a corresponding degree of unpredictability. In particular, creative thought should involve something akin to the chance combinations hypothesized in Chapter 3. Because highly creative scientists are so open to novelty, complexity, and diversity in their already changeable environments, they necessarily have all sorts of ideas popping to mind unexpectedly. Their greater associative richness then expands and develops this unpredictable influx into equally unanticipated directions. This expansion and development of even the most insignificant stimulus is illustrated by what Francis Darwin said of his father, Charles:

> it was as though he were charged with theorizing power ready to flow into any channel on the slightest disturbance, so that no fact, however small, could avoid releasing a stream of theory, and thus the fact became magnified into importance. In this way it naturally happened that many untenable theories occurred to him; but fortunately his richness of imagination was equalled by his power of judging and condemning the thoughts that occurred to him. (F. Darwin, 1892/1958, p. 101)

The latter part of this quote makes a useful point: the profusion of ideas and images notwithstanding, most of these thoughts lead nowhere. Fruitful pathways to solutions, or even partial solutions, are always extremely rare. The economist William S. Jevons expressed it well in *The Principles of Science*:

> it would be an error to suppose that the great discoverer seizes at once upon the truth, or has any unerring method of divining it. In all probability the errors of the great mind exceed in number those of the less vigorous one. Fertility of imagination and abundance of guesses at truth are among the first requisites of discovery; but the erroneous guesses must be many times as numerous as those that prove well founded. The weakest analogies, the most whimsical notions, the most apparently absurd theories, may pass through the teeming brain, and no record remain of more than the hundredth part.... The truest theories involve suppositions which are inconceivable, and no limit can be placed to the freedom of hypotheses. (Jevons, 1877/1900, p. 577)

Hence, the subjective experience of the creative process is no less probabilistic than the objective behavior that results. According to Jevons's estimate, the odds of coming up with a good combination are 1 in 100.

Actually, these remarks greatly understate the unpredictability of the underlying mental process. After all, these comments concentrate on the conscious experience of creative problem solving. Yet creativity largely takes place below the threshold of awareness. It is in this unconscious realm that much of the hypothesized combinatorial process occurs. In this level subliminal priming effects and diffuse spreading activation become heavily involved. Only when these operations obtain possible good combinations will one of their products pop into focal awareness. Hence, the chaos of the creativity in the conscious mind is no more than the tip of the iceberg. Below the surface is a far more extensive world of even more chaotic processes. The probabilistic nature of this cognitive unconscious is propelled all the more by the scientist's openness to even irrelevant experiences and the capacity for generating numerous and varied associations. When these operations are combined with those happening in the conscious mind, a good combination probably appears in solely one of a thousand or more transient thoughts.

In a nutshell, at the highest levels of scientific creativity, chance and genius become synonymous.

IMPLICATIONS

The integrative perspective has significant consequences for future research on creativity in science. Perhaps the foremost implication is the dire need to conduct research that deliberately combines two or more of the four perspectives. For example, a complete understanding of scientific creativity is impossible so long as there are two isolated psychologies of science, one adopting the logic perspective and the other the genius perspective. Instead of going their separate ways, psychologists should combine experimental and correlational methods. Specifically, intellectual and dispositional variables should become an integral part of laboratory studies of creative problem solving. For instance, laboratory experiments can be used to assess how individual differences in openness to experience influences the extent of opportunistic assimilation that takes place during the incubation period.

Another potential line of inquiry involves the integration of the chance and logic perspectives. Although the so-called discovery programs operate totally according to a preordained linear logic, the computer programs that

179

most unequivocally evince human creativity – such as genetic algorithms and programming – invariably contain a random component. Therefore, it seems advisable to devise discovery programs that incorporate a similar component. It would then seem more likely that the resulting programs might make genuine discoveries rather than confining themselves to re-discoveries. Perhaps the only real obstacle to creating bona fide discovery programs is the need to provide the resulting system with the rich associative networks that underlie human creativity. This would require the development of connectionist models of the mind that operate on a very grand scale.

Research Framework. Nonetheless, if I had to identify the single most critical topic for research, it would probably concern the characteristics of the creative scientist. More specifically, we need to know more about how various developmental and dispositional factors determine the type of creativity displayed by any individual. According to the thesis elaborated in this book, the interconnections should follow the pattern represented in Figure 7.2. Developmental and dispositional variables are placed along an underlying dimension that reflects the relative proportions of constraint and chance required for creativity in a given endeavor. Development factors include home environment, birth order, education and training, mentors and role models, and sociocultural zeitgeist, whereas dispositional factors include cognitive processes, openness to experience, and psychopathology. Corresponding to these contrasts are parallel contrasts in the forms that creativity is most likely to take. Besides the major distinction between the sciences and the arts, discrepancies also appear within each general domain. On the scientific side, paradigmatic sciences (e.g., physics) tend to be more constrained than nonparadigmatic sciences (e.g., sociology). And within the paradigmatic disciplines, practitioners of normal science operate under more constraint than do revolutionary scientists. A comparable situation holds for artistic creators, such as the contrast between highly formal endeavors (e.g., classical music) and highly expressive endeavors (e.g., lyric poetry).

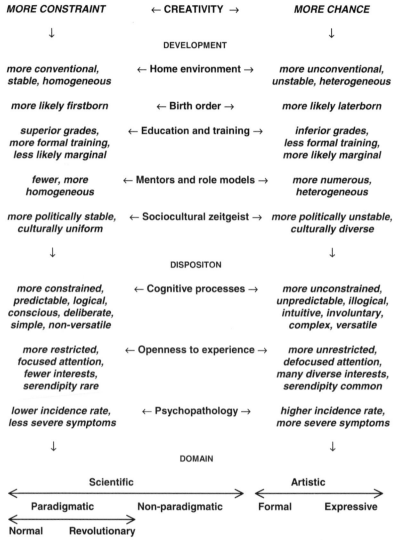

MORE CONSTRAINT   ← CREATIVITY →   MORE CHANCE

↓   DEVELOPMENT   ↓

more conventional, stable, homogeneous	← Home environment →	more unconventional, unstable, heterogeneous
more likely firstborn	← Birth order →	more likely laterborn
superior grades, more formal training, less likely marginal	← Education and training →	inferior grades, less formal training, more likely marginal
fewer, more homogeneous	← Mentors and role models →	more numerous, heterogeneous
more politically stable, culturally uniform	← Sociocultural zeitgeist →	more politically unstable, culturally diverse

↓   DISPOSITON   ↓

more constrained, predictable, logical, conscious, deliberate, simple, non-versatile	← Cognitive processes →	more unconstrained, unpredictable, illogical, intuitive, involuntary, complex, versatile
more restricted, focused attention, fewer interests, serendipity rare	← Openness to experience →	more unrestricted, defocused attention, many diverse interests, serendipity common
lower incidence rate, less severe symptoms	← Psychopathology →	higher incidence rate, more severe symptoms

↓   DOMAIN   ↓

Scientific   Artistic
←————————————————→ ←————————————————→
Paradigmatic   Non-paradigmatic   Formal   Expressive
←————————————→
Normal   Revolutionary

FIGURE 7.2. Representation of the developmental and dispositional variables that determine the type of creativity displayed by a given individual. On the left side are developmental and dispositional circumstances that impose more constraint, whereas on the right side are circumstances that reserve a greater role for chance. At the bottom of the figure are the expectations regarding the most probable domain of creativity implied by placement along the underlying dimension of constraint versus chance.

181

In earlier chapters, and especially in Chapter 5, I have presented sufficient evidence for believing that Figure 7.2 provides a reasonable consolidation of what has been learned so far. Even so, prior research has been
piecemeal and incomplete. Although many studies have examined the
differences between scientific and artistic creators, hardly any have tried
to document the developmental and dispositional variables that distinguish revolutionary and normal scientists. Certainly no investigator has
yet attempted to scrutinize this distinction in the larger context of the
differences between scientific and artistic creativity. So many more investigations remain to be done to substantiate the details of the scheme
presented in the figure.

Of course, the hypothesized pattern of relationships would operate in a
probabilistic rather than deterministic fashion. Few scientists would conform perfectly to theoretical expectation. Nevertheless, I would argue that
those scientists who fit the pattern most closely would enjoy a higher likelihood of exhibiting creativity. For example, a scientist who is best equipped
to do revolutionary science will probably not do as well in normal science as
a colleague whose development and disposition are best suited to highly
constrained scientific creativity. Similarly, a scientist who follows most
closely the developmental and dispositional pattern expected of paradigmatic disciplines will probably attain higher eminence as a physicist or
chemist than as a psychologist or sociologist. These expectations are also
deserving of systematic empirical inquiry.

Potential Applications. Increased knowledge about the creative scientist
can have practical repercussions. In particular, such information can provide the basis for identifying scientific talent and for encouraging the
creative development of those identified as talented. In addition, practicing scientists can certainly benefit by deliberately making their activities
conform more closely to the research programs that drive high-impact
science – such as is schematically represented in Figure 7.1. Nevertheless,
the integrative framework also suggests that these applications must be
carried out with some caution. To concentrate the effort on individual

scientists is to exalt the genius perspective above the rest. The other perspectives cannot be ignored. For example, the zeitgeist perspective imposes the obligatory reminder that discoveries and inventions emerge not just from individual scientists, but also from scientific communities. By introducing a field of scientists into the calculations, we are forced to recognize some of the misleading implications of a totally individualistic account.

To illustrate the last point, let us consider individual differences in research output. Judging from the highly skewed distribution, it would seem possible to reduce the number of active scientists with minimal cost to the scientific enterprise. If the bottom half of the distribution accounts for only about 15% of the total productivity, then a cost-effective policy might be to fire half the world's scientists. The result should be 85% of the original output at merely half the cost. The flaw in this argument is that it treats each individual scientist as if he or she were isolated from a community of scientists. It thus overlooks the possibility that the most prolific scientists – the creative geniuses of their fields – constitute the apex of a pyramid of which their less productive but more numerous colleagues form the base. Removing the base may thus lower the apex. Newton once said that he saw farther than other scientists because he "stood on the shoulders of giants." He should have added that those giants stood on the shoulders of scientists of more ordinary stature, thereby contributing to the range of his vision.

Indeed, according to the Price Law, the elitism at the top is a direct function of the quantity at the bottom, an effect that was explained in terms of the richer information exchange that occurs in larger fields. Even the lone article published by an otherwise unknown scientist may stimulate the thinking of the most illustrious scientist in the same discipline. The odds are not high, but they are not zero either. Moreover, the immense number of scientists who contribute solely one idea each compensates for the low odds. Thus, if we deleted the output of all scientists who cited at least once the publication of someone in the lower half of the distribution, it is likely that we would lose much more than a mere 15% of the total output.

This might seem to be a wasteful process, but no viable alternative exists. Although scientific creativity is certainly more logical than artistic creativity, it nonetheless remains invariably messy and inefficient. In fact, that may be the single most consequential point to deduce from the chance perspective. Creativity, scientific or otherwise, is not the kind of deterministic process that is implied by the logic, genius, and zeitgeist perspectives. No logical method, no inspired genius, no sociocultural or disciplinary zeitgeist has the absolute power to ensure the discovery of a scientific truth. Instead, logic, genius, and zeitgeist must all participate by means of combinatorial processes that emerge out of multiple, interacting, and uncertain minds. At the level of the individual scientist this necessity requires the proliferation of uncited publications, whereas at the level of the scientific community it demands the profusion of unsung scientists.

This inescapable reality must insert an immense amount of serendipity into the history of scientific achievement. Any attempt to extirpate or deny the infusion of chance would harm rather than enhance creativity in science.

References

Adams, C. W. (1946). The age at which scientists do their best work. *Isis, 36*, 166–169.

Adler, A. (1938). *Social interest: A challenge to mankind* (J. Linton & R. Vaughan, Trans.). London: Faber & Faber.

Albert, R. S. (1971). Cognitive development and parental loss among the gifted, the exceptionally gifted and the creative. *Psychological Reports, 29*, 19–26.

Allison, P. D., Long, J. S., & Krauze, T. K. (1982). Cumulative advantage and inequality in science. *American Sociological Review, 47*, 615– 625.

Allison, P. D., Price, D. S., Griffith, B. C., Moravcsik, M. J., & Stewart, J. A. (1976). Lotka's law: A problem in its interpretation and application. *Social Studies of Science, 6*, 269–276.

Allison, P. D., & Stewart, J. A. (1974). Productivity differences among scientists: Evidence for accumulative advantage. *American Sociological Review, 39*, 596–606.

Altus, W. D. (1966, January 7). Birth order and its sequelae. *Science, 151*, 44–48.

Amabile, T. M. (1982). Social psychology of creativity: A consensual assessment technique. *Journal of Personality and Social Psychology, 43*, 997–1013.

American heritage electronic dictionary (3rd ed.). (1992). Boston: Houghton Mifflin.

Andrews, F. M. (1979). Motivation, diversity, and the performance of research units. In F. M. Andrews (Ed.), *Scientific productivity: The effectiveness of research groups in six countries* (pp. 253–289). Cambridge, England: Cambridge University Press.

Ansburg, P. I., & Hill, K. (2003). Creative and analytic thinkers differ in their use of attentional resources. *Personality & Individual Differences, 34*, 1141–1152.

Ashton, S. V., & Oppenheim, C. (1978). A method of predicting Nobel prizewinners in chemistry. *Social Studies of Science, 8*, 341–348.

Austin, J. H. (1978). *Chase, chance, and creativity: The lucky art of novelty*. New York: Columbia University Press.

185

References

Baer, J. (1993). *Creativity and divergent thinking: A task-specific approach*. Hillsdale, NJ: Erlbaum.

Baer, J. (1994). Divergent thinking is not a general trait: A multidomain training experiment. *Creativity Research Journal, 7*, 35–46.

Baer, J. (1996). The effects of task-specific divergent-thinking training. *Journal of Creative Behavior, 30*, 183–187.

Bain, A. (1977). *The senses and the intellect* (D. N. Robinson, Ed.). Washington, DC: University Publications of America. (Original work published 1855.)

Barron, F. X. (1963). The needs for order and for disorder as motives in creative activity. In C. W. Taylor & F. X. Barron (Eds.), *Scientific creativity: Its recognition and development* (pp. 153–160). New York: Wiley.

Barron, F. X. (1969). *Creative person and creative process*. New York: Holt, Rinehart & Winston.

Barron, F. X., & Harrington, D. M. (1981). Creativity, intelligence, and personality. *Annual Review of Psychology, 32*, 439–476.

Barsalou, L. W., & Prinz, J. J. (1997). Mundane creativity in perceptual symbol systems. In T. B. Ward, S. M. Smith, & J. Vaid (Eds.), *Creative thought: An investigation of conceptual structures and processes* (pp. 267–309). Washington, DC: American Psychological Association.

Bayer, A. E., & Dutton, J. E. (1977). Career age and research – Professional activities of academic scientists: Tests of alternative non-linear models and some implications for higher education faculty policies. *Journal of Higher Education, 48*, 259–282.

Bayer, A. E., & Folger, J. (1966). Some correlates of a citation measure of productivity in science. *Sociology of Education, 39*, 381–390.

Bell, E. T. (1937). *Men of mathematics*. New York: Simon & Schuster.

Bell, E. T. (1951). *Mathematics: Queen and servant of science*. New York: McGraw Hill.

Bernal, J. D. (1971). *Science in history* (4 vols., 3rd. ed.). Cambridge, MA: MIT Press.

Berry, C. (1981). The Nobel scientists and the origins of scientific achievement. *British Journal of Sociology, 32*, 381–391.

Berry, C. (1999). Religious traditions as contexts of historical creativity: Patterns of scientific and artistic achievement and their stability. *Personality & Individual Differences, 26*, 1125–1135.

Beveridge, W. I. B. (1957). *The art of scientific investigation* (3rd ed.). New York: Vintage.

Blackburn, R. T., Behymer, C. E., & Hall, D. E. (1978). Correlates of faculty publications. *Sociology of Education, 51*, 132–141.

Bliss, W. D. (1970). Birth order of creative writers. *Journal of Individual Psychology, 26*, 200–202.

References

Bloom, B. S. (1963). Report on creativity research by the examiner's office of the University of Chicago. In C. W. Taylor & F. X. Barron (Eds.), *Scientific creativity: Its recognition and development* (pp. 251–264). New York: Wiley.

Boden, M. A. (1991). *The creative mind: Myths & mechanisms.* New York: BasicBooks.

Boden, M. A. (1995). What is creativity? In M. A. Boden (Ed.), *Dimensions of creativity* (pp. 75–117). Cambridge, MA: MIT Press.

Bohr, H. (1967). My father. In S. Rozental (Ed.), *Niels Bohr: His life and work as seen by his friends and colleagues* (pp. 325–335). Amsterdam: North-Holland Publishing.

Boring, E. G. (1963). *History, psychology, and science* (R. I. Watson & D. T. Campbell, Eds.). New York: Wiley.

Bowen, D. D., Perloff, R., & Jacoby, J. (1972). Improving manuscript evaluation procedures. *American Psychologist, 27,* 221–225.

Bowerman, W. G. (1947). *Studies in genius.* New York: Philosophical Library.

Bowers, K. S., Farvolden, P., & Mermigis, L. (1995). Intuitive antecedents of insight. In S. M. Smith, T. B. Ward, & R. A. Finke (Eds.), *The creative cognition approach* (pp. 27–51). Cambridge, MA: MIT Press.

Bradshaw, G. F., Langley, P. W., & Simon, H. A. (1983). Studying scientific discovery by computer simulation. *Science, 222,* 971–975.

Bramwell, B. S. (1948). Galton's "Hereditary" and the three following generations since 1869. *Eugenics Review, 39,* 146–153.

Brannigan, A. (1981). *The social basis of scientific discoveries.* Cambridge, England: Cambridge University Press.

Brannigan, A., & Wanner, R. A. (1983a). Historical distributions of multiple discoveries and theories of scientific change. *Social Studies of Science, 13,* 417–435.

Brannigan, A., & Wanner, R. A. (1983b). Multiple discoveries in science: A test of the communication theory. *Canadian Journal of Sociology, 8,* 135–151.

Brimhall, D. R. (1922). Family resemblances among American Men of Science. *American Naturalist, 56,* 504–547.

Brimhall, D. R. (1923a). Family resemblances among American Men of Science. II. Degree of resemblance in comparison with the generality: Proportion of workers in each science and distribution of replies. *American Naturalist, 57,* 74–88.

Brimhall, D. R. (1923b). Family resemblances among American Men of Science. III. The influence of the nearness of kinship. *American Naturalist, 57,* 137–152.

Bringmann, W. G., & Balk, M. M. (1983). Wilhelm Wundt's publication record: A re-examination. *Storia e Critica della Psichologia, 4,* 61–86.

Brown, F. (1968). Bereavement and lack of a parent in childhood. In E. Miller (Ed.), *Foundations of child psychiatry* (pp. 435–455). Oxford, England: Pergamon.

References

Brown, V. R., & Paulus, P. B. (2002). Making group brainstorming more effective: Recommendations from an associative memory perspective. *Current Directions in Psychological Science, 11*, 208–212.

Burt, C. (1943). Ability and income. *British Journal of Educational Psychology, 12*, 83–98.

Burt, C. (1963). Is intelligence distributed normally? *British Journal of Statistical Psychology, 16*, 175–190.

Busse, T. V., & Mansfield, R. S. (1984). Selected personality traits and achievement in male scientists. *Journal of Psychology, 116*, 117–131.

Campbell, D. T. (1960). Blind variation and selective retention in creative thought as in other knowledge processes. *Psychological Review, 67*, 380–400.

Candolle, A. de (1873). *Histoire des sciences et des savants depuis deux siècles.* Genève: Georg.

Cannon, W. B. (1940). The role of chance in discovery. *Scientific Monthly, 50*, 204–209.

Carringer, D. C. (1974). Creative thinking abilities in Mexican youth. *Journal of Cross-Cultural Psychology, 5*, 492–504.

Carson, S., Peterson, J. B., & Higgins, D. M. (2003). Decreased latent inhibition is associated with increased creative achievement in high-functioning individuals. *Journal of Personality and Social Psychology, 85*, 499–506.

Cassandro, V. J. (2001). *Versatility, creative products, and the personality correlates of eminent creators.* Unpublished doctoral dissertation, University of California, Davis.

Cattell, R. B., & Drevdahl, J. E. (1955). A comparison of the personality profile (16 P. F.) of eminent researchers with that of eminent teachers and administrators, and of the general population. *British Journal of Psychology, 46*, 248–261.

Chambers, J. A. (1964). Relating personality and biographical factors to scientific creativity. *Psychological Monographs: General and Applied, 78* (7, Whole No. 584).

Charlton, S., & Bakan, P. (1988–89). Cognitive complexity and creativity. *Imagination, Cognition and Personality, 8*, 315–322.

Christensen, H., & Jacomb, P. A. (1992). The lifetime productivity of eminent Australian academics. *International Journal of Geriatric Psychiatry, 7*, 681–686.

Cicchetti, D. V. (1991). The reliability of peer review for manuscript and grant submissions: A cross-disciplinary investigation. *Behavioral and Brain Sciences, 14*, 119–186.

Clark, R. D., & Rice, G. A. (1982). Family constellations and eminence: The birth orders of Nobel Prize winners. *Journal of Psychology, 110*, 281–287.

Cohen, J. M., & Cohen, M. J. (Eds.). (1960). *The Penguin dictionary of quotations.* Baltimore: Penguin Books.

References

Cole, J. R. (1987). Women in science. In D. N. Jackson & J. P. Rushton (Eds.), *Scientific excellence: Origins and assessment* (pp. 359–375). Beverly Hills, CA: Sage Publications.

Cole, J., & Cole, S. (1972, October 27). The Ortega hypothesis. *Science, 178*, 368–375.

Cole, S. (1979). Age and scientific performance. *American Journal of Sociology, 84*, 958–977.

Cole, S. (1983). The hierarchy of the sciences? *American Journal of Sociology, 89*, 111–139.

Cole, S., & Cole, J. R. (1967). Scientific output and recognition: A study in the operation of the reward system in science. *American Sociological Review, 32*, 377–390.

Cole, S., & Cole, J. R. (1973). *Social stratification in science*. Chicago: University of Chicago Press.

Cole, S., Cole, J. R., & Simon, G. A. (1981). Chance and consensus in peer review. *Science, 214*, 881–886.

Comte, A. (1855). *The positive philosophy of Auguste Comte* (H. Martineau, Trans.). New York: Blanchard. (Original work published 1839–1842.)

Constant, E. W., II (1978). On the diversity of co-evolution of technological multiples: Steam turbines and Pelton water wheels. *Social Studies of Science, 8*, 183–210.

Corry, L., Renn, J., & Stachel, J. (1997, November 14). Belated decision in the Hilbert-Einstein priority dispute. *Science, 278*, 1270–1273.

Cox, C. (1926). *The early mental traits of three hundred geniuses*. Stanford, CA: Stanford University Press.

Crane, D. (1967). The gatekeepers of science: Some factors affecting the selection of articles for scientific journals. *American Sociologist, 2*, 195–201.

Crane, D. (1972). *Invisible colleges*. Chicago: University of Chicago Press.

Cronbach, L. J. (1957). The two disciplines of scientific psychology. *American Psychologist, 12*, 671–684.

Cropper, W. H. (1970). *The quantum physicists*. New York: Oxford University Press.

Csikszentmihalyi, M. (1990). The domain of creativity. In M. A. Runco & R. S. Albert (Eds.), *Theories of creativity* (pp. 190–212). Newbury Park: Sage.

Csikszentmihalyi, M. (1999). Implications of a systems perspective for the study of creativity. In R. J. Sternberg (Ed.), *Handbook of creativity* (pp. 313–338). Cambridge: Cambridge University Press.

Daintith, J., Mitchell, S., & Tootill, E. (1981). *A biographical encyclopedia of scientists* (Vol. 1). New York: Facts on File.

Darwin, F. (Ed.). (1958). *The autobiography of Charles Darwin and selected letters*. New York: Dover. (Original work published 1892.)

References

Davis, G. A. (1975). In frumious pursuit of the creative person. *Journal of Creative Behavior, 9,* 75–87.

Davis, R. A. (1987). Creativity in neurological publications. *Neurosurgery, 20,* 652–663

Dennis, W. (1954a, September). Bibliographies of eminent scientists. *Scientific Monthly, 79,* 180–183.

Dennis, W. (1954b). Productivity among American psychologists. *American Psychologist, 9,* 191–194.

Dennis, W. (1955, April). Variations in productivity among creative workers. *Scientific Monthly, 80,* 277–278.

Dennis, W. (1966). Creative productivity between the ages of 20 and 80 years. *Journal of Gerontology, 21,* 1–8.

Dennis, W., & Girden, E. (1954). Current scientific activities of psychologists as a function of age. *Journal of Gerontology, 9,* 175–178.

Dewing, K., & Battye, G. (1971). Attention deployment and nonverbal fluency. *Journal of Personality and Social Psychology, 17,* 214–218.

Diamond, A. M., Jr. (1980). Age and the acceptance of cliometrics. *Journal of Economic History, 40,* 838–841.

Díaz de Chumaceiro, C. L. (1995). Serendipity or pseudoserendipity? Unexpected versus desired results. *Journal of Creative Behavior, 29,* 143–147.

Diehl, M., & Stroebe, W. (1987). Productivity loss in brainstorming groups: Toward the solution of a riddle. *Journal of Personality and Social Psychology, 53,* 497–509.

Dirac, P. A. M. (1963). The physicist's picture of nature. *Scientific American, 208* (5), 45–53.

Downs, R. B. (1983). *Books that changed the world* (rev. ed.). New York: New American Library.

Dryden, J. (1885). Epistle to Congreve. In W. Scott & G. Saintsbury (Eds.), *The works of John Dryden* (Vol. 11, pp. 57–60). Edinburgh: Paterson. (Original work published 1693)

Dugosh, K. L., Paulus, P. B., Roland, E. J., & Yang, H.-C. (2000). Cognitive stimulation in brainstorming. *Journal of Personality and Social Psychology, 79,* 722–735.

Dunbar, K. (1995). How scientists really reason: Scientific reasoning in real-world laboratories. In R. J. Sternberg & J. E. Davidson (Eds.), *The nature of insight* (pp. 365–396). Cambridge, MA: MIT Press.

Dunbar, K. (1997). How scientists think: On-line creativity and conceptual change in science. In T. B. Ward & S. M. Smith (Eds.), *Creative thought: An investigation of conceptual structures and processes* (pp. 461–493). Washington, DC: American Psychological Association.

Eiduson, B. T. (1962). *Scientists: Their psychological world.* New York: Basic Books.

References

Eisenman, R. (1964). Birth order and artistic creativity. *Journal of Individual Psychology, 20*, 183–185.

Eisenstadt, J. M. (1978). Parental loss and genius. *American Psychologist, 33*, 211–223.

Ellis, H. (1926). *A study of British genius* (rev. ed.). Boston: Houghton Mifflin.

Ericsson, K. A. (1996). The acquisition of expert performance: An introduction to some of the issues. In K. A. Ericsson (Ed.), *The road to expert performance: Empirical evidence from the arts and sciences, sports, and games* (pp. 1–50). Mahwah, NJ: Erlbaum.

Eysenck, H. J. (1993). Creativity and personality: Suggestions for a theory. *Psychological Inquiry, 4*, 147–178.

Eysenck, H. J. (1994). Creativity and personality: Word association, origence, and psychoticism. *Creativity Research Journal, 7*, 209–216.

Eysenck, H. J. (1995). *Genius: The natural history of creativity*. Cambridge, England: Cambridge University Press.

Faust, D. (1984). *Limits of scientific reasoning*. Minneapolis: University of Minnesota Press.

Feist, G. J. (1993). A structural model of scientific eminence. *Psychological Science, 4*, 366–371.

Feist, G. J. (1994). Personality and working style predictors of integrative complexity: A study of scientists' thinking about research and teaching. *Journal of Personality and Social Psychology, 67*, 474–484.

Feist, G. J. (1997). Quantity, quality, and depth of research as influences on scientific eminence: Is quantity most important? *Creativity Research Journal, 10*, 325–335.

Feist, G. J. (1998). A meta-analysis of personality in scientific and artistic creativity. *Personality and Social Psychology Review, 2*, 290–309.

Feist, G. J., & Barron, F. X. (2003). Predicting creativity from early to late adulthood: Intellect, potential, and personality. *Journal of Research in Personality, 37*, 62–88.

Feist, G. J., & Gorman, M. E. (1998). The psychology of science: Review and integration of a nascent discipline. *Review of General Psychology, 2*, 3–47.

Ferber, M. A. (1986). Citations: Are they an objective measure of scholarly merit? *Signs, 11*, 381–389.

Fernberger, S. W. (1946, August 23). Scientific publication as affected by war and politics. *Science, 104*, 175–177.

Finke, R. A., Ward, T. B., & Smith, S. M. (1992). *Creative cognition: Theory, research, applications*. Cambridge, MA: MIT Press.

Fiske, S. T., & Taylor, S. E. (1991). *Social cognition* (2nd ed.). New York: McGraw-Hill.

Fowler, R. G. (1987). Toward a quantitative theory of intellectual discovery (especially in physics). *Journal of Scientific Exploration, 1*, 11–20.

References

Furumoto, L. (1989). The new history of psychology. In I. S. Cohen (Ed.), *The G. Stanley Hall lecture series* (Vol. 9, pp. 9–34). Washington, DC: American Psychological Association.

Gabora, L. (2002). Cognitive mechanisms underlying the creative process. In T. Hewett & T. Kavanagh (Eds.), *Proceedings of the Fourth International Conference on Creativity and Cognition* (pp. 126–133). United Kingdom: Loughborough University.

Galton, F. (1869). *Hereditary genius: An inquiry into its laws and consequences*. London: Macmillan.

Galton, F. (1874). *English men of science: Their nature and nurture*. London: Macmillan.

Galton, F. (1972). *Hereditary genius: An inquiry into its laws and consequences* (2nd ed.). Gloucester, MA: Smith. (Original work published 1892.)

Gardner, H. (1983). *Frames of mind: A theory of multiple intelligences*. New York: Basic Books.

Gardner, H. (1993). *Creating minds: An anatomy of creativity seen through the lives of Freud, Einstein, Picasso, Stravinsky, Eliot, Graham, and Gandhi*. New York: Basic Books.

Garfield, E. (1987). Mapping the world of science: Is citation analysis a legitimate evaluation tool? In D. N. Jackson & J. P. Rushton (Eds.), *Scientific excellence: Origins and assessment* (pp. 98–128). Beverly Hills, CA: Sage Publications.

Garvey, W. D., & Tomita, K. (1972). Continuity of productivity by scientists in the years 1968–1971. *Science Studies, 2*, 379–383.

Ghadirian, A.-M., Gregoire, P., & Kosmidis, H. (2001). Creativity and the evolution of psychopathologies. *Creativity Research Journal, 13*, 145–148.

Gholson, B., Shadish, Jr., W. R., Neimeyer, R. A., & Houts, A. C. (Eds.). (1989). *The psychology of science: Contributions to metascience*. Cambridge: Cambridge University Press.

Gibson, J., & Light, P. (1967). Intelligence among university scientists. *Nature, 213*, 441–443.

Gieryn, T. F., & Hirsh, R. F. (1983). Marginality and innovation in science. *Social Studies of Science, 13*, 87–106.

Goertzel, M. G., Goertzel, V. & Goertzel, T. G. (1978). *300 eminent personalities: A psychosocial analysis of the famous*. San Francisco: Jossey-Bass.

Goertzel, V., & Goertzel, M. G. (1962). *Cradles of eminence*. Boston: Little, Brown.

Goldberg, D. E. (1989). *Genetic algorithms in search, optimization, and machine learning*. Reading, MA: Addison-Wesley.

Gooding, D. C. (1996). Scientific discovery as creative exploration: Faraday's experiments. *Creativity Research Journal, 9*, 189–205.

References

Gottfredson, S. D. (1978). Evaluating psychological research reports: Dimensions, reliability, and correlates of quality judgments. *American Psychologist, 33,* 920–934.

Gough, H. G. (1976). Studying creativity by means of word association tests. *Journal of Applied Psychology, 61,* 348–353.

Gough, H. G. (1979). A creative personality scale for the adjective check list. *Journal of Personality and Social Psychology, 37,* 1398–1405.

Greenwald, A. G., & Schuh, E. S. (1994). An ethnic bias in scientific citations. *European Journal of Social Psychology, 24,* 623–639.

Gruber, H. E. (1974). *Darwin on man: A psychological study of scientific creativity.* New York: Dutton.

Gruber, H. E. (1989). Networks of enterprise in creative scientific work. In B. Gholson, W. R. Shadish, Jr., R. A. Neimeyer, & A. C. Houts (Eds.), *The psychology of science: Contributions to metascience* (pp. 246–265). Cambridge: Cambridge University Press.

Gruszka, A., & Necka, E. (2002). Priming and acceptance of close and remote associations by creative and less creative people. *Creativity Research Journal, 14,* 193–205.

Guilford, J. P. (1967). *The nature of human intelligence.* New York: McGraw-Hill.

Hadamard, J. (1945). *The psychology of invention in the mathematical field.* Princeton, NJ: Princeton University Press.

Hagstrom, W. O. (1974). Competition in science. *American Sociological Review, 39,* 1–18.

Haight, F. A. (1967). *Handbook of the Poisson distribution.* New York: Wiley.

Han, K. S. (2003). Domain-specificity of creativity in young children: How quantitative and qualitative data support it. *Journal of Creative Behavior, 37,* 117–142.

Hargens, L. L. (1978). Relations between work habits, research technologies, and eminence in science. *Sociology of Work and Occupations, 5,* 97–112.

Hargens, L. L., McCann, J. C., & Reskin, B. F. (1978). Productivity and reproductivity: Fertility and professional achievement among research scientists. *Social Forces, 57,* 154–163.

Hart, M. H. (1987). *The 100: A ranking of the most influential persons in history.* Secaucus, NJ: Citadel Press.

Helmholtz, H. von (1898). An autobiographical sketch. In *Popular lectures on scientific subjects, second series* (E. Atkinson, Trans., pp. 266–291). New York: Longmans, Green.

Helmholtz, H. von (1971). An autobiographical sketch. In R. Kahl (Ed.), *Selected writings of Hermann von Helmholtz* (pp. 466–478). Middletown, CT: Wesleyan University Press. (Original work published 1891.)

Helmreich, R. L., Spence, J. T., Beane, W. E., Lucker, G. W., & Matthews, K. A. (1980). Making it in academic psychology: Demographic and personality correlates of attainment. *Journal of Personality and Social Psychology, 39*, 896–908.

Helmreich, R. L., Spence, J. T., & Thorbecke, W. L. (1981). On the stability of productivity and recognition. *Personality and Social Psychology Bulletin, 7*, 516–522.

Helson, R. (1980). The creative woman mathematician. In L. H. Fox, L. Brody, & D. Tobin (Eds.), *Women and the mathematical mystique* (pp. 23–54). Baltimore: Johns Hopkins University Press.

Helson, R., & Crutchfield, R. S. (1970). Mathematicians: The creative researcher and the average Ph.D. *Journal of Consulting and Clinical Psychology, 34*, 250–257.

Hoffman, B. (1972). *Albert Einstein: Creator and rebel.* New York: Plume.

Holland, J. (1975). *Natural and artificial systems.* Ann Arbor, MI: University of Michigan Press.

Holland, J. H. (1992). Genetic algorithms. *Scientific American, 267* (1), 66–72.

Holton, G. (1971–72). On trying to understand the scientific genius. *American Scholar, 41*, 95–110.

Holton, G. (1982). Toward a theory of scientific progress. In G. A. Almond, M. Chodorow, & R. H. Pearce (Eds.), *Progress and its discontents* (pp. 202–225). Berkeley: University of California Press.

Hook, E. B. (2002). *Prematurity in scientific discovery: On resistance and neglect.* Berkeley: University of California Press.

Horner, K. L., Rushton, J. P., & Vernon, P. A. (1986). Relation between aging and research productivity of academic psychologists. *Psychology and Aging, 1*, 319–324.

Horner, K. L., Murray, H. G., & Rushton, J. P. (1994). Aging and administration in academic psychologists. *Social Behavior and Personality, 22*, 343–346.

Horvitz, L. A. (2000). *The quotable scientist: Words of wisdom from Charles Darwin, Albert Einstein, Richard Feynman, Galileo, Marie Curie, and more.* New York: McGraw-Hill.

Huber, J. C. (1998a). Invention and inventivity as a special kind of creativity, with implications for general creativity. *Journal of Creative Behavior, 32*, 58–72.

Huber, J. C. (1998b). Invention and inventivity is a random, Poisson process: A potential guide to analysis of general creativity. *Creativity Research Journal, 11*, 231–241.

Huber, J. C. (1999). Inventive productivity and the statistics of exceedances. *Scientometrics, 45*, 33–53.

Huber, J. C. (2000). A statistical analysis of special cases of creativity. *Journal of Creative Behavior, 34*, 203–225.

References

Huber, J. C. (2001). A new method for analyzing scientific productivity. *Journal of the American Society for Information Science and Technology, 52*, 1089–1099.

Huber, J. C. (2002). A new model that generates Lotka's Law. *Journal of the American Society for Information Science and Technology, 53*, 209–219.

Huber, J. C., & Wagner-Döbler, R. (2001a). Scientific production: A statistical analysis of authors in mathematical logic. *Scientometrics, 50*, 323–337.

Huber, J. C., & Wagner-Döbler, R. (2001b). Scientific production: A statistical analysis of authors in physics, 1800–1900. *Scientometrics, 50*, 437–453.

Hudson, L. (1958). Undergraduate academic record of Fellows of the Royal Society. *Nature, 182*, 1326.

Hudson, L. (1966). *Contrary imaginations*. Baltimore: Penguin.

Hudson, L., & Jacot, B. (1986). The outsider in science. In C. Bagley & G. K. Verma (Eds.), *Personality, cognition and values* (pp. 3–23). London: Macmillan.

Hull, D. L., Tessner, P. D., & Diamond, A. M. (1978, November 17). Planck's principle: Do younger scientists accept new scientific ideas with greater alacrity than older scientists? *Science, 202*, 717–723.

Illingworth, R. S., & Illingworth, C. M. (1969). *Lessons from childhood*. Edinburgh: Livingston.

James, W. (1880, October). Great men, great thoughts, and the environment. *Atlantic Monthly, 46*, 441–459.

Jeans, J. (1942). Newton and the science of to-day. *Nature, 150*, 710–715.

Jevons, W. S. (1900). *The principles of science: A treatise on logic and scientific method* (2nd ed.). London: Macmillan. (Original work published 1877.)

Johnson, S. (1781). *The lives of the most eminent English poets* (Vol. 1). London: Bathurst et al.

Johnson-Laird, P. N. (1993). *Human and machine thinking*. Hillsdale, NJ: Lawrence Erlbaum.

Juda, A. (1949). The relationship between highest mental capacity and psychic abnormalities. *American Journal of Psychiatry, 106*, 296–307.

Jungk, R. (1958). *Brighter than a thousand suns* (J. Cleugh, Trans.). New York: Harcourt Brace.

Kahneman, D., Slovic, P., & Tversky, A. (Eds.). (1982). *Judgment under uncertainty: Heuristics and biases*. Cambridge, England: Cambridge University Press.

Kantorovich, A., & Ne'eman, Y. (1989). Serendipity as a source of evolutionary progress in science. *Studies in History and Philosophy of Science, 20*, 505–529.

Kaplan, R. (Ed.). (2001). *Science says: A collection of quotations on the history, meaning, and practice of science*. New York: Freeman.

Karlson, J. I. (1970). Genetic association of giftedness and creativity with schizophrenia. *Hereditas, 66*, 177–182.

Kasof, J. (1997). Creativity and breadth of attention. *Creativity Research Journal, 10*, 303–315.

King, L. A., McKee Walker, L., & Broyles, S. J. (1996). Creativity and the five-factor model. *Journal of Research in Personaltiy, 30*, 189–203.

Klahr, D. (2000). *Exploring science: The cognition and development of discovery processes.* Cambridge, MA: MIT Press.

Klahr, D., & Simon, H. A. (1999). Studies of scientific creativity: Complementary approaches and convergent findings. *Psychological Bulletin, 125*, 524–543.

Koestler, A. (1964). *The act of creation.* New York: Macmillan.

Köhler, W. (1925). *The mentality of apes* (E. Winter, Trans.). New York: Harcourt, Brace.

Koza, J. R. (1992). *Genetic programming: On the programming of computers by means of natural selection.* Cambridge, MA: MIT Press.

Koza, J. R. (1994). *Genetic programming II: Automatic discovery of reusable programs.* Cambridge: MIT Press.

Koza, J. R., Bennett III, F. H., Andre, D., & Keane, M. A. (1999). *Genetic programming III: Darwinian invention and problem solving.* San Francisco: Morgan Kaufmann.

Kroeber, A. L. (1917). The superorganic. *American Anthropologist, 19*, 163–214.

Kroeber, A. L. (1944). *Configurations of culture growth.* Berkeley: University of California Press.

Kroeber, A. L. (1963). *Anthropology: Culture patterns and processes.* New York: Harbinger Book.

Kuhn, T. S. (1970). *The structure of scientific revolutions* (2nd ed.). Chicago: University of Chicago Press.

Kuhn, T. S. (1977). *The essential tension.* Chicago: University of Chicago Press.

Kulkarni, D., & Simon, H. A. (1988). The process of scientific discovery: The strategy of experimentation. *Cognitive Science, 12*, 139–175.

Kyvik, S. (1989). Productivity differences, fields of learning, and Lotka's law. *Scientometrics, 15*, 205–214.

Kyvik, S. (1990). Motherhood and scientific productivity. *Social Studies of Science, 20*, 149–160.

Lamb, D., & Easton, S. M. (1984). *Multiple discovery.* Avebury, England: Avebury.

Lambert, W. E., Tucker, G. R., & d'Anglejan, A. (1973). Cognitive and attitudinal consequences of bilingual schooling: The St. Lambert project through grade five. *Journal of Educational Psychology, 65*, 141–159.

Langley, P., Simon, H. A., Bradshaw, G. L., & Zythow, J. M. (1987). *Scientific discovery.* Cambridge, MA: MIT Press.

References

Lee, J. D., Vicente, K. J., Cassano, A., & Shearer, A. (2003). Can scientific impact be judged prospectively? A bibliometric test of Simonton's model of creative productivity. *Scientometrics, 56*, 223–232.

Lehman, H. C. (1953). *Age and achievement.* Princeton, NJ: Princeton University Press.

Lehman, H. C. (1947). The exponential increase of man's cultural output. *Social Forces, 25*, 281–290.

Lehman, H. C. (1958, May 23). The chemist's most creative years. *Science, 127*, 1213–1222.

Lehman, H. C., & Witty, P. A. (1931). Scientific eminence and church membership. *Scientific Monthly, 33*, 544–549.

Levin, S. G., & Stephan, P. E. (1989). Age and research productivity of academic scientists. *Research in Higher Education, 30*, 531–549.

Levin, S. G., & Stephan, P. E. (1991). Research productivity over the life cycle: Evidence for academic scientists. *American Economic Review, 81*, 114–132.

Levin, S. G., & Stephan, P. E. (1999, August 20). Are the foreign born a source of strength for U.S. science? *Science, 285*, 1213–1214.

Lindsey, D. (1988). Assessing precision in the manuscript review process: A little better than a dice roll. *Scientometrics, 14*, 75–82.

Long, J. S. (1992). Measures of sex differences in scientific productivity. *Social Forces, 71*, 159–178.

Lopez, E. C., Esquivel, G. B., & Houtz, J. C. (1993). The creative skills of culturally and linguistically diverse gifted students. *Creativity Research Journal, 6*, 401–412.

Lotka, A. J. (1926). The frequency distribution of scientific productivity. *Journal of the Washington Academy of Sciences, 16*, 317–323.

Ludwig, A. M. (1992). Creative achievement and psychopathology: Comparison among professions. *American Journal of Psychotherapy, 46*, 330–356.

Ludwig, A. M. (1995). *The price of greatness: Resolving the creativity and madness controversy.* New York: Guilford Press.

Ludwig, A. M. (1998). Method and madness in the arts and sciences. *Creativity Research Journal, 11*, 93–101.

Mach, E. (1896, January). On the part played by accident in invention and discovery. *Monist, 6*, 161–175.

MacKinnon, D. W., & Hall, W. B. (1972). Intelligence and creativity. *Proceedings of the XVIIth International Congress of Applied Psychology, Liege, Belgium* (Vol. 2, 1883–1888). Brussels: EDITEST.

Mandler, G. (1995). Origins and consequences of novelty. In S. M. Smith, T. B. Ward, & R. A. Finke (Eds.), *The creative cognition approach* (pp. 9–25). Cambridge, MA: MIT Press.

Manis, J. G. (1951). Some academic influences upon publication productivity. *Social Forces, 29*, 267–272.

Mansfield, R. S., & Busse, T. V. (1981). *The psychology of creativity and discovery: Scientists and their work.* Chicago: Nelson-Hall.

Marsh, H. W., & Ball, S. (1989). The peer review process used to evaluate manuscripts submitted to academic journals: Interjudgmental reliability. *Journal of Experimental Education, 57*, 151–169.

Martindale, C. (1989). Personality, situation, and creativity. In J. A. Glover, R. R. Ronning, & C. R. Reynolds (Eds.), *Handbook of creativity* (pp. 211–232). New York: Plenum Press.

Martindale, C. (1990). *The clockwork muse: The predictability of artistic styles.* New York: Basic Books.

Martindale, C. (1995). Creativity and connectionism. In S. M. Smith, T. B. Ward, & R. A. Finke (Eds.), *The creative cognition approach* (pp. 249–268). Cambridge, MA: MIT Press.

Martindale, C., Brewer, W. F., Helson, R., Rosenberg, S., Simonton, D. K., Keeley, A., Leigh, J., & Ohtsuka, K. (1988). Structure, theme, style, and reader response in Hungarian and American short stories. In C. Martindale (Ed.), *Psychological approaches to the study of literary narratives* (pp. 267–289). Hamburg: Buske.

McCrae, R. R. (1987). Creativity, divergent thinking, and openness to experience. *Journal of Personality and Social Psychology, 52*, 1258–1265.

McCrae, R. R. & Costa, P. T. (1997). Conceptions and correlates of openness to experience. In R. Hogan, J. Johnson, & S. Briggs (Eds.), *Handbook of personality.* (pp. 825–847). San Diego, CA: Academic Press.

McCurdy, H. G. (1960). The childhood pattern of genius. *Horizon, 2*, 33–38.

McReynolds, P. (1971). Reliability of ratings of research papers. *American Psychologist, 26*, 400–401.

Mednick, S. A. (1962). The associative basis of the creative process. *Psychological Review, 69*, 220–232.

Mendelsohn, G. A. (1976). Associative and attentional processes in creative performance. *Journal of Personality, 44*, 341–369.

Mendelsohn, G. A. & Griswold, B. B. (1966). Assessed creative potential, vocabulary level, and sex as predictors of the use of incidental cues in verbal problem solving. *Journal of Personality and Social Psychology, 4*, 423–431.

Merton, R. K. (1961a). The role of genius in scientific advance. *New Scientist, 12*, 306–308.

References

Merton, R. K. (1961b). Singletons and multiples in scientific discovery: A chapter in the sociology of science. *Proceedings of the American Philosophical Society, 105,* 470–486.

Merton, R. K. (1968, January 5). The Matthew effect in science. *Science, 159,* 56–63.

Miles, C. C., & Wolfe, L. S. (1936). Childhood physical and mental health records of historical geniuses. *Psychological Monographs, 47,* 390–400.

Miller, A. I. (2000). *Insights of genius: imagery and creativity in science and art.* Cambridge, MA: MIT Press.

Molina, E. C. (1942). *Poisson's exponential binomial limit.* Princeton, NJ: Van Nostrand.

Moulin, L. (1955). The Nobel Prizes for the sciences from 1901–1950: An essay in sociological analysis. *British Journal of Sociology, 6,* 246–263.

Mullins, C. J. (1963). Prediction of creativity in a sample of research scientists. *IEEE Transactions on Engineering Management, EM-10* (2), 52–57.

Mumford, M. D., Marks, M. A., Connelly, M. S., Zaccaro, S. J., & Johnson, T. F. (1998). Domain based scoring of divergent thinking tests: Validation evidence in an occupational sample. *Creativity Research Journal, 11,* 151–164.

Myers, C. R. (1970). Journal citations and scientific eminence in contemporary psychology. *American Psychologist, 25,* 1041–1048.

Nemeth, C. J., & Kwan, J. (1985). Originality of word associations as a function of majority vs. minority influence. *Social Psychology Quarterly, 48,* 277–282.

Nemeth, C. J., & Kwan, J. (1987). Minority influence, divergent thinking and detection of correct solutions. *Journal of Applied Social Psychology, 17,* 788–799.

Nemeth, C. J., & Wachtler, J. (1983). Creative problem solving as a result of majority vs. minority influence. *European Journal of Social Psychology, 13,* 45–55.

Newell, A., Shaw, J. C., & Simon, H. A. (1958). Elements of a theory of human problem solving. *Psychological Review, 65,* 151–166.

Newell, A., & Simon, H. A. (1972). *Human problem solving.* Englewood Cliffs, NJ: Prentice-Hall.

Nisbett, R. E., & Wilson, T. D. (1977). Telling more than we can know: Verbal reports on mental processes. *Psychological Review, 84,* 231–259.

Ochse, R. (1989). A new look at primary process thinking and its relation to inspiration. *New Ideas in Psychology, 7,* 315–330.

Ogburn, W. K., & Thomas, D. (1922). Are inventions inevitable? A note on social evolution. *Political Science Quarterly, 37,* 83–93.

Olby, R. (1979). Mendel no Mendelian? *History of Science, 17,* 53–72.

Oromaner, M. (1977). Professional age and the reception of sociological publications: A test of the Zuckerman-Merton hypothesis. *Social Studies of Science, 7,* 381–388.

199

Ortega y Gasset, J. (1957). *The revolt of the masses* (M. Adams, Trans.). New York: Norton. (Original work published 1932.)

Over, R. (1981). Affiliations of psychologists elected to the National Academy of Sciences. *American Psychologist, 36,* 744–752.

Over, R. (1982). Research productivity and impact of male and female psychologists. *American Psychologist, 37,* 24–31.

Over, R. (1988). Does scholarly impact decline with age? *Scientometrics, 13,* 215–223.

Over, R. (1989). Age and scholarly impact. *Psychology and Aging, 4,* 222–225.

Over, R. (1990). The scholarly impact of articles published by men and women in psychology journals. *Scientometrics, 18,* 71–80.

Patinkin, D. (1983). Multiple discoveries and the central message. *American Journal of Sociology, 89,* 306–323.

Perkins, D. N. (1981). *The mind's best work.* Cambridge, MA: Harvard University Press.

Perkins, D. N. (2000). *The eureka effect: The art and logic of breakthrough thinking.* New York: Norton.

Peters, D. P., & Ceci, S. J. (1982). Peer-review practices of psychological journals: The fate of published articles, submitted again. *Behavioral & Brain Sciences, 5,* 187–255.

Peterson, J. B., & Carson, S. (2000). Latent inhibition and openness to experience in a high-achieving student population. *Personality and Individual Differences, 28,* 323–332.

Peterson, J. B., Smith, K. W., & Carson, S. (2002). Openness and extraversion are associated with reduced latent inhibition: Replication and commentary. *Personality & Individual Differences, 33,* 1137–1147.

Petty, R. E., Fleming, M. A., & Fabrigar, L. R. (1999). The review process at *PSPB:* Correlates of interreviewer agreement and manuscript acceptance. *Personality and Social Psychology Bulletin, 25,* 188–203.

Planck, M. (1949). *Scientific autobiography and other papers* (F. Gaynor, Trans.). New York: Philosophical Library.

Platt, W., & Baker, R. A. (1931). The relation of the scientific "hunch" to research. *Journal of Chemical Education, 8,* 1969–2002.

Platz, A. (1965). Psychology of the scientist: XI. Lotka's law and research visibility. *Psychological Reports, 16,* 566–568.

Platz, A., & Blakelock, E. (1960). Productivity of American psychologists: Quantity versus quality. *American Psychologist, 15,* 310–312.

Poincaré, H. (1921). *The foundations of science: Science and hypothesis, the value of science, science and method* (G. B. Halstead, Trans.). New York: Science Press.

Popper, K. (1959). *The logic of discovery.* New York: Basic Books.

References

Post, F. (1994). Creativity and psychopathology: A study of 291 world-famous men. *British Journal of Psychiatry, 165,* 22–34.

Price, D. (1963). *Little science, big science.* New York: Columbia University Press.

Price, D. (1965, July 9). Networks of scientific papers. *Science, 149,* 510–515.

Price, D. (1978). Ups and downs in the pulse of science and technology. In J. Gaston (Ed.), *The sociology of science* (pp. 162–171). San Francisco: Jossey-Bass.

Proctor, R. A. (1993). Computer stimulated associations. *Creativity Research Journal, 6,* 391–400.

Rainoff, T. J. (1929). Wave-like fluctuations of creative productivity in the development of West-European physics in the eighteenth and nineteenth centuries. *Isis, 12,* 287–319.

Raskin, E. A. (1936). Comparison of scientific and literary ability: A biographical study of eminent scientists and men of letters of the nineteenth century. *Journal of Abnormal and Social Psychology, 31,* 20–35.

Reber, A. S. (1993). *Implicit learning and tacit knowledge: An essay on the cognitive unconscious.* Oxford, England: Oxford University Press.

Redner, S. (1998). How popular is your paper? An empirical study of the citation distribution. *European Physical Journal B, 4,* 131–134.

Reichenbach, H. (1938). *Experience and prediction: an analysis of the foundations and the structure of knowledge.* Chicago: University of Chicago Press.

Roberts, R. M. (1989). *Serendipity: Accidental discoveries in science.* New York: Wiley.

Roe, A. (1953). *The making of a scientist.* New York: Dodd, Mead.

Roe, A. (1965, October 15). Changes in scientific activities with age. *Science, 150,* 113–118.

Roe, A. (1972, May 26). Patterns of productivity of scientists. *Science, 176,* 940–941.

Rodgers, R. C., & Maranto, C. L. (1989). Causal models of publishing productivity in psychology. *Journal of Applied Psychology, 74,* 636–649.

Root-Bernstein, R. S., Bernstein, M., & Garnier, H. (1993). Identification of scientists making long-term, high-impact contributions, with notes on their methods of working. *Creativity Research Journal, 6,* 329–343.

Root-Bernstein, R. S., Bernstein, M., & Garnier, H. (1995). Correlations between avocations, scientific style, work habits, and professional impact of scientists. *Creativity Research Journal, 8,* 115–137.

Rothenberg, A. (1983). Psychopathology and creative cognition: A comparison of hospitalized patients, Nobel laureates, and controls. *Archives of General Psychiatry, 40,* 937–942.

Rothenberg, A. (1986). Artistic creation as stimulated by superimposed versus combined-composite visual images. *Journal of Personality and Social Psychology, 50,* 370–381.

Rothenberg, A. (1987). Einstein, Bohr, and creative thinking in science. *History of Science, 25,* 147–166.

Rothenberg, A. (1996). The Janusian process in scientific creativity. *Creativity Research Journal, 9,* 207–231.

Rubinstein, G. (1999). Authoritarianism and its relation to creativity: A comparative study among students of design, behavioural sciences and law. *Personality & Individual Differences, 34,* 695–705.

Rushton, J. P. (1990). Creativity, intelligence, and psychoticism. *Personality and Individual Differences, 11,* 1291–1298.

Rushton, J. P. (2000). Individual differences and scientific productivity. In R. D. Goffin & E. Helmes (Eds.), *Problems and solutions in human assessment: Honoring Douglas N. Jackson at seventy* (pp. 173–194). New York: Kluwer Academic.

Scarr, S., & Weber, B. L. R. (1978). The reliability of reviews for the *American Psychologist. American Psychologist, 33,* 935.

Schaefer, C. E., & Anastasi, A. (1968). A biographical inventory for identifying creativity in adolescent boys. *Journal of Applied Psychology, 58,* 42–48.

Schachter, S. (1963). Birth order, eminence, and higher education. *American Sociological Review, 28,* 757–768.

Schlipp, P. A. (Ed.). (1951). *Albert Einstein: Philosopher-scientist.* New York: Harper.

Schmookler, J. (1966). *Invention and economic growth.* Cambridge, MA: Harvard University Press.

Schneider, J. (1937). The cultural situation as a condition for the achievement of fame. *American Sociological Review, 2,* 480–491.

Schooler, J. W., & Melcher, J. (1995). The ineffability of insight. In S. M. Smith, T. B. Ward, & R. A. Finke (Eds.), *The creative cognition approach* (pp. 97–133). Cambridge, MA: MIT Press.

Schubert, D. S. P., Wagner, M. E., & Schubert, H. J. P. (1977). Family constellation and creativity: Firstborn predominance among classical music composers. *Journal of Psychology, 95,* 147–149.

Scott, W. A. (1974). Interreferee agreement on some characteristics of manuscripts submitted to the *Journal of Personality and Social Psychology. American Psychologist, 29,* 698–702.

Seelig, C. (1958). *Albert Einstein: A documentary biography* (M. Savill, Trans.). London: Staples Press.

Segal, S. M., Busse, T. V., & Mansfield, R. S. (1980). The relationship of scientific creativity in the biological sciences to predoctoral accomplishments and experiences. *American Educational Research Journal, 17,* 491–502.

Seifert, C. M., Meyer, D. E., Davidson, N., Patalano, A. L., & Yaniv, I. (1995). Demystification of cognitive insight: Opportunistic assimilation and the prepared-mind

References

perspective. In R. J. Sternberg & J. E. Davidson (Eds.), *The nature of insight* (pp. 65–124). Cambridge, MA: MIT Press.

Shadish, W. R., Jr. (1989). The perception and evaluation of quality in science. In B. Gholson, W. R. Shadish, Jr., R. A. Neimeyer, & A. C. Houts (Eds.), *The psychology of science: Contributions to metascience* (pp. 383–426). Cambridge: Cambridge University Press.

Shapiro, G. (1986). *A skeleton in the darkroom: Stories of serendipity in science*. San Francisco: Harper & Row.

Shockley, W. (1957). On the statistics of individual variations of productivity in research laboratories. *Proceedings of the Institute of Radio Engineers, 45,* 279–290.

Shrager, J., & Langley, P. (Eds.). (1990). *Computational models of scientific discovery and theory formation*. San Mateo, CA: Kaufmann.

Silverman, S. M. (1974). Parental loss and scientists. *Science Studies, 4,* 259–264.

Simon, H. A. (1955). On a class of skew distribution functions. *Biometrika, 42,* 425–440.

Simon, H. A. (1973). Does scientific discovery have a logic? *Philosophy of Science, 40,* 471–480.

Simon, H. A. (1986). What we know about the creative process. In R. L. Kuhn (Ed.), *Frontiers in creative and innovative management* (pp. 3–20). Cambridge, MA: Ballinger.

Simon, R. J. (1974). The work habits of eminent scientists. *Sociology of Work and Occupations, 1,* 327–335.

Simonton, D. K. (1975). Sociocultural context of individual creativity: A transhistorical time-series analysis. *Journal of Personality and Social Psychology, 32,* 1119–1133.

Simonton, D. K. (1976a). Biographical determinants of achieved eminence: A multivariate approach to the Cox data. *Journal of Personality and Social Psychology, 33,* 218–226.

Simonton, D. K. (1976b). Do Sorokin's data support his theory?: A study of generational fluctuations in philosophical beliefs. *Journal for the Scientific Study of Religion, 15,* 187–198.

Simonton, D. K. (1976c). Philosophical eminence, beliefs, and zeitgeist: An individual-generational analysis. *Journal of Personality and Social Psychology, 34,* 630–640.

Simonton, D. K. (1976d). The sociopolitical context of philosophical beliefs: A transhistorical causal analysis. *Social Forces, 54,* 513–523.

Simonton, D. K. (1977). Creative productivity, age, and stress: A biographical time-series analysis of 10 classical composers. *Journal of Personality and Social Psychology, 35,* 791–804.

References

Simonton, D. K. (1978). Independent discovery in science and technology: A closer look at the Poisson distribution. *Social Studies of Science, 8*, 521–532.

Simonton, D. K. (1979). Multiple discovery and invention: Zeitgeist, genius, or chance? *Journal of Personality and Social Psychology, 37*, 1603–1616.

Simonton, D. K. (1980a). Intuition and analysis: A predictive and explanatory model. *Genetic Psychology Monographs, 102*, 3–60.

Simonton, D. K. (1980b). Techno-scientific activity and war: A yearly time-series analysis, 1500–1903 A.D. *Scientometrics, 2*, 251–255.

Simonton, D. K. (1980c). Thematic fame and melodic originality in classical music: A multivariate computer-content analysis. *Journal of Personality, 48*, 206–219.

Simonton, D. K. (1980d). Thematic fame, melodic originality, and musical zeitgeist: A biographical and transhistorical content analysis. *Journal of Personality and Social Psychology, 38*, 972–983.

Simonton, D. K. (1983). Formal education, eminence, and dogmatism: The curvilinear relationship. *Journal of Creative Behavior, 17*, 149–162.

Simonton, D. K. (1984a). Artistic creativity and interpersonal relationships across and within generations. *Journal of Personality and Social Psychology, 46*, 1273–1286.

Simonton, D. K. (1984b). Creative productivity and age: A mathematical model based on a two-step cognitive process. *Developmental Review, 4*, 77–111.

Simonton, D. K. (1984c). *Genius, creativity, and leadership: Historiometric inquiries.* Cambridge, Mass.: Harvard University Press.

Simonton, D. K. (1984d). Is the marginality effect all that marginal? *Social Studies of Science, 14*, 621–622.

Simonton, D. K. (1984e). Scientific eminence historical and contemporary: A measurement assessment. *Scientometrics, 6*, 169–182.

Simonton, D. K. (1985). Quality, quantity, and age: The careers of 10 distinguished psychologists. *International Journal of Aging and Human Development, 21*, 241–254.

Simonton, D. K. (1986a). Biographical typicality, eminence, and achievement style. *Journal of Creative Behavior, 20*, 14–22.

Simonton, D. K. (1986b). Multiple discovery: Some Monte Carlo simulations and Gedanken experiments. *Scientometrics, 9*, 269–280.

Simonton, D. K. (1986c). Multiples, Poisson distributions, and chance: An analysis of the Brannigan-Wanner model. *Scientometrics, 9*, 127–137.

Simonton, D. K. (1986d). Stochastic models of multiple discovery. *Czechoslovak Journal of Physics, B 36*, 138–141.

Simonton, D. K. (1987). Multiples, chance, genius, creativity, and zeitgeist. In D. N. Jackson & J. P. Rushton (Eds.), *Scientific excellence: Origins and assessment* (pp. 98–128). Beverly Hills, CA: Sage Publications.

References

Simonton, D. K. (1988a). Age and outstanding achievement: What do we know after a century of research? *Psychological Bulletin, 104,* 251–267.

Simonton, D. K. (1988b). *Scientific genius: A psychology of science.* Cambridge: Cambridge University Press.

Simonton, D. K. (1989a). Age and creative productivity: Nonlinear estimation of an information-processing model. *International Journal of Aging and Human Development, 29,* 23–37.

Simonton, D. K. (1989b). The chance-configuration theory of scientific creativity. In B. Gholson, W. R. Shadish, Jr., R. A. Neimeyer, & A. C. Houts (Eds.), *The psychology of science: Contributions to metascience* (pp. 170–213). Cambridge: Cambridge University Press.

Simonton, D. K. (1989c). Shakespeare's sonnets: A case of and for single-case historiometry. *Journal of Personality, 57,* 695–721.

Simonton, D. K. (1990). Lexical choices and aesthetic success: A computer content analysis of 154 Shakespeare sonnets. *Computers and the Humanities, 24,* 251–264.

Simonton, D. K. (1991a). Career landmarks in science: Individual differences and interdisciplinary contrasts. *Developmental Psychology, 27,* 119–130.

Simonton, D. K. (1991b). Latent-variable models of posthumous reputation: A quest for Galton's G. *Journal of Personality and Social Psychology, 60,* 607–619.

Simonton, D. K. (1992a). Leaders of American psychology, 1879–1967: Career development, creative output, and professional achievement. *Journal of Personality and Social Psychology, 62,* 5–17.

Simonton, D. K. (1992b). The social context of career success and course for 2,026 scientists and inventors. *Personality and Social Psychology Bulletin, 18,* 452–463.

Simonton, D. K. (1994). *Greatness: Who makes history and why.* New York: Guilford Press.

Simonton, D. K. (1995). Foresight in insight? A Darwinian answer. In R. J. Sternberg & J. E. Davidson (Eds.), *The nature of insight* (pp. 465–494). Cambridge, MA: MIT Press.

Simonton, D. K. (1997a). Creative productivity: A predictive and explanatory model of career trajectories and landmarks. *Psychological Review, 104,* 66–89.

Simonton, D. K. (1997b). Foreign influence and national achievement: The impact of open milieus on Japanese civilization. *Journal of Personality and Social Psychology, 72,* 86–94.

Simonton, D. K. (1999a). Creativity and genius. In L. A. Pervin & O. John (Eds.), *Handbook of personality theory and research* (2nd ed.). New York: Guilford Press.

Simonton, D. K. (1999b). Matthew effects. In M. A. Runco & S. Pritzker (Eds.), *Encyclopedia of creativity* (Vol. 2, pp. 185–192). San Diego: Academic Press.

References

Simonton, D. K. (1999c). *Origins of genius: Darwinian perspectives on creativity*. New York: Oxford University Press.

Simonton, D. K. (1999d). Talent and its development: An emergenic and epigenetic model. *Psychological Review, 106*, 435–457.

Simonton, D. K. (2000a). Creativity: Cognitive, developmental, personal, and social aspects. *American Psychologist, 55*, 151–158.

Simonton, D. K. (2000b). Methodological and theoretical orientation and the long-term disciplinary impact of 54 eminent psychologists. *Review of General Psychology, 4*, 1–13.

Simonton, D. K. (2002). *Great psychologists and their times: Scientific insights into psychology's history*. Washington, DC: American Psychological Association.

Simonton, D. K. (2003a). Creativity as variation and selection: Some critical constraints. In M. Runco (Ed.), *Critical creative processes* (pp. 3–18). Cresskill, NJ: Hampton Press.

Simonton, D. K. (2003b). Scientific creativity as constrained stochastic behavior: The integration of product, process, and person perspectives. *Psychological Bulletin, 129*, 475–494.

Simonton, D. K. (2004). Psychology's status as a scientific discipline: Its empirical placement within an implicit hierarchy of the sciences. *Review of General Psychology, 7*.

Skinner, B. F. (1959). A case study in scientific method. In S. Koch (Ed.), *Psychology: A study of a science* (Vol. 2, pp. 359–379). New York: McGraw-Hill.

Smith, W. J., Albright, L. W., & Glennon, J. R. (1961). The prediction of research competence and creativity from personal history. *Journal of Applied Psychology, 45*, 59–62.

Sobel, R. S., & Rothenberg, A. (1980). Artistic creation as stimulated by superimposed versus separated visual images. *Journal of Personality and Social Psychology, 39*, 953–961.

Sorokin, P. A. (1969). *Society, culture, and personality*. New York: Cooper Square. (Original work published 1947)

Stavridou, A., & Furnham, A. (1996). The relationship between psychoticism, trait-creativity and the attentional mechanism of cognitive inhibition. *Personality & Individual Differences, 21*, 143–153.

Stent, G. S. (1972). Prematurity and uniqueness in scientific discovery. *Scientific American, 227*, 84–93.

Sternberg, R. J. (1989). Computational models of scientific discovery: Do they compute? [Review of Scientific discovery: Computational explorations of the creative process.] *Contemporary Psychology, 34*, 895–897.

References

Sternberg, R. J. (1998). A propulsion model of types of creative contributions. *Review of General Psychology, 3*, 83–100.

Sternberg, R. J. (2004). *WICS: A theory of wisdom, intelligence, and creativity synthesized*. New York: Cambridge University Press.

Sternberg, R. J., & Davidson, J. E. (Eds.). (1995). *The nature of insight*. Cambridge, MA: MIT Press.

Sternberg, R. J., & Gordeeva, T. (1996). The anatomy of impact: What makes an article influential? *Psychological Science, 7*, 69–75.

Stewart, J. A. (1983). Achievement and ascriptive processes in the recognition of scientific articles. *Social Forces, 62*, 166–189.

Stumpf, H. (1995). Scientific creativity: A short overview. *Educational Psychology Review, 7*, 225–241.

Suedfeld, P. (1985). APA presidential addresses: The relation of integrative complexity to historical, professional, and personal factors. *Journal of Personality and Social Psychology, 47*, 848–852.

Suedfeld, P., & Coren, S. (1992). Cognitive correlates of conceptual complexity. *Personality and Individual Differences, 13*, 1193–1199.

Suler, J. R. (1980). Primary process thinking and creativity. *Psychological Bulletin, 88*, 144–165.

Sulloway, F. J. (1996). *Born to rebel: Birth order, family dynamics, and creative lives*. New York: Pantheon.

Taylor, D. W. (1963). Variables related to creativity and productivity among men in two research laboratories. In C. W. Taylor & F. X. Barron (Eds.), *Scientific creativity: Its recognition and development* (pp. 228–250). New York: Wiley.

Taylor, M. S., Locke, E. A., Lee, C., & Gist, M. E. (1984). Type A behavior and faculty research productivity: What are the mechanisms? *Organizational Behavior and Human Performance, 34*, 402–418.

Terman, L. M. (1954). Scientists and nonscientists in a group of 800 gifted men. *Psychological Monographs: General and Applied, 68* (7, Whole No. 378), 1–44.

Thagard, P. (1992). *Conceptual revolutions*. Princeton, NJ: Princeton University Press.

Tweney, R. D. (1989). Fields of enterprise: On Michael Faraday's thought. In D. B. Wallace & H. E. Gruber (Eds.), *Creative people at work: Twelve cognitive case studies* (pp. 90–106). New York: Oxford University Press.

Tweney, R. D. (1990). Five questions for computationalists. In J. Shrager & P. Langley (Eds.), *Computational models of scientific discovery and theory information* (pp. 471–484). San Mateo, CA: Kaufmann.

Tweney, R. D., Doherty, M. E., & Mynatt, C. R. (Eds.). (1981). *On scientific thinking*. New York: Columbia University Press.

References

Van Zelst, R. H., & Kerr, W. A. (1951). Some correlates of technical and scientific productivity. *Journal of Abnormal and Social Psychology, 46,* 470–475.

Visher, S. S. (1947, Autumn). Starred scientists: A study of their ages. *American Scientist, 35,* 543, 570, 572, 574, 576, 578, 580.

Wagman, M. (2000). *Scientific discovery processes in humans and computers: Theory and research in psychology and artificial intelligence.* Westport, CT: Praeger.

Walberg, H. J., Rasher, S. P., & Parkerson, J. (1980). Childhood and eminence. *Journal of Creative Behavior, 13,* 225–231.

Wallas, G. (1926). *The art of thought.* New York: Harcourt, Brace.

Wan, W. W. N., & Chiu, C.-Y. (2002). Effects of novel conceptual combination on creativity. *Journal of Creative Behavior, 36,* 227–240.

Wechsler, J. (Ed.). (1978). *On aesthetics in science.* Cambridge, MA: MIT Press.

Weisberg, R. W. (1992). *Creativity: Beyond the myth of genius.* New York: Freeman.

Weller, A. C. (2001). *Editorial peer review: Its strengths and weaknesses.* Medford, NJ: Information Today.

Wertheimer, M. (1982). *Productive thinking* (M. Wertheimer, Ed.). Chicago: University of Chicago Press. (Original work published 1945.)

Whaples, R. (1991). A quantitative history of the *Journal of Economic History* and the cliometric revolution. *Journal of Economic History, 51,* 289–301.

White, L. (1949). *The science of culture.* New York: Farrar, Straus.

White, K. G., & White, M. J. (1978). On the relation between productivity and impact. *Australian Psychologist, 13,* 369–374.

Wilson, T. D., DePaulo, B. M., Mook, D. G., & Klaaren, K. J. (1993). Scientists' evaluations of research: The biasing effects of the importance of the topic. *Psychological Science, 4,* 322–325.

Wolff, W. M. (1970). A study of criteria for journal manuscripts. *American Psychologist, 25,* 636–639.

Wolff, W. M. (1973). Publication problems in psychology and an explicit evaluation schema for manuscripts. *American Psychologist, 28,* 257–261.

Woodward, W. R. (1974). Scientific genius and loss of a parent. *Science Studies, 4,* 265–277.

Wuthrich, V., & Bates, T. C. (2001). Schizotypy and latent inhibition: Non-linear linkage between psychometric and cognitive markers. *Personality and Individual Differences, 30,* 783–798.

Xie, Y., & Shauman, K. A. (2003). *Women in science: Career processes and outcomes.* Cambridge, MA: Harvard University Press.

Yuasa, M. (1974). The shifting center of scientific activity in the West: From the sixteenth to the twentieth century. In. N. Shigeru, D. L. Swain, & Y. Eri (Eds.), *Science and society in modern Japan* (pp. 81–103). Tokyo: University of Tokyo Press.

References

Zajonc, R. B. (1976, April 16). Family configuration and intelligence. *Science, 192,* 227–235.

Zhao, H. (1984). An intelligence constant of scientific work. *Scientometrics, 6,* 9–17.

Zhao, H., & Jiang, G. (1985). Shifting of world's scientific center and scientist's social ages. *Scientometrics, 8,* 59–80.

Zuckerman, H. (1977). *Scientific elite.* New York: Free Press.

Zuckerman, H., Cole, J. R., & Bruer, J. T. (Eds.). (1991). *The outer circle: Women in the scientific community.* New York: Norton.

Zusne, L. (1976). Age and achievement in psychology: The harmonic mean as a model. *American Psychologist, 31,* 805–807.

Index

The 100: A Ranking of the Most Influential Persons in History, 2
algorithmic problem solving and creativity, 140–141
associative process, constraints, 108–110
associative richness and creativity, 105–111
a symbol defined, xiii
α symbol defined, xiv, 57

BACON software and scientific creativity experiments, 5, 152
Beethoven, Ludwig von (*Fifth Symphony*), 1–3
bias, 85–87, 89
Bohr, Niels and Janusian thinking, 118
brainstorming, 154
breakthroughs, scientific, 144–145
b symbol defined, xiii
β symbol defined, xiv, 57

career trajectories
  and the combinatorial process, 60–64
  differences by discipline, 68
  individual differences, 64–67
chance combination model. *See also* combinatorial model
  assumptions, 43–49
  and creativity, 173–179

general discussion, 8–10
vs. logic perspective, 138
and multiples, 39
Pasteur, Louis on, 10
problem solving, 142–143
processes, 144–157
chance defined, 41
civilization, 1, 2
cognitive psychology, 139
combinatorial model. *See also* chance combination model
  advantages of, 73–74
  age function, 61
  career trajectories and, 60–64
  general discussion, 41–43, 135
  objections to, 75
  output, 61
  and research programs, 83
  variances explained, 68–70
computer problem solving, 150–153
context of discovery, 164
context of justification, 164
creative person. *See* person, creative
creative process. *See* process, creative
creative production. *See* production, creative
creative products. *See* products, creative

creativity. *See also* scientists, individual,
     creativity of
algorithmic problem solving and, 140–141
applications of research, 182–184
and associative richness, 105–111
BACON software and scientific creativity
     experiments, 5, 152
basis for, i
chance combination model, 173–179
and cognitive complexity, 109
consequences of, 3
discovery programs and, 5, 138, 179
domain and, 97
environment, shared and, 119–125
fostering, 131
gender differences in, 23
Geneplore model, 149
group, 153–157
Hadamard, Jacques and, 41, 43
hierarchies theory of, 105–108
high *vs.* low, 172–173
incubation period of, 145–146
intelligence and, 103–105
Janusian thinking and, 116–118
journal articles, 17
network of enterprise, 79
openness to experience, 111–113
Ortega y Gasset and the logic perspective, 6
Poincaré, Henri, 41–43
primary process, 109
product focus of, 15
psychopathology and, 113–116, 122, 123
research framework, 180–182
research programs and, 77–84
scientific
     appreciation of, 2–3
     environment and, 119
     foundations of, 103–118, 162
     and genetic heritage, 118–119
     peer review and, 88–91
     perspectives on, x, 3–12
     and priority disputes, 56
     requirements of, 7
     restrictions on, 101
     traits, 52, 141–142
     scientific vs artistic, 99, 100, 102, 127–128
     secondary process, 109
     stimulation of and problem solving,
          148–149
     stochastic processes and, 41
     warfare and, 131
Creativity: Beyond the Myth of Genius, 137
c symbol defined, xiii
$C_i(t)$ symbol defined, xiii

Darwin, Charles
     multiple participation and, 34, 37
     and openness to experience, 112
     output as a function of concerted effort,
          82–83
     research projects, acceptance of, 80–81
     scientific versatility of, 79–80
defocused attention defined, 111
disciplines, constraints upon, 101–102
discoveries, simultaneous and multiples, 33
discovery programs and creativity, 5, 138,
     179
divergent thought defined, 110
domain, scientific defined, 44
domain and creativity, 97
duplicates, rarity of, 55

Edison, Thomas and career output, 70
education and creative development,
     125–130
Einstein, Albert
     on education and the creative impulse,
          125
     and the genius perspective, 7
     on his creative process, 164
     scientific versatility of, 79
elaboration defined, 60
environment and creative development,
     119–125
epochs, creative, 131–133
epochs, scientific, 133–134

Index

equal-odds rule, , 22–24, 38, 50–52, 67, 84, 140

Erdös, Paul and career output, 63

e symbol defined, xiii

Exploring Science, 15

family experiences and creative development, 119–125

Faraday, Michael on the creative process, 43

field, scientific defined, 44

Fifth Symphony (Beethoven), 1–3

firstborns and classical composition, 124

flat hierarchy of associations, 105–108

gender differences in creativity, 23

Geneplore model of creativity, 149

generalists defined, 45

genetic algorithms, 151, 180

genetic programming, 151–152, 180

genius and individual variation, 18–19

genius and zeitgeist, 11

genius perspective

and career output distribution, 28

general discussion, 6–8, 135, 171–179

and multiples, 37

Gestalt psychology, 138–139

grade (multiple) defined, 31

group creativity. *See* creativity, group

γ symbol defined, xv

Hadamard, Jacques and mathematical creativity, , 41, 43

Hamlet (Shakespeare), 1–3

Helmholtz, Hermann von, 40, 129, 130

heuristic methods of problem solving, 142–143

hierarchies theory of creativity, 105–108

Hilbert, David and the independence criterion for singleton discovery, 36

H_i symbol defined, xiii, 51

hit rates

mass producers and, 23, 24

and perfectionists, 23, 24

publication and, 22, 23

H_{it} symbol defined, xiii

Human Problem Solving, 139–140

ideas

origin of, 77

closed system, 62

influx of new, 62–64

Pasteur, Louis, 81

parallel processing of, 79

ideation defined, 60

incubation period, length of, 147

incubation period of creativity, 145–146

initial creative potential defined, 60

insight problems, 144–148

intellect, human and bias, 85–87, 89

intelligence and creativity, 103–105

intuition and problem solving, 147–148

I symbol defined, xiv

Janusian thinking and creativity, 116–118

journal articles and defining creativity, 17

Kant, Immanuel, 4

k symbol defined, xiv, 61

Last Supper (Vinci), 1–3

latent inhibition defined, 114

laterborns and revolutionary science, 124

Law of Parsimony and scientific activity, 76

Locke, John, 4

logic perspective

and career output distribution, 28

vs. chance, 138

general discussion, 4–6, 163–168

vs. genius, 138

and insight problems, 147

limitations, 166–168

Ortega y Gasset on, 6

processes, 138–144, 165–166

role of, 164–166

Lotka's Law, 20

213

Index

Mach, Ernst and cognitive capacities, 105

mass producers and hit rates, 23, 24

mathematical notation, xiii-xv

Matthew Effect, 73–74

Merton, Robert K.
multiples and, 55
and zeitgeist, 10

metasciences, differences among, 4

Mill, John Stewart, 4

m_i symbol defined, xiv, 60

μ symbol defined, xv

multiples
categorization of, 31
chance combination model, 39
characteristics of, 29
Darwin, Charles, 34, 37
discoveries, 33, 53–59
distribution of grades, 29–33, 38
doublets and, 58
examples of, 11
genius perspective, 37
grade defined, 31
grades
Poisson distribution, 53
and singletons, 31, 53, 54
identity, degree of, 35–38
individual variation in participation, 34–35
Merton, Robert K., 55
Newton, Isaac, 34
occurrence of, 29
and scientific communities, 28–38
scientists participation in, 34
temporal separation, 33–34, 57
variance, 37
vs singletons, rarity, 35
zeitgeist and, 32, 33, 35, 91–96

network of enterprise and creativity, 79

Newton, Isaac
and multiples participation, 34
Principia Mathematica, 1, 4

and scientific community, 28–29
and versatility in study, 79

N symbol defined, xiv

n symbol defined, xiv

null hypothesis defined, 76

nulltons vs. singletons, 53

Ockham's razor and scientific activity, 76

On The Part Played by Accident in Invention and Discovery, 8

openness to experience and creativity, 111–113

opportunistic assimilation defined, 146

Ortega y Gasset, José and the logic perspective of scientific creativity, 6

output
career, individual, 70–71
career distribution, 25, 28, 71
career landmarks, 67
combinatorial, 61
Darwin, Charles, 82–83
individual scientist, 71–72
interdisciplinary contrasts, 67–72
longitudinal fluctuations in, , 24, 59–60
and scientific community, 97–98
scientists, individual, 71–72
skewed distribution of, 52

paradigm defined, 101

parallel processing of ideas, 79

Pasteur, Louis
and the chance perspective, 10
ideas, origin of, 81

peer evaluations, impact on the discipline, 87

peer reviews and the creative process, 84–91

perfectionists and hit rates, 23, 24

person, creative defined, 15

perspectives, integration of, 12–13

$P(j)$ symbol defined, xiv,

Planck, Max and the genius perspective, 7

Planck's Principle, 64

Plato (Republic), 1–3

214

Index

Poincaré, Henri and creativity, 41–43
Poisson distribution
  contagious, 56–57
  and multiple grades, 53
  nature of, 25–27, 52
political instability and creative
    development, 132, 133
Price's Law, 98, 183
Principia Mathematica (Newton), 1, 4
problems, reasonable defined, 144
problems, unreasonable, 144
problem solving, 139–140, 147–148, 150–153
process, creative defined, 15
product focus of scientific creativity, 15
production, creative, 148–150
productivity and citation counts,
    correlation, 25
productivity distribution, 28
products, creative, 16, 17
The Psychology of Creativity and Discovery, 14
*The Psychology of Science: Contributions to
    Metascience*, ix
psychopathology and creativity, 113–116,
    122, 123
p symbol defined, xiv
publications
  distribution, quality *vs.* quantity, 22, 23
  distribution of, 21, 22
  history of, 16
  lifetime output, 20–21
  and scientific careers, 16–28
published articles, criteria for, 17

radioactivity and serendipity, 8
recognition, variation in, 19
Republic (Plato), 1–3
research programs and scientific creativity,
    77–84
revolts, nationalistic and creative
    development, 132–133
The Role of Chance in Discovery, 8
r symbol defined, xiv
ρ symbol defined, xv, 51

science, psychology of, 14
*Scientific Creativity as Constrained Stochastic
    Behavior: The Integration of Product,
    Process, and Person Perspectives*, x
Scientific Genius: A Psychology of Science, ix
scientific products, analysis of, 16
scientific psychology. *See* science,
    psychology of
scientists
  creative vs noncreative, 128–130
  individual, creativity of, 98, 102, 175, 181
  and multiples participation, 34
  output, individual, 71–72
  study of, 99, 183
  and versatility, 79, 110
serendipity
  defined, 8
  episodes of, 9
  forms of, 9
  and radioactivity, 8
  X-rays and, 8
  and zeitgeist, 10
Shakespeare, William (*Hamlet*), 1–3
Simon, Herbert, 4–6
Simonton, Dean Keith, i
singletons
  criteria for, 36–37
  and multiples grades, 31, 53
  nulltons and, 53
sociocultural context and creative
    development, 130–134
sociocultural determinism. *See* zeitgeist
specialists defined, 45
spirit of the times. *See* zeitgeist
spreading activation defined, 146
σ^2 symbol defined, xv
statistical expectation, departures from,
    23
steep hierarchy of associations, 105–108
stochastic defined, 41
stochastic processes and creativity, 41
strong methods of problem solving defined,
    140

Index

style, individual creative, 38
symbols, definitions of, xiii

thinkers, mental processes of, 7–8
T_i symbol defined, xiv, 51
T_{it} symbol defined, xiv
training and creative development,
125–130
T symbol defined, xiv
t symbol defined, xiv, 61

u_i symbol defined, xiv, 51
u_{it} symbol defined, xiv
Vinci, Leonardo da (*Last Supper*), 1–3

warfare and creativity, 131

weak methods of problem solving, 142–143
White, Leslie and zeitgeist, 11

X-rays and serendipity, 8

zeitgeist
calculus and, 94
and career output distribution, 28, 71
general discussion, 10–12, 135, 168–171
genius and, 11
Merton, Robert K., 10
and multiples, 32, 33, 35, 91–96
serendipity and, 10
and singletons, 36
vs genius perspective, 134
White, Leslie, 11